YOUTH UNEMPLOYMENT

Youth Unemployment:

A socio-psychological study of disadvantaged 16-19 year-olds

C. Murray,
Centre for Youth Studies,
University of Manchester,

NFER Publishing Company

Published by the NFER Publishing Company Ltd.,
Darville House, 2 Oxford Road East,
Windsor, Berks, SL4 1DF
Registered Office: The Mere, Upton Park, Slough, Berks, SL1 2DQ.
First published 1978

ISBN 0 85633 172 4

Typeset by Yale Press Ltd., London SE25
Printed in Great Britain by
Lonsdale Universal Printing, Bath
Distributed in the USA by Humanities Press Inc.,
Atlantic Highlands, New Jersey 07716 USA.

Acknowledgements

The assistance of colleagues at the University of Manchester was of considerable importance with regard to the implementation of the research which forms the substance of this book. In terms of overseeing the contractual arrangements for the research, Ken Wallace and Ken Tittle of the Bursar's Department, and David Richardson of the Vice-Chancellor's Office, were quietly effective. Professor John Turner, sometime Dean of the Faculty of Education, provided valuable support at Faculty level during the initial period of the research, and Professor Brian Rodgers, Head of the Geography Department, furnished assistance with regard to work describing the geographical setting of CI as outlined in the original report.

Full-time research staff were recruited at short notice, September 1973, for the project but their sustained effort and co-operative attitude contributed indispensably to the conduct of the project. David Haran was closely involved in the quantitative aspect of the research but also involved himself in observational work; he assisted in the construction of scales, oversaw their administration to the CI samples and contributed substantially to the interpretation of results. Ian McNab was largely responsible for the qualitative aspect of the research though he also helped in scale construction and test administration; he visited all eight CI areas, established guidelines for the observational work and undertook participant observation in three areas.

Part-time assistance was provided by Duncan Scott who joined the University as Van Leer Lecturer in Youth Studies in January 1974 and undertook participant observation in two areas in addition to helping with the administration of tests. Stephen Howarth gave generously of his time in interviewing employers and following up ex-CI employees, and Enid Clapcott undertook some observational work with regard to CI provision for girls; both these part-time helpers were postgraduate students. Stephen Kenny, postgraduate geography student, undertook much of the work relating to the geographical context of CI and with the assistance of Anne Lowcock drew up a series of maps showing the distribution of CI projects which were included in the original report but which have not been used in this text. Tom Sharp of the Manchester University Medical Computing Centre and Jenny Lalor of the University of London Computing Centre provided valuable assistance during the analysis of the quantitative data. The help afforded by Principal Careers Officers, Heads of Schools and Principals of FE Colleges and their staff in the areas chosen for the research, greatly facilitated the selection of comparison groups of young people.

It must be remarked that throughout the research period there was generous co-operation from CI employees at all levels of the organization and unstinting support from Department of Employment officials; without such co-operation and support the research programme could not have been completed. The agreement of the Department of Employment to extend the one-year contractual period for a further three months so that the full-time research workers could complete their own reports is indicative of the measure of support we received.

Florence, Kath, June, Margaret and Norma transcribed tapes and typed working papers, interim reports and the final manuscript; their help is gratefully acknowledged.

Finally I must acknowledge my debt to Dr Tom Fitzpatrick, a colleague at the University of Manchester, who read an earlier draft of this book and suggested changes in the presentation of material to enhance readability. This essentially involved the removal of much statistical material which was originally presented in tabular form. The interested reader may refer to the original report, reference copies are held at the Department of Employment and Manchester University Libraries, in order to familiarize himself with this and other relevant material.

Papers based on the research reported in this book were given at the 70th Annual General Metting of the American Sociological Association (San Francisco, August 1975), and the XXIst International Congress of Psychology (Paris, July 1976). Chapter three includes material contained in an editorial for the London Educational Review (Volume 4, Number 3, 1975), and a general account of the Community Industry scheme has been previously published in Paedagogica Europaea X/1975/2 and in Youth in Contemporary Society published by the NFER.

Contents

List of Tables

List of Figures

Chapter 1

The Origin and Development of Community Industry

Introduction

There has been little research into the characteristics of special groups of young people who may be thought to be 'at risk' in an employment sense. This book is about such young people and draws on data from a research project into the effectiveness of an experimental scheme known as Community Industry (CI) which was established to provide meaningful employment in a caring organizational environment for disadvantaged young people under the age of 18. Though focused on such organizational provision it has a much broader concern in that CI provides a window through which to observe adjustment to work of various groups of young manual workers. Thus while the great majority of young people successfully cope with the demands of schooling and experience the transition from school to work as a relatively smooth process, there are others who may have neither the inner and/or external resources to perform effectively in either school or work situations.

While the emphasis of our research rests on a description of such special groups we cannot ignore the structural factors associated with the individual's adjustment or non-adjustment to the world of work. In brief, disadvantaged groups may obtain employment of kinds systematically different from those considered advantaged. The characteristics of these differing employment experiences may be set down in terms of those related to disadvantaged groups, *viz.* low pay, poor working conditions, unstable employment, limited job advancement and little if any provision for training. The employment pattern in this secondary sector of the labour market is seen to be self-reinforcing with the absence of enterprise — specific training affecting and being affected by high labour turnover, the reverse situation applying in the primary sector.

A general difficulty lies in the fact that extension of the period of formal education tends to build up employment related aspirations which are inevitably disappointed when the expansion in education is not matched by changes in the employment structure; a number of employers, particularly in times of recession, simply raise the educational requirements for entry to a given occupation without changing the nature of the jobs involved. Such a dislocation between schools and work may lead to an under-employment of young people who become disillusioned and bored with unchallenging work and resentful for the poor returns on their extended investment in schooling. The mounting of programmes geared to the needs of the unqualified school leaver which incorporate both educational and industrial philosophies may be one answer but it is certainly no simple task. There is an ever present danger that the 'educational element' will be lost and that such programmes will revert to an industrial emphasis which is inappropriate to the task in hand. It is made even more difficult by the rather different ideological inclinations of youth/community workers, teachers and workers and by the political pressure put on civil servants to develop and expand 'experimental' programmes without adequate evaluation of what has been achieved in their pilot phases.

It is against this background that we view the emergence of an active manpower policy involving a job creation and adjustment programme for young people who are at risk in an employment and social sense. This policy has been recently described (MSC 1977) as meeting the individual needs of unemployed young people as they seek to secure permanent employment. It is reflected in a programme, estimated to cost some £170M per year when fully operational, which is made up of two kinds of opportunities; courses designed to prepare young people for work and different kinds of work experience. Encompassing both these elements, but at the same time offering a distinctive kind of provision is the scheme known as Community Industry. In the words of the MSC report this form of provision

> 'Offers a distinctive kind of assessment, employment, rehabilitation and training for some of the most seriously disadvantaged amongst the young unemployed and those who find it most difficult to obtain and hold down normal jobs.' (p.38)

This book is about Community Industry (CI). In that it reports research which terminated some four years ago it is something of a historical account.[1] On the other hand some of the processes which are described at both individual and organizational levels constitute the very bases of social behaviour and as such are as relevant today as when the material was first collected. It is no simple matter to analyze[2] such social behaviour and related social processes particularly as they are moulded and shaped into organizational forms. However it is hoped that this account will fairly present some of the problems which men face when they engage in social experiments designed to alleviate particular social problems and at the same time serve as an introduction to the study of social-psychological processes.

Having made the reader aware of the context and procedures associated with the research we must now turn to the major purpose of this chapter which is to describe how an 'idea' develops into a social reality: more specifically with the birth and early development of the organization which came to be known as Community Industry.

Early Initiatives

In the spring and summer of 1971 a growing concern was apparent among voluntary and statutory agencies with a responsibility for young people about the concentration of the young unemployed in certain areas of the UK. The difficult employment situation facing school leavers was highlighted in a press release from the Institute of Careers Officers during May of that year which urged the optimum utilization of this section of the labour force:

> 'It now seems certain that many thousands of these young people will spend the first few months of post-school life "unwanted" by the working world. In the development areas of Northern Ireland, Scotland, Wales and Northern England, the school leavers will join the already considerable numbers of their unemployed older brothers and sisters. The prospects for many are that they will still be seeking their first job at the end of the year. This happened to the 1962 school leavers when the national unemployment level was lower than at present. In many other areas of the country the quest for a "career" is likely to be cast aside in the immediate necessity of finding a "job" . . . "any job". If any industrial organization received such scant return on capital investment it would go bankrupt.' (Press release: Institute of Careers Officers: May, 1971).

This theme was taken up and developed in the national press, and the National Association of Youth Clubs (NAYC), following a recommendation of their development committee, decided to call a conference on the 'young unemployed' with a view to co-ordinating and initiating action designed to help ameliorate the situation. A one-day conference with this title was held at Sheffield on 28th July, 1971 with representatives in attendance from the Youth Service, Youth Employment Service, Careers Service, Further Education and Industry.[3]

The orientation of the conference is perhaps best given by a member's retrospective reply to criticisms that the proposals then under consideration were 'irrelevant'.[4]

> 'The purpose of this conference was not to pursue long term policies, but to seek some immediate short term and hastily asembled support for young people who now face hardship . . .; unrealized expectations of being accepted as adult wage-earners; and a depressing blow to morale at a time which could be an exacting and challenging step forward into young adult life. In this situation we have a choice of two evils: do nothing because the root cause of the problem is basic inequality in the system, or to offer some support services, albeit palliative, which may, quite wrongly in my view, suggest acceptance of the situation, but which may make some profit from what we all recognize to be a bad job.' (New Society, 12th August, 1971).

Arising from the conference a working party was set up on the 'young unemployed' which circulated a Newsletter (9th August, 1971) to all Youth Employment Offices and youth officers in the UK. The purpose of the newsletter was to provide momentum for the embryonic movement and produce details of local initiatives designed to help unemployed boys and girls. It contained brief comparative statistics of the number of registered unemployed school leavers in the month of July for 1970 and '71 and provided a number of suggestions for action and brief accounts of existing local arrangements. Local groups were invited to apply for funds, set aside by the NAYC, in order to maintain projects already underway for consideration at a subsequent meeting of the working party.[5] Thus at this early stage there appeared to be local initiative and support for projects designed to help unemployed young people and three of the many ideas put forward, under the headings of voluntary service projects, workshop communes and involvement of retired or unemployed adults, contained the seed for further developments.

These ideas were taken further in a press release describing the projects which the action group hoped to support (NAYC press information sheet 18th August, 1971). The projects in question were centred on 'community work' which would be undertaken on a paid basis with sympathetic adults associated in a caring-supervisory role. Further discussion took place between interested parties and by mid-September, 1971 the basis of a scheme described as Community Industry (CI) began to crystallize. In proposing this scheme a certain reformulation of the original position of the working group is discernible particularly with regard to a stress on the need for tackling the long-term unemployment situation and to concentrate efforts in helping the less able young person. This position is illustrated by reference to the second newsletter issued by the working party:

> 'As a result of its discussion and of information received the NAYC working party now sees its role, particularly in relation to the areas of highest need, to the less able group and in more particular to the 17+ group. It will continue to provide information about measures taken to improve opportunities for the young unemployed in the short-term situation but sees its major task to assist in those areas where the problem is long-term.
> To this end a paper has been submitted to the depts. of employment, environment and education and science where it is receiving careful attention. The paper does not pretend to approach anything like a total situation, rather to make a deliberate and precise move towards a solution of the problems of the less able in the depressed regions.' (Action Young Unemployed: Issue 2nd September, 1971. p.8).

Though Parliament was in recess at this time considerable efforts were made to obtain political support for some form of co-ordinated action with regard to the proposals contained in the newsletter. These proposals suggested the establishment of teams of workers operating at local level who would help the less able unemployed young people develop a new 'community industry'. It was emphasized that the work undertaken would not be voluntary but paid at a 'realistic' rate on the basis of a 'proper job for a proper wage'. Participatory democracy with a strong educational bias was seen as being the characteristic theme of CI with full worker involvement helping to develop a new form of industry. A radical alternative to the present occupational structure was evidently in the minds of the CI protagonists and is made rather explicit in the following passage:

> 'We are advocating the recognition of a new *'industry* of community work' which like any other industry would pay appropriate rates and in which would

> emerge a career structure.'
> (Action Youth Unemployed: Issue 2: September, 1971, p.13)

The 'new industry' was seen both in terms of helping youngsters who might be broadly termed socially and economically disadvantaged but also those of average or above average ability who were employed in unchallenging jobs:

> 'Whilst the main recruiting ground for these schemes would be amongst the less academically able we would not see them as restricted to this group. We referred earlier to the under-employment of some more able young people in industry. Some of these might also be attracted to such schemes, leaving opportunities in industry for the less able peers who have been currently squeezed out. This could be achieved without productive loss to the industrial sector.'
> (Action Young Unemployed: Issue 2: September, 1971, p.14.).

Thus at this point Community Industry was clearly seen as a scheme providing a form of long-term sheltered employment for seriously disadvantaged young people and as an alternative to short term 'dead end' jobs for the academically able.

Though CI, seen in these terms, would appear to be a rather radical alternative to the present employment pattern, it was criticized at the time for not being radical enough! Inspection of correspondence by the working group reflects a preoccupation with arguments for changing the system rather than supporting it. In these terms the scheme was seen as being reactionary in that employment situations were to be presented in a duly constituted and approved form to young people. A sample of such thinking is presented in the following extract:

> 'The major point to make perhaps is that the scheme is reactionary and conservative in the extreme and adopts an unacceptably patronizing attitude towards the young people it purports to serve . . . What is required is the establishment of a real community industry where young people have an opportunity to create new employment on their own behalf, not undertake tasks for the benefit of others. If we are talking about education we should talk about far more than our next steps into the status quo, we should talk about the creation of new structures rather than a propping up of existing ones.'
> (Correspondence: dated 19th October, 1971).

Formal Establishment of CI

The proposals for CI were eventually lodged with the Department of Employment (DE) and in a written answer to a question raised in the House of Commons Mr Robert Carr, then Secretary of State for Employment, announced on the 23rd November, 1971 that the government would make half a million pounds available for an experimental scheme designed to employ young people on work of social value. The substance of the reply may be given as follows:

> 'The National Association of Youth Clubs has put forward a proposal for an experimental scheme for employing young people on work of social value, especially in the environmental and community field. The aim is to see what scope there is for organized arrangements designed to bring together young people who are having difficulty in finding steady employment and work of lasting value which would otherwise not be done. I have agreed to make half a million pounds available for this scheme. It will be run by the NAYC who will work in close co-operation with local authorities and others concerned. It is intended to select for the experiment six places in development or intermediate areas. The scheme is being introduced on a pilot basis for 12 months and will then be reviewed to see what lessons can be drawn.'
> (Hansard: Vol. 826, p.334).

It is clear that in adopting the scheme government viewed the arrangements as 'experimental' and thus the model of CI as employed by the working party, involving a long-term alternative career structure, could not be put into immediate operation.

The DE press release associated with the announcement indicated that the NAYC would administer the scheme through a central co-ordinating unit under the direction of a National Co-ordinator. The deputy co-ordinator and finance officer appointed to CI were to be seconded officials from the DE and were established in post by January, 1972, with the National Co-ordinator taking up his appointment on 1st February.[6] The nucleus of the central co-ordinating team (CI HQ) was thus established early in 1972 and occupied office accommodation rented from NAYC at their London headquarters. It was envisaged that CI HQ would oversee the arrangements for the recruitment of 500 young people under the age of 18 who would be employed in six areas chosen on the basis of agreed criteria and be responsible to a national management group.

The national management structure for CI arose directly out of the NAYC working party on the young unemployed. The working party became in fact the National Management Group for CI (NMG) and consequently throughout this initial period had the dual function of operating in this capacity and as the NAYC working party. The task which confronted the NMG was to provide a workable administrative framework for the implementation of CI by developing procedures and deciding on operating policies which would make an innovative idea a reality. Interviews with members who were involved in establishing CI indicate that the NMG at this time was a fairly large body with a very wide representation of interests and hence found it difficult to act as a management group for a national scheme. It met very infrequently during the first year of the scheme[7] and a member recalls:

> 'Quite frankly it was a group which was far more concerned with spending hours when it did meet discussing abstruse points of philosophy rather than deciding on wage rates.'

The consequences of a weak national management structure meant that day-to-day decisions affecting CI were taken by representatives of the DE, CI HQ and the Chairman of the NMG. At the early stages of the development of CI there was thus no readily available arena in which to discuss policy or obtain support for policy-related decisions. This situation was somewhat aggravated by the rather ill-defined purposes of the developing organization, there being a broad conceptual basis on which to build but little specificity of goals designed to provide a particular operational set. Some loss of communication was also apparent at this time in terms of the original model proposed for CI by the action group and the limited experimental nature of the scheme envisaged by government. In the words of a CI HQ member:

> 'The CI idea as set out in all the published documents and the papers put up to government was the setting up of an alternative source of employment which would be capable of offering some degree of career structure for young people. It would be a long-term thing homing in on the disadvantaged young people as a source of labour and on environmental and community work tasks as a source of work because there was a tremendous gap in both types of provision. It became clear, however, that government never really accepted the basic concept of CI as put forward by its protagonists. Let me add that this was not made clear to those who were appointed as staff, it only became clear as CI began to operate.'

The six original areas chosen for CI located in England and Wales, were later supplemented by an additional two areas in Scotland. These areas were chosen by DE on the recommendation of the

NAYC working group. The criteria used in selecting areas are set out in an explicit fashion in a draft handbook for CI (February, 1972). It is suggested that CI teams should be set up in 'assisted areas' characterized by high youth unemployment yet where opportunities existed for suitable work projects to be undertaken by young people who might be interested in joining the scheme. An important further consideration governing selection of an area was that local bodies, particularly the local authority, should be 'enthusiastic and committed' to operating CI.

In recommending that teams be appointed to serve the chosen areas the existence of local support was emphasized. This may be illustrated by reference to the relevant correspondence between the action group and the DE:

> *South Wales:* 'The four authorities involved (Newport BC, Cwmbran UDC, Cwmbran DC, and Pontypool RDC) all guaranteed firm support for the proposals and the consequent level of material commitment.'
> *North West:* 'A strong support team has already done a great deal of work in Liverpool and have a high level of commitment to the scheme . . . There is a definite commitment from the Liverpool City Authority and a formal request for a team through the Director of Education.'
> *South Yorkshire:* 'Attention should be paid to the area around Mexborough and Hemsworth, centred on South Elmsall . . . A special sub-group in the West Riding was in existence and a firm request for a team has been submitted by the West Riding CC through the Chief Education Officer. Firm guarantees of assistance had been offered locally . . .'
> *North East:* 'A strong local group had been established in Teesside, firm commitment by the LEA . . . In Newcastle a similar situation prevailed . . . A strong case was also presented for Sunderland and Wearside and a firm commitment from Sunderland CB had been received.' (Letter from Action Group to CYEE 10th December, 1971).

The importance of enlisting local support as a criteria for selection of an area for CI is highlighted by the fact that at this point Sunderland was not included as a CI area because it did not have a strong support group which contrasted with the reported situation for Teesside and Newcastle.[8]

Organizational Development During the Experimental Year

It was assumed that in each of the areas chosen for CI a local initiative had indicated backing for the scheme and local authority involvement suggested that the implications of adopting CI in that area had been understood. It is clear however that this was not the case. Area arrangements for the reception of CI, where they had been made, were of an informal character and no formal letters of intent had been received or issued by the action group. The full implications of this situation were not fully realized until management staff had taken up their positions in each area. A member involved in the establishment of area staff at the time describes the dilemma:

> 'One of the few bits of briefing we could give them (area staff) was that local authority support in terms of office facilities and transport was guaranteed . . . when they came to start operating it became patently obvious that in no area was the local authority really aware of the practical implications for it of CI going into that area. None were really aware, some more aware than others. Nobody had bothered to tell them or brief them and everyone assumed they'd been briefed.'

Discussion with area staff who had been in post from the inception of CI illustrates the problems associated with local reception at this time. In May, 1972 the staff in area . . . found that CI office accommodation consisted of one large room in a converted school serving as a local community centre. Transport was provided and efforts were made to meet CI requirements but the local authority was in a difficult position because it had not budgeted for the facilities required for CI. In October, 1973 CI HQ were still trying to obtain satisfactory office accommodation in this area. Other areas report that little provision was made for accommodation, transport, or tools, and this situation in part resulted from poor communication between the action group and local authorities in terms of a failure to specify the implications of adopting the scheme. An area member reports:

> 'When we arrived in . . . the local authority hadn't any idea whatsoever what was implied, they had no provision for accommodation or transport, no tools or anything.'

The pattern repeats and it becomes clear that insufficient groundwork had been done with regard to ensuring adequate local provision before area staff were appointed.[9]

The end result of this was that a major portion of the experimental year, particularly in terms of the time spent by CI HQ staff, was largely involved in retrieval processes which essentially involved lobbying influential individuals in local authorities in order to obtain the necessary backing for CI. A CI HQ member reports this process:

> 'Take the . . . area situation, it eventually resulted in a meeting with local authority officers and the only thing we could do in the circumstances was to be completely honest and apologize for the mess which had been made with the preparations and indicating that it arose purely because of inadequate briefing of all parties. We stated that we hoped for their co-operation and stressed CI was a good concept and as a result, this was late 1972, . . .area find an office and begin to find tools which we can work with. This retrieval process had to be very much a person to person contact business in all areas using whatever political or local influence we could muster.'

Though such a situation resulted in area staff having to allocate a major proportion of their time to securing the necessary facilities for local 'survival', it appears to have had little tangible effect in terms of holding up the development of CI, for area staff remained with the organization during this difficult period and young people were gradually recruited.[10]

The interviewing panels for the appointment of area staff included the National Co-ordinator, Deputy National Co-ordinator, representatives of local interests and the Principal Careers Officer or his representative. Thus local people had a voice in initial appointments, and though the National Co-ordinator preserved the right of veto this wasn't in fact used and in all cases of initial appointment the majority opinion was accepted.[11] The advertisement setting out a description of the area staff jobs is given below:

NATIONAL ASSOCIATION OF YOUTH CLUBS
TEAM LEADERS AND TEAM
MEMBERS
required for
COMMUNITY INDUSTRY.

This is initially a one year scheme, aimed at providing paid opportunities for young people under 18 in environmental and community work projects in the areas experiencing highest levels of youth unemployment.

Eight local teams of three (a leader and two members) will arrange projects involving the employment of young people. The scheme is particularly aimed at those young people who have left school with no qualification and whose potential has not yet been realized. The scheme is under the direction of the National Association of Youth Clubs, and sponsored by the Department of Employment. Team leaders will require organizational skill and will be chiefly responsible for liaison with local agencies and the support of the team. Team

> members will be working closely with young people, and with adults with craft skills who will be specially employed as scheme consultants. The appointments are for one year in the first instance, and candidates able to obtain secondment from existing agencies will be considered.
> Preference will be given to applicants who can start soon. The team leaders are expected to be in the age group 28-45, but the team members may be younger. Teams will be based on the following places: Newcastle, Sunderland, Teesside, Liverpool, the area around Mexborough (South Yorkshire), Newport and S.W. Monmouthshire. Scotland (2).

Observation of the wording of the advertisement indicates that the job requirements are cast in very general terms and it appears that the individuals making up the appointment committees had little idea as to the nature or scope of the work involved. In the words of a member of an appointing committee:

> 'Initially there were titles, there were broad distinctions as to who did what but in terms of any detailed analysis this was not available nor could it have been because essentially we were interviewing people for jobs, the like of which, in a sense, had not existed before.'

The eight team leaders initially appointed were all men, three having a youth service background and the remainder possessing industrial or related experience; team members were drawn equally from both sexes. In selecting the team a number of errors of judgment appear to have been made which in part reflected an extension of CI's 'caring role' to adults as well as young employees. Thus it appears that a number of adults were employed as 'calculated risks' in that they had had a previous health or emotional problem but which at the time of appointment were thought to have been overcome, whereas others were in some senses more immature than the youngsters they were employing. Examination of these early appointments suggests that in only three of the eight areas were 'satisfactory' teams established. The problem was particularly acute in one area with two of the three team members finding themselves in difficulty and eventually resigning from CI.

Once appointed the area teams were to engage 'scheme consultants' as 'appropriate projects' emerged, who would be adults with skills appropriate to the particular projects. It was envisaged that projects would be chosen so that there would be continuity of employment for the consultant, thus as one project requiring a particular type of skill closed down another project requiring the same skill would replace it. In addition to offering skilled help to the

Fig. 1: **Illustration of CI Structure**
(From Draft CI Handbook. Appendix 1. Feb. 1972).

(A) *Headquarters*

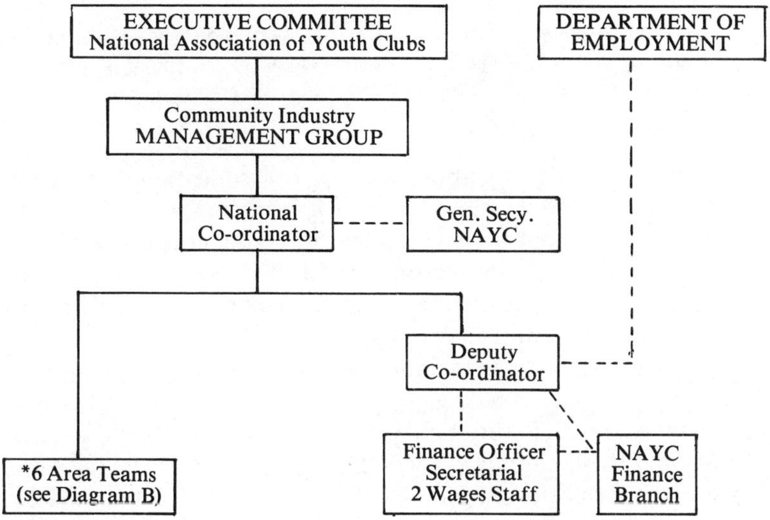

*Subsequently increased to 8

(B) *Local*

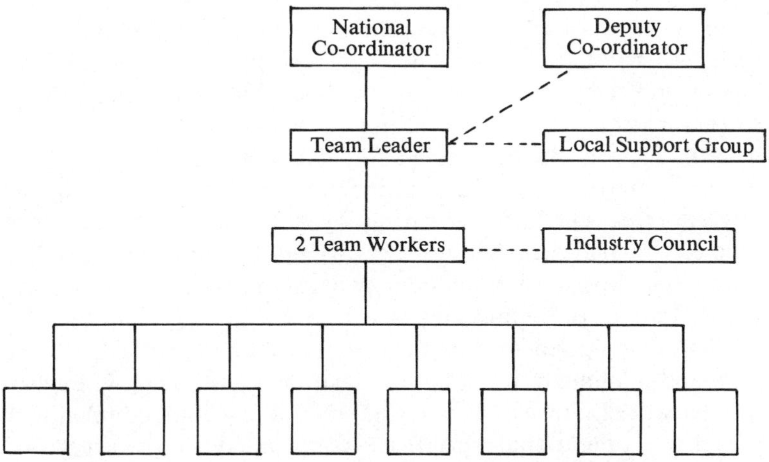

Projects (up to 8) with scheme consultants and young workers.

young people working on a project and imparting elements of that skill, the scheme consultant was also seen as having an educational role. The scheme consultants were to avoid

> 'As far as possible . . . a supervisor or foreman role, since the educational element of the project entails the greatest scope for the young people to be involved in decision making, target setting and group co-ordination.'
> (Draft CI handbook, February, 1972).

In order to provide an opportunity for this educational as well as instrumental role the ratio of scheme consultants to young people was fixed at 1:10 and the involvement of young people was seen in both instrumental, 'a proper job for a proper wage properly done', and expressive/educational terms embracing community involvement and a share in decision making.

The team leader, team members and scheme consultants were to be helped by local support groups, some of which were already in existence, and which were representative of local authorities, trade unions, industry, churches, social and youth work agencies. Additionally the local support groups were seen as being instrumental in encouraging the formation of Industry Councils which, with appropriate representation from the young people, were intended to provide each area with a forum for discussion and planning. The young people themselves were to be actively involved in arrangements for setting up such Councils.

Final responsibility for recruitment of young employees was vested in the local teams who would select from a number of prospective employees sent by the local careers officer. Thus careers officers were to be tied in with the scheme as sources who would refer young people for employment with CI. There was to be positive discrimination in recruitment, selection being weighted towards those who had been unemployed for the longest periods of time or who had personal or other difficulties. The structure of CI during this experimental period may be given in diagrammatic form in Fig. 1 on the preceding page.

CI thus struggled into existence with material support at local level and administrative support at national level being somewhat problematic. Diffuse and somewhat conflicting goals coupled with a lack of operational specificity contributed to the 'teething' problems experienced by the embryonic organization. In the face of these difficulties it is somewhat remarkable that the target figure of young employees was reached and that a structure developed which allowed CI to provide paid employment opportunities within a sheltered and caring environment. The words of a CI HQ member summarize the organizational orientation during this period:

> 'You can take it from me that in the year January through December (1972) it was a question of retrieving as much as we could and making do where we couldn't.'

The build up in recruitment of young employees accompanied by the retrieval process previously referred to might be expected to have had a demoralizing effect on organizational personnel; however an area member recalls that it operated in a positive way helping to bond the relationships between area staff and young people. We may quote in rather extended fashion to illustrate this point:

> 'J. and I were crushed up in a corner of a small room but they (CI employees) could see our conditions and they were a lot worse than their's were which you know was most unusual. In other words somebody else was trying to work in conditions which they might not have stood for. That year in this area there wasn't any money put in by the local authority and as for buying or finding tools and equipment, there was no provision so what you couldn't get out of your sponsors you had to scrounge around for. We even used to go to the housing and maintenance depot to get paint brushes which the L A painters had traded in. We used to get old paint which the corporation didn't want and which had to be knocked up or stirred for two hours to make it into anything like useful. This was the ridiculous set-up that we had, but somehow the young people went along with us. They bore all this with us; we used our own cars a lot dashing here and there and everywhere to get such and such . . . and we'd either get it or not. Whichever way it was the young people were with us and they'd say "Ah well, never mind you know" but they'd be thinking with us, weighing up *our* problems.'

An Interim Period

CI was requested to report on its operations during the first year of its existence by 15th September, 1972 and hence the report really reflects four months of operation from May through to August and in parts is largely symbolic in content.[12] A reply to the report was promised for mid-November indicating whether CI would be funded for a further period; the timing of this reply being rather critical as all area staff contracts were due to terminate on 31st December. A decision as to the continuance of CI was not in fact made by that date and the ensuing interim period was a difficult time in the development of CI. The organization was still able to function however as agreement had been reached that the outstanding balance from the initial grant should be drawn until the end of the financial rather than calendar year, that is, until 31st March, 1973 and all staff were informed that their contracts were to be extended for a further three monthly period. A practical consequence of the delay in deciding the future of CI was that it was not possible for CI HQ to officially inform local authorities of the support facilities required for 1973-74 in time for them to make the necessary budgetary allowance. In the words of a CI HQ member:

> 'In fact they (L.A.s) were saying "What do you want for 73-74?" and we had to say that we didn't know whether we were carrying on. Not until mid-February, 1973 could we officially begin the round of negotiations with L.A.s to guarantee their support for the next financial year.'

In fact some local authorities had anticipated the continuance of CI and had provided for the necessary finance; however, others hadn't and in some areas this support had to be secured at a later date.

This interim period also appears to have had consequences in human terms being a time of great disorientation at all levels of the organization. The NMG did not meet during this time and CI HQ staff made decisions on a day to day basis having no guidance as to overall policy. Similarly communication between HQ and area staff seems to have been adversely affected with CI HQ staff remaining in London in readiness for an announcement about the future of CI rather than visiting the areas to provide some measure of reassurance. A certain amount of mistrust appears to have resulted from this situation and is illustrated by a CI HQ member's recollection of area staff's reactions during this period:

> 'Their confidence in CI as an employer received a certain hammering at that time. Their relationship with HQ was somewhat affected because there were certain members of area staff who were convinced that HQ knew much more than they would let on. You have a chain reaction with scheme consultants losing confidence in area management, areas staff's confidence in HQ being sapped and HQ's confidence in both NAYC and DE being sapped. This happened, although at an intellectual level all parties recognized the difficulty the next above were in. The end result was yet another retrieval process but in a different sphere.'

To help bolster morale a national conference of CI staff

employees was called for December, 1972 at which all areas were represented. It was thought that by this date definite proposals could be put forward and enthusiasm regenerated; however, a decision had not in fact been communicated and the conference became, in the words of a member, a 'grouse shop'. Similarly a meeting of the NMG was scheduled for the 9th February, 1973 in the belief that some indication of the future of CI would be received by that date. The meeting was in fact cancelled as no such indication had been given and a letter from the National Co-ordinator informing members of this sets out in some detail the difficulties that CI was facing at this period. These mainly related to the imminent departure of area staff to permanent employment and the inability of CI to fill the posts until the future of the scheme was ensured. It was also stressed that to terminate contracts abruptly — CI were only legally required to allow the contracts of existing employees to lapse — would be bad for the image of an organization posing as a caring employer seeking to help the unemployed. The pressure from media sources for CI officials to comment on press reports regarding its uncertain future is referred to in correspondence and underlines the point previously made:

> 'It is unfortunate that reports in local papers often appear to be based on information which neither we nor the areas possess. You will appreciate that this causes, on the one hand, further consternation in the areas and, on the other, a growing lack of confidence by areas in their HQ as they presume that we are deliberately withholding information from them. I am not sure we can go on much longer without giving a mere "No comment" answer to press enquiries.'

It was further pointed out that the departure of scheme consultants, resulting in a lack of adequate supervision, and the non-availability of short-term projects might result in redundancies.

Renewal and Expansion of CI

On the 15th February 1973 the Parliamentary Under-Secretary for the DE replied to a question raised in the House with regard to the continuance of CI as follows:

> 'My department will continue to support Community Industry and increase the grant to make available at least 2,000 places under the scheme. Discussions about the detailed arrangements for 1973-74 will now be held with the organizers. I should like to congratulate the NAYC and those connected with Community Industry for what has been achieved to date.'
> (Hansard: Vol.850, p.417).

A memorandum issued by CI HQ dealing with priority issues to be discussed in the light of the above statement suggests that the first priority is to establish 'What is to be the declared aim(s) of CI?' (Memo. 73/9, 15th February 1973).

Inspection of correspondence between the relevant parties during early March 1973 indicates the emergence of a more pronounced emphasis on the 'rehabilitative' nature of the scheme. The emphasis is on the help which CI might give to young people within a given geographical area who are likely to experience more difficulty than their contemporaries in finding and keeping a job; such help being in the provision of work experience which would improve their prospects in the employment field. It is stressed that:

> 'As CI cannot itself offer a career of long-term employment for its young employees it is in their own best interest that their experience of work with CI should help prepare them for subsequent employment.'
> (Letter 6th March 1973).

In order to help achieve this objective it is suggested that a limit of one year should normally be established for a young person's employment with CI; that such a limit be applied in a flexible fashion, and that regular reviews of the young employees' progress should be undertaken. A further suggestion relates to the establishment of a wage rate for young people which would be distinct from local authority manual rates and at a lower level than those then being applied.

Difficulties in reconciling the organizational 'model' of CI as initially proposed and the emphasis now required in terms of the renewal of the grant became clearly apparent at this stage. To those responsible for its early development it now seemed clear that the government was not ready to accept their views of the 'basic premises' on which CI had been founded; a member involved in the discussion expresses disquiet at what is considered a new emphasis and recollects:

> 'We presented a particular socio-economic analysis of the unemployment problems facing young people now and in the future. Essentially this saw the causes of unemployment as two-fold: a recession in the economy which is now being rectified and is bringing unemployment figures down, and, much more importantly, a switch from labour intensive to capital intensive industry, leaving a permanent pool of unwanted, unskilled labour . . . we believed that despite policies encouraging solutions there would remain a pool of unwanted,

> unqualified labour. The CI scheme was designed for this purpose and we saw it having an on-going requirement in our society.'
> (Letter, 7th March).

Similarly the emphasis on 'throughput' of young employees, though phrased in moderate fashion, was seen largely in emotional terms as 'a sword of Damocles over the heads of already insecure young people' rather than as a means of serving their best interests. These and other issues were discussed at a meeting of a newly constituted body responsible for the national management of CI. At this meeting it was agreed that the former National Management Group should be reconstituted as a National Advisory Panel with the oversight of the scheme delegated to a National Management Board (NMB). The NMB was made up of three members nominated by the NAYC, two by the Secretary of State and one each by the TUC and CBI under an independent chairman nominated by the NAYC. Meetings were to be held at least six times a year. The first meeting was held on 6th June, 1973. Examination of the minutes and accompanying documentation[13] of this and subsequent board meetings, supplemented by interviews with Board members, provides a picture of the growth and development of CI during its phase of renewal and expansion.

A member recollects that the NMB's first meeting involved the establishment of the 'identities' of the various parties and a marking out of areas of interest. Thus the TUC representative raised the question of union membership for the young people and the NAYC representatives emphasized their watching brief with regard to CI's educational aspect by reference to a projected CI HQ appointment on the training side. The DE's concern with creating a realistic employment situation was underlined by discussion on the review of progresss of CI's young employees and stress on the legal liabilities of CI as an employing organization. A draft on the agreed conditions attached to the renewed grant for CI was brought to the attention of members so that any amendments could be made before it was ratified by the NAYC executive.

The agreed conditions make explicit the tightening up of the aims of CI and emphasize the 'rehabilitative' nature of the scheme:

> 'The broad aim shall be to assist young people to cope more effectively with life in society, both in terms of overcoming personal problems and by making a positive contribution to their communities.

The particular aim of the scheme shall be to prepare for regular employment (in as short a time as practicable) unemployed young people who for various reasons find it more difficult than their contemporaries to obtain and keep jobs, with special emphasis on the needs of those who are socially or personally disadvantaged. The method of operation shall take the form of work experience in full-time but temporary employment embodying a style of working which is industrially realistic and capable of turning out products economically to the standard of quality required by sponsors; the work situation shall be used to develop the educational and vocational potential of each young employee so that:

(i) his standard of skill, basic knowledge and social attitude can be advanced to the extent that given the opportunity he could take on other full-time employment;

(ii) experience of work in the scheme will lead to a more positive and responsible attitude to society;

(iii) through an experience of participating in the organization of the work project in which he is engaged he may gain social organizational skill of wider community application.'

(NMB/73/5).

In these terms CI is seen as an organization providing a period of stabilisation for young people who for various reasons have problems in securing and holding down employment. This point is further re-inforced in a progress report furnished by CI HQ where there is an explicit recognition that in terms of operating policy:

'CI cannot realistically offer a career of long-term employment. Positive incentives to throughput are to be instituted, including a more deliberate use of the betterment register, regular reviews of young employees by CI in conjunction with careers officers, the greater availability of training provision and the recognition that only in exceptional circumstances is it anticipated that a young person will need to remain in CI's employ for more than 12 months although there will be flexibility in interpreting this general position.'

(NMB/73/1).

This specification of goals is accompanied by a change in the nomenclature of area staff with the label 'management' being substituted for that of 'leadership'. The team leader is now referred to as an area manager (AM) and the tasks of the team members are reflected in terms of the new titles of projects officer (Pr. O) and personnel officer (PO). The management structure of CI thus reflects the construct of a 'model area' employing 100 young people with the team leader's function being the responsibility of an area manager and the tasks of the two team members being formally differentiated in the persons of a projects officer and personnel officer.[14] In addition each area is allocated an office manager and a clerk typist with areas employing over 100 young people being entitled to an additional personnel post. The CI HQ staff complement was expanded by the addition of two further posts, a national personnel officer (NPO) and a national training officer (NTO).

The arrangements governing the employment of area staff were still subject to discussion at this stage and a 'rules roles' framework began to emerge covering such points as procedures for governing the computation and allocation of annual leave, the salaries of existing staff and their conditions of employment, the justification of salary differentials for AMs and POs in areas employing more than 100 young people and the form of the contractual statement issued to staff. It is of interest to note that an additional area of policy agreement still outstanding at this time, eighteen months after the inception of CI, is the role of 'community'; more specifically the nature and extent of involvement of local support groups.

The development of local support groups had reflected the patterns of local interests and initiatives associated with helping unemployed young people which has previously been discussed. Consequently the range of interests represented on them, their structure and the degree of commitment of members reflected these early preoccupations. An illustration of how local support groups may become organized in order to resist the implementation of a particular policy may be given as follows. At the time of the renewal of grant to CI a decision had to be made with regard to which area employees were to receive new contracts. A certain area manager was informed that his contract would not be renewed and on being so informed appeared to accept this; a member of CI HQ recalls however that:

> 'Within the space of a week we had official representatives from the local support group including a trades union official demanding to see the executive of the NAYC.'

The executive appointed a commission of enquiry into the affair which found that there were grounds for not renewing the contract but suggested that it be renewed for a trial period of six months. In the opinion of the CI HQ member the local support group in the area had, until this incident, seldom met and

'. . . had been virtually none-effective . . . all the reports we received from staff in the area were that the support group was virtually a cipher and that the most effective contact was with individual members. The support group only really came to prominence with the intended dismissal of the area manager . . . I think it's also important to bear in mind the area manager's strong affiliation with local affairs.'

A further illustration of the tensions relating to local support in relation to the implementation of national policy relates to the monthly returns made by the area in question. Examination of these returns (NMB/73/30) revealed that for the month in question the ratio of scheme consultants to young people was lower than that generally accepted. This situation appears to have arisen from the recruitment of additional scheme consultants before establishing that sufficient young people would be available to justify the appointments. Instructions were issued by CI HQ indicating that the number of scheme consultants should be reduced by three. The area manager convened a meeting of the area's scheme consultants and reports as follows:

'The scheme consultants to a man appreciated the problem and agreed with the difficulty but felt strongly that there should be no redundancies at this stage because (1) they felt that the numbers could fluctuate indeterminantly and that the period involved was too short to assess a true picture; (2) the potato harvest was to finish very soon; (3) if notices were issued on the date in question this could mean a termination of scheme consultants' employment only two to three weeks prior to the school leaving date; (4) the hardship which could be caused to scheme consultants just prior to Christmas.

The area manager also reports that:

'I personally secured the offer of alternative employment for all three consultants at their own trade locally with the opportunity of much higher income, better hours and overtime, in permanent jobs but they stated they would rather be with CI for the job satisfaction and interest which they have in the young people.'

These incidents bring into prominence the relationship between CI HQ and local support. The extent of involvement of support groups in CI matters as seen by CI HQ during the initial development of CI is set out in retrospective fashion (NMB73/2) as follows:

(1) To help in the selection of area staff by providing the chairman and one or two

members for the appointing committee.
(2) To offer personal support to CI area staff.
(3) To facilitate the operation of the scheme locally by assisting in the provision of both useful personal contacts, materials and equipment.
(4) To liaise with local industry councils.

In these terms the role of the local support group was perceived by CI HQ to be largely supportive and advisory rather than managerial. However, in the majority of the areas the groups had increasingly developed an 'executive' rather than supportive role and this lies at the centre of the recommendation that support groups should be dissolved and replaced by advisory panels. It is suggested that:

> 'The proposed panels would have no executive functions and would not be involved in staff appointments or management processes . . . they would be composed of local people on whose individual expertise CI could draw from time to time.'
> (NMB/73/2).

These recommendations embody a proposed solution to the organizational strains associated with attempts by local groups to assert their assumed 'authority', and incidently preserve their identity and independence, in the face of policy decisions reached at national level by CI HQ. In addition to 'buffering' the organization from pressures at local level the advisory panels are seen as necessary for maintaining the credibility of CI as a community venture:

> 'Without the involvement of local people in the scheme in a formal way CI is likely to appear as a national organization with a number of branches . . . It might be useful to have formally associated with the scheme local people who cannot only advise the area managers of possible criticisms or antagonisms but also be able to defend the scheme if necessary.'
> (NMB/73/2).

The replacement of 'support groups' by 'advisory panels', which would neither have a committee structure nor issue formal minutes, is thus seen as a means of preserving 'community' and at the same time as a mechanism for reducing the tensions engendered by local groups interposing in developing administrative processes. In effect then advisory panels were lists of people who might be consulted on an individual basis at the request of area management and thus possessed no formal structure.

This attempt at redefinition received rather an uneven reception at local level, a member recalls:

> 'When this was communicated by the Board to support groups there was a howl of protest from a number of areas.'

This is underlined by the Chairman of NMB who visited the areas and reports:

> 'It was clear in all areas that the Board's decision had aroused considerable feeling ranging from aggressive hostility in one area, to polite but reasoned comments in most others.'
> (NMB/73/14).

Interviews with an influential member of the local support group, who was also a senior officer of the local authority, in the area which had reacted with 'aggressive hostility' suggests that this support group had seen itself from the onset of CI as being a 'management group' and was not prepared to reconstitute itself as an advisory panel: the support group member reports in rather definite fashion:

> 'We formed a management group in . . . right from the outset . . . when the decision was taken at national level that management groups didn't exist, they'd only existed for about two years but they didn't exist! So we called for the chairman to come up and explain the situation (Chairman of NMB) and he said "Well of course if you want management committees then you can have them but we're not going to call them management committees." So we've got this rather silly system of the area manager being able to call upon individuals and we pointed out what a nonsense this was.'

The member went on to point out that if a paid official of a local authority was consulted as an 'individual' rather than in his official capacity as representative on a committee he would not be able to use the influence associated with that position. By attending a support group as a representative of a local authority committee an official could report back to that committee and thus be better placed to put the case for any resources which might be required.

More generally the reaction of local support groups to their proposed demise, as given in NMB documents, reflected a notion that consultation on an individual basis was not adequate to meet all contingencies. It was pointed out that occasional meetings were necessary to facilitate a sharing of information between local bodies concerned with supporting CI. Similarly it was thought that where officials of local authorities were involved there was a need for the establishment of formal procedures as the commitment of public monies involved the principle of 'accountability'. It was reported that area managers found the support groups of some value as 'sounding boards' for local opinion and the groups were also seen as being a useful 'irritant element' of the CI structure, acting to challenge national policy in the light of local knowledge by conveying their feelings to the NMB.

The outcome of this conflict as to the structure and function of support groups is reflected in a rather uneasy compromise. It was left to local decision as to the style and mode of operation of local advisory panels, the label 'support groups' no longer being used with their broad functions being defined by the NMB. Thus NMB accepted that:

> 'In some areas there would be panels invited by the area manager to offer support on an individual basis (as previously proposed). In others, the panels or groups will meet from time to time informally. In others, the panels or groups will have a more formal structure of chairman, secretary, minutes etc.' (NMB/73/14).

In new areas, however it was decided to encourage advisory panels with the initiative for forming such panels coming from the local area manager, though in special circumstances

> 'A panel might form itself into a support group if it so wished.' (NMB minutes).

This action was intended to help ease what was seen as the growing 'problem of communication' and to help 'personalize' the expanding organization. Such problems were inferred from the NMB Chairman's observation that local groups felt CI was becoming too autocratic and too centrally controlled and hence in their view adopting an inappropriate operational set for an organization which had a community basis. A paper outlining the purposes of advisory groups was sent to each area and it was further decided that they should receive a bulletin recording the main business of each NMB meeting.

The formalization and delineation of procedures associated with the expansion of CI is also discernible in attempts to make explicit the criteria governing its central operating processes and by the expressed need to develop structures designed to ensure the maintenance of the organization. With regard to the former it will be recalled that the scope of work projects was defined rather loosely, though pointed up by examples, in the early phase of CI, as 'new jobs that would not otherwise get done'. How this should be interpreted in an operational sense is now set out in explicit fashion as follows:

> 'It is necessary to establish that the sponsor of a project has no resources available to undertake the work and there is sufficient evidence to indicate that without intervention the work would not be undertaken within the next few years. The work has to be judged worthwhile in community terms and it is necessary to establish that the sponsor will not gain financially as a result of CI undertaking the work rather than another contractor. *Contracting* to undertake the work brings home to the sponsor that the working group is not only paid by CI but is also responsible for management and control. It is necessary to establish that a suitably qualified scheme consultant is available to supervise the project and that the sponsor will provide the required tools and materials necessary for its implementation. The work undertaken must be of a kind which will allow group participation and provide jobs that are judged worthwhile. Worthwhile jobs are thought to be those which provide an opportunity for varied and interesting work giving the young person the opportunity to develop his 'work potential' without departing from realistic industrial practices.' (NMB/73/4).

Details of proposed projects were to be submitted to CI HQ for approval before being undertaken, thus providing a standard policy with regard to the type of work undertaken and establishing control over the implementation of work schedules. The overall strategy with regard to approval or disapproval of work projects is seen in terms of the need to maintain a balance between the 'educational' aims of CI and the provision of a context for work involvement which is sufficiently realistic to provide a basis for introducing young people to 'open' employment. This is reflected in an operational sense by the existence of a spread of projects in each area from the physical-centred, environment-improvement type schemes on the one hand to the person-centred project, best illustrated perhaps by the pre-school play group, on the other. The productive tension in maintaining the balance between 'the people v things' work involvement is illustrated by reference to an area which was thought by CI HQ to be 'out of balance', in this respect being geared towards the 'people' side of the continuum. The illustration is derived from interviews with area and CI HQ staff.

The projects in this area tended to be largely of the person-centred type and were justified by a strong emphasis on 'social education' from the management side which reflected a 'participative' approach to the young person's involvement in CI. This orientation appears to reflect two major influences; one being the rather radical nature of community self-help schemes which had become characteristic of the area and the other being the interests of the area staff which essentially involved an inclination to work with young people in informal contexts. The characteristics of the work situation are highlighted by the situation facing a new area manager on the resignation of the original incumbent. On Fridays one work group wouldn't work as there had been mutual agreement with a scheme consultant that Fridays would be a free day; the time sheets being adjusted accordingly. Another group, engaged in cleaning out a canal, was under the supervision of a scheme consultant who undertook some part-time swimming instruction and on three afternoons a week the group would accompany him to the baths; the trips being justified on grounds of 'social education'. These practices, characteristic of this area but by no means general, reflect the difficulties associated with a rather loose approach to management which interprets 'social education' and 'participation' in rather an idiosyncratic fashion. The new manager was chosen with a view to 'redressing the balance'; a member of the appointing committee recalls:

> 'We wanted somebody in there who would sort the situation out, redress the balance, get a bit of realism into the situation and who was tough enough to stand up to the inevitable brickbats which would come from local concerns.'

This illustration points up the desire to secure what is considered an appropriate mix of projects and the mechanisms, at some cost to the individual involved, used to obtain it.

With regard to the generation of structures relating to the maintenance of CI a centrally organized training system is seen to be required (NMB/73/10); the following needs being singled out for attention: (i) induction and initial job training for area staff; (ii) training to meet special or individual needs. Induction training is intended to provide an introduction to CI for the area staff, the pattern being varied according to the particular position involved.

The proposed content of job training for area staff is set down in general fashion as follows:

(i) Area managers: functioning as a manager: involving a consideration of (a) decision making (b) supervising staff (c) recognizing and handling problems.
(ii) Personnel and projects officers: (a) the organization and function of the Youth Employment Service and local government (b) working in groups (c) effective interviewing (d) maintaining personnel records (e) project planning and scheduling (Pr.O. only) (f) supervising staff (Pr.O. only).
(iii) Scheme consultants: (a) Young employees' adjustment to work and the community, (b) working in groups (c) problems in the work situation.
(Discussion with NTO).

Training for young employees is set out under the heading of 'social education' (NMB/73/26) and is said to reflect the application of two criteria:

(a) The course must offer an important learning experience to the young employee . . . aspects of this could be things such as improving his ability to function socially, learning to speak and act with confidence and listening to and understanding others.
(b) The course must be conducted in a way that will promote this learning . . . it should be organized and structured so that it is likely to achieve its objectives and it should be under responsible supervision.'

A half day per week was originally set aside for the social education of YEs but the paper indicates that this had not generally been used and response to the provision of additional non-vocational courses was thought to be disappointing.[15] A self-reflected criticism of the provision in this area is given in the following terms:

'A general criticism which could be made of CI's efforts in providing social education is that too little thought was given to what the young employees could be expected to gain from training. Social education should be used to provide young employees with experiences and information which will promote their development in areas where they are thought deficient; this must involve more careful consideration of the needs of the employees and the aims of the courses than has been given to date.'
(NMB/73/26).

A further central concern of the growing organization relates to staff pay and their conditions of service and is reflected in discussions about superannuation and the formation of a staff association. A superannuation scheme for adult staff was supported by the NMB on an optional and contributary basis and the question was brought to the fore by an agreement in principle[16] that government support for CI would be continued until 31st

March, 1975. Arrangements for such superannuation were discussed in relation to the Social Workers Pension Fund (SWPF) to which all members of NAYC could apply after a minimum period of service;[17] it being argued that CI employees were de-facto employees of NAYC. Additionally the Board agreed that:[18]

> 'We should get away from the unsatisfactory system under which the first staff were appointed, namely "a rate for the man within an agreed range for the job" to a consistent policy throughout CI of a "rate for the job".'
> (NMB/73/7).

It is further suggested that:

> 'CI stands or falls on our ability to recruit and keep good scheme consultants. AMs are reporting an increasing number of resignations because of the low wage and are experiencing growing difficulties in filling vacancies.'
> (NMB/73/9).

The whole question of salaries and conditions of service was deferred pending a review by the Civil Service Dept. However, a further indication of the move towards 'rationality' in CI is seen in the emergence of an employee negotiating group with responsibility for ensuring agreement over the pay and conditions of service of CI employees. A conference, attended by AMs and POs, was convened to sound the opinion of members with regard to the appropriate form of procedure for representing staff views. The general reaction of the conference (NMB/73/27) was in favour of a Staff Association for adult employees[19] and it was recommended that liaison be established with the TUC concerning recognition of such an association and the position of members belonging to unions.[20] The initiative in actually forming a Staff Association appears to have arisen in informal discussion between area managers; eleven of the thirteen areas had expressed themselves in favour of such an arrangement. The NMB was informed that a Staff Association had been formed and an executive committee elected:

> 'Our members have asked me to write to you with the request that the NMB afford us sole negotiating rights. It is envisaged, subject to this agreement, that a meeting between the Board and our committee can take place. I look forward to receiving your reply at your earliest convenience.'
> (Letter to NMB from AM 23rd October, 1973).

Though the young people were to be excluded from participation in the Staff Association another means was ostensibly open to them for ensuring their involvement in organizational process.

The avenue for ensuring participation by young people in the operation of CI lay in the establishment of area industry councils (AIC). In these councils it was intended that rank and file personnel could debate matters relating to the principles and practice of their organization and communicate their observations to CI HQ or the NMB. The councils were thus seen as providing a structure through which the young people could discuss their interests and be realistically involved in organizational planning and management processes. A thumbnail sketch of the operation of local industry councils submitted to NMB by CI HQ provides an indication of how they were perceived to be operating during this period:

Area (i) '. . . (the area) considers that participation of young employees is good and the results of action taken from meetings support the need for industry councils.'

Area (ii) 'It became doubtful whether the meetings provided any real benefit. Monthly meetings in the initial stages were changed to quarterly meetings and the industry council has now not met for 5 months.'

Area (iii) 'There is an apparent lack of interest of young employees in . . . towards an industry council. This may be due to lack of initiative, imagination and motivation of the management team in the past and more recently representatives of the projects have refused to attend meetings.'

Area (iv) 'The young employees are not really interested and needed to be pushed into attending meetings.'

Area (v) 'Due to lack of interest from the young employees meetings were dropped until September this year when a very satisfactory meeting was held. One young employee represents each project and one of the POs sits in on the meetings. It is intended to hold meetings monthly.'

Area (vi) 'The management staff find difficulty in identifying the effective and meaningful role of an industry council bearing in mind the existing means for individual young people to express opinions and concern to scheme consultants and PO.'

Area (vii) 'Young employees appear to feel that because the works council has no power to influence the terms and conditions of work the meetings lack purpose.'

Area (viii) 'The meetings appear to have lost their usefulness as the young employees now have their own shop steward through their union membership. They feel this to be a more effective form of representation as grievances about pay, hours of work and holidays are out of area management hands.'
(NMB/73/29)

The involvement of young people in the processes of their organization through area industrial councils thus appears to be rather marginal. The factors contributing to this situation are summarized as follows: (NMB/73/29) Young employees feel that the councils have little or no influence in organizational decision making and consequently find other, non institutional, means of airing their views and grievances. The rate of turnover of young employees mitigates against the effective functioning of the type of structure developed to encourage participation and communication. The purposes of the councils are somewhat ill-defined and may reflect an ideological commitment to press young people into 'participative democracy' because it is regarded as a 'good thing', rather than reflecting the fact that the young people see this as a means whereby their views receive careful consideration and are actually acted upon. Somewhat at a loss to deal with effective participation by young employees in their operation of their organization the NMB decided to encourage 'flexible arrangements to suit an area's needs'.

Reflections on the development of CI during the first two years of its operation and resolutions with regard to its future development are contained in documents prepared by DE (NMB/73/39) and by the NMB Chairman (NMB/74/1). The thinking associated with both papers is reflected in the New Year Message from the NMB to area staffs which is of interest as it reveals in explicit fashion a preoccupation with the degree of 'bureaucracy' in CI; concern is expressed about the degree of centralized control and the need to devolve more decision making functions to area staff is emphasized. It is stated that the debate about the goals of CI, the 'career for life' as against the 'preparation for work' positions, is 'now regarded as buried'; however, the importance of the social education aspect of CI is stressed and it is of interest to note that the parent document (NMB/73/39) suggests that:

'There has perhaps never been a clearly agreed and understood plan for what

social education in a CI context was all about.'
(Para. 16).

Three levels of social education are then distinguished:

(i) A basic level associated with the development of YEs' characteristics as expressed in the phrase 'help them stand on their own feet'.

(ii) The development of an understanding and interest in 'community' by being part of an organization capable of 'responding to community needs'.

(iii) The widening of the YEs' interests.

With regard to the latter point a realistic note is struck in the following terms:

'Social education might also seek to develop other interests. However imaginatively organized CI might be, many of its employees are likely to end up in routine jobs which might attract high wages. The future life style of youngsters might assume a familiar pattern of work, flat life, children, football and TV. There is nothing worse perhaps than the patronage of liberals who would attempt to change that in the belief that they know what is *right* for others, but given the opportunities many youngsters might want to develop hobbies or other interests. Youth clubs might fail to attract them but within CI, given a sensible working out and arrangement of projects, scope might be created to help youngsters discover interests.' (Para. 17. NMB/73/39).

Social education is seen (NMB/74/5) as a means of assisting each individual to social and personal maturity by

'(i) helping him to value himself as a human being with a positive contribution to make to his company;

(ii) assisting him to self-knowledge and to increased understanding of others and the society in which he lives;

(iii) making him aware of opportunities for his development as a person, and more able to use them.'
(Para. 2).

It is pointed out that these notions are built into CI and it is suggested that they 'largely determine the whole approach of the staff to their work'. The need for sensitizing staff, particularly scheme consultants, to opportunities for learning which take place in the work situation is recognized and it is suggested that a programme of staff development should be started which has as its aims 'to increase awareness in all staff of the need to actively seek improvements in their skill as social educators and to suggest ways in which this could be done'.

Thus the onset of 1974 for CI was a time of organizational re-appraisal coupled with a growing realization that the young people in its employ required considerable skill and expertise from those most immediately concerned with them and that this should be recognized in their training.

Theoretical overview

It is perhaps useful to conclude a discussion of the origin and development of Community Industry by considering some theoretical implications embodied in the term 'organization'. There is a voluminous inter-disciplinary literature on the topic of organizational structure and behaviour (Pugh, 1966; March, 1965) and Silverman devotes the first chapter of his 'Theory of Organizations' to the question of definitions. In attempting to synthesize the distinguishing characteristics of organizations from such definitions he suggests that:

> 'an ideal type of formal organization should stress at least three distinguishing features . . .
>
> 1. Organizations, unlike other social arrangements, arise at an ascertainable point in time. They are easier to perceive as artefacts, consciously established to serve certain purposes which are generally stated at the time. Their founder(s) further provide them with a set of rules which generally lay down clear lines of authority and communication with the intention of ensuring that those purposes may most readily be attained.
>
> 2. As artefacts, organizations will be characterized by a patterning of relationships which is less taken for granted by the participants who seek to co-ordinate and control.
>
> 3. It follows that a relatively great amount of attention will be paid in organizations to the discussion and execution of planned changes in social relations and the 'rules of the game' upon which they are based.'
> (Silverman, 1970, p.14).

These views reflect a literature which focuses on relatively permanent kinds of organizations and tend to neglect what Palisi (1970) calls 'transitory associations' which have a limited life span.

Such transitory associations may serve as the carrier of ideas and provide a stimulus for organizations of a more permanent kind. In such circumstances the first distinguishing feature mentioned by Silverman is rather too tidy a description even in the ideal case of how normative organizations might originate and move along the transitory-permanence dimension. Such a movement clearly has implications for structure, and in the development of CI we have seen how an 'ideal' is given organizational form embodying a co-ordinated system of positions and functions. In this development we may discern how the pressures referred to by Selznick, bring about 'the institutionalization of relationships which are thus removed from the uncertainties of individual fealty or sentiment' (Selznick, 1948, p.25). CI is, however, officially committed in its goal orientation to 'non-rationality', the term being used in a sociological sense, and this element is seen as an integral part of its formal structure. The organization thus represents an interesting departure from other organizations where the 'non-rational element' is normally seen as part of informal processes.

In attempting to understand the emerging organizational disposition of CI we may turn to Etzioni's paper (1960) which provides an important corrective to the view which uses organizational goals as 'yardsticks' for measuring organizational performance. The substance of his critique of the goal model approach as related to organizational effectiveness, is that goals are 'cultural entities' or ideal end states and consequently, since the resources for achieving these end states nearly always fall short of those required, 'social units are less perfect than their cultural anticipations'. The alternative position advocated by Etzioni addresses the question 'under the given conditions how close does the organizational allocation of resources approach an optimum distribution' rather than 'how devoted is the organization to its goals'. Thus our attention is directed towards resource distribution, and we see that CI during its initial phase had to devote considerable resources to mere survival. It did this by attracting human material 'inputs', by creating an administrative structure consonant with its legal liability as an employer, and by coping with environmental pressures at local and national level. The growth of CI points up the processes of accommodation and compromise associated with environmental adaptation. This is particularly well illustrated at local level where, as we have seen, the visible results of projects completed to a 'satisfactory' standard, with all that this implies in terms of the continuing allocation of human and material resources, was a necessary means of securing further work and support, which in turn affected recruitment. We may note, however, that the tension between 'social' and 'work' emphases, often described in conflict terms, may be a productive force (Coser, 1968) constituting the essential dynamic of the organization, and this will be a reoccurring theme as we develop our account in subsequent chapters.

Notes

1. At the onset of the research Community Industry employed approximately 650 young people in eight geographical areas: Dundee, Glasgow, Liverpool, Mexborough, Newcastle, Newport, Sunderland and Teesside. Though expansion into additional areas had been authorized and the process of recruiting additional young people begun, the research brief restricted the investigation to the eight original areas during the period October 1973 to September 1974. At the time of writing it has been announced that Community Industry will expand to accommodate 5,500 places.

2. The research strategy developed for examining the personal and employment circumstances of the samples of young people described in this book reflect a commitment to what has been termed 'multiple operationism' in social science. This refers to the adoption of a number of methods which complement one another in order to overcome the weaknesses inherent in reliance on any one technique. Both 'soft' and 'hard' methods were employed with the investigators moving from unstructured individual and group interviews to initial on side monitoring and subsequent periods of extended observation to quantitive techniques involving scale construction; a content analysis of available information located in files at Community Industry Headquarters was also undertaken. Guidelines which were developed for the implementation of the research strategy reflected three major considerations. It was thought desirable that the field work in each area for the 'qualitative' aspect should cover a reasonably extended period of time and yet allow for replication; a month was thought to be an appropriate period in this respect. Secondly, as many geographical areas as possible should be covered in the time available for this aspect of the work; two field workers being assigned to make parallel studies in different geographical areas. Finally, it was decided that CI staff and young employees in each area would complete a questionnaire administered by research staff in accommodation arranged by area personnel. The questionnaire information was used to furnish measures for the 'quantitative' aspect of the research. It was also decided that comparison groups of young people in open employment and those in the

last year of school, drawn from each geographical area, would also complete the questionnaire.

To meet the first two points two members of the research staff spent periods of participant observation in five areas for a period of five months. Appropriate liaison was established between research workers during the first period of observation to ensure a unified approach to this aspect of field work. With regard to the latter point a limited amount of pre-testing of possible questions for inclusion in the questionnaires was undertaken during the initial phase of the research. This preliminary work of questionnaire construction was supplemented by visits to a local CI area where discussion groups of young people were set up in order to assess the level of verbal responses to particular questions and estimate the degree of co-operation expected for this aspect of the study. Three questionnaire booklets were prepared for administration to the various groups involved in the research; one for school leavers, one for CI young employees and apprentices, and one for CI adult employees. They are to be found in an appendix. For a discussion of some of the methodological issues associated with this research strategy the interested reader is referred to Murray (1978).

3. Local initiatives were also underway at this time; the Sheffield branch of the Community and Youth Service Association called a meeting of interested parties on 1st July 1971 to see how unemployed youngsters in that area might be helped.

4. The proposals were deemed irrelevant in that they did not consider the inequalities of opportunity which were seen by the author to discriminate between those staying on at school and those leaving early. (New Society, 5th August 1971.)

5. Held in Sheffield on 17th August 1971.

6. This was the earliest date at which release could be secured from previous employment, and the fact that the CI HQ team was not in post on the same date is quite fortuitous.

7. Dates of meetings: 20th January 1972; 25th May 1972; 11th September 1972.

8. The eight original areas eventually chosen for CI as described in Note 1.

9. The originator of 'Enterprise Ulster' visited CI areas towards the end of the experimental year and provides 'external' validation for this point. In a letter dated 6th December 1972, he writes: '. . . my visit brought home to me the need to have the close co-operation of the LA in each area . . . At present a great deal of valuable time of the area staff has to be devoted to finding, indeed even scrounging, stores and equipment'.

10. The first two recruits were employed in the week beginning 17th April 1972,

and the end of month totals for the following five months were 225 (May); 368 (June); 449 (July); 505 (August).

11. There were 822 applications for the 24 area posts which were advertised in the press.

12. This report was compiled by the National Co-ordinator for CI and the Chairman of the NMG.

13. Papers accompanying minutes are referred to in sequence as NMB/73/1, 2, . . .

14. In areas employing less than 50 young people a personnel officer would not be appointed. Standard salaries for new appointments to these posts were agreed, being £2,370 for area managers and £1,685 for PrOs. The office manager received £1,350 with the young people being paid on a scale based on that for local government manual workers: £8.06 at 15 years, £9.85 at 16 years, £11.64 at 17 years, £13.43 at 18 years.

15. Listed in order of the number of YEs in attendance, the non-vocational courses included (i) Conflicts in Society (WEA course of 1 week initially, then 4 hours per week for 8 weeks; 58 YEs attending); (ii) Scottish Association of Youth Clubs weekend courses (6 courses with 44 YEs attending); (iii) an FE liberal studies course (4 hours per week for 10 weeks with 36 YEs attending).

16. Reported at NMB on 7th August 1973.

17. A minimum length of service, fixed at 6 months, was required before application could be made to join the scheme with NAYC operating on a 6 per cent contribution from both employer and employee. The amount of pension payable was determined by multiplying the average salary over the last three years of work by $\frac{1}{60}$ th of the number of years served under the scheme.

18. It is further suggested that AMs should receive an additional £100 per annum in areas employing 150 young people and £200 in areas employing 200 young people. (NMB/73/8)

19. Young employees were to be excluded on the grounds of the short-term nature of their employment and their apparent lack of interest.

20. The TUC indicated that it would not recognize a Staff Association as having negotiating rights except on the basis of it being an interim non-registered organization awaiting appropriate union representation. Affiliation to the Civil and Public Services Association was discussed but came to nothing.

References

COSER, O.F. (1968). *The functions of social conflict.* London: Routledge and Kegan Paul.

ETZIONI, A. (1960). Two approaches to organizational analysis: a critique and suggestion. *Administrative Science Quarterly.* 5. 257-278.

Manpower Services Commission (1977). Young People and Work. London.

MARCH, J.G. (ed.) (1965). *Handbook of organizations.* Chicago: Rand McNally.

MURRAY, C. (1978). (In Press). Methods and Measures. In Murray, C. (ed.) *Youth in Contemporary Society.* Windsor: NFER Publishing Co. Ltd.

PALISI, B.J. (1971). Some suggestions about the transitory permanence dimension of organizations. *British Journal of Sociology.* 20. 200-206.

PUGH, D.S. (1966). Modern organization theory: a psychological and sociological study. *Psychological Bulletin.* 66. 235-251.

SELZNICK, P. (1948). Foundations of the theory of organizations *American Sociological Review.* 13. 25-35.

SILVERMAN, D. (1970). *The theory of organizations.* London: Heinemann.

Chapter 2

Goals, operational commitments and environmental constraints

Values and ideologies

An examination of the way in which the 'caring role' of CI is interpreted in terms of observations of day-to-day activities provides an insight into the general system of values and ideological commitments which characterize the operating set of CI. The term 'caring role' as used by members of the area staff* refers to a range of functions which are not directly related to the tasks involved in projects. Translated into behavioural terms it frequently simply means the non-rigid application of rules. For example, YEs are supposed to have their pay docked for lateness; but if a SC knows that the person is having difficulties at home, such as his parents don't work and don't get him up for work, the sanction may be waived. Similarly, it may mean discussing problems with the person and even helping him to reach a solution; thus a SC may use the situations of a young person's repeated lateness to initiate a discussion of the reasons for and possible solution of a personal problem. Finally 'the caring role' also refers to discussion with the young people on matters which are important to them or which are seen as relevant to their relationships with other people. It should be noted, however, that the area in which things are *done* is the area of work and that with respect to 'the caring role' what happens is that people *talk*. Furthermore, when this occurs, it is because of the SC's personality and interpersonal skills; it is not a planned part of the organizational structure.

The staff and SCs show a sincere desire to help the young people through the context of the job. Values about what constitutes a 'proper job' and ideologies about work in general thus partially determine what 'helping the young people' means in practice. A 'proper job' which is of benefit to the community is seen as meaning, in the main, some sort of material task involving manual

* The following abbreviations are used: SC, scheme consultant; ASM, area staff member; AM, area manager; PO, personnel officer; PrO, projects officer; RO, research officer; YE, young employee.

work. Projects involving this kind of work are readily available and it makes sense to the staff to look for sponsors who will provide this sort of activity; some of the projects for girls are, however, exceptions to this general case. It is felt to be important that CI should have some visible material effect on the community by building, renovating, decorating or otherwise physically influencing the surroundings so that more sponsors will accept CI's services. Jobs which involve such physical modifications of the surroundings are also readily seen, both inside and outside CI, as being 'real work'; in particular the fact that local authority functionairies *see* that CI does 'real work' is important to the maintenance of CI at the area level. It is, therefore, not surprising that most of CI's SCs are skilled or semi-skilled manual workers; these men are needed so that the types of projects which are obtained can be executed to an acceptable standard so that further projects of a similar kind will be forthcoming. Thus SCs are hired as joiners or bricklayers with some knowledge of young people rather than group workers with some knowledge of joinery or brickwork.

The end result of this orientation is that the meaning of 'helping' the young people and the perception of their problems reflects the background experiences of the staff involved. Varying degrees of sophistication exist amongst the staff and SCs in accounting for these problems and in suggesting ways of overcoming them. One thing is common though to almost all accounts; the problems tend to be seen in psychologistical terms referring to the individual characteristics of the particular young person. The young people are said to have low self-esteem, to lack self-confidence, to be lacking in discipline or respect for authority:

ASM: 'I see CI as giving an opportunity for a youngster to come out of a poor environment or from bad social circumstances and find a relationship with someone they can trust and find a job they can do well even if it's only making tea, and somebody says "Well done . . ., that was a super cup of tea you made" and then building on that, finding his latent potential and putting it to work in ordinary work, nothing sophisticated — nothing special about it. And then the youngster gets confidence 'cos I think a youngster wants to work, and I think every youngster wants a discipline in life. It might not be the discipline that I've got, but they want some discipline, some controls . . . Even the toughest youngster likes to be *guided* in what he wants to do. Likes to have someone to come to so he can ask "What do I do next?" He wants to know, he wants guidance, he wants help, he wants support, he wants a friend!'

The suggestion made here is that the antecedents of 'the problem' are deficiencies in the physical and social environmental of the young person which somehow give rise to 'a lack of confidence' and a generalized uncertainty. In other words, the problem itself is some sort of deficiency in the individual which is to be rectified by a certain kind of social relationship with another person. Attention might also be drawn to the apparent paternalism of the remarks and the implied passivity of the YE, matters which will be referred to subsequently. In a conversation between a staff member and a member of the local support group, the perceived nature of the 'problem' was implicitly conveyed in terms of a definition of successful outcomes:

ASM: 'Whether you do anything to the home background, I doubt very much, but I think we can get them to attend 40 hours and apply themselves 40 hours. Find work and stay in work, then that in itself is as much as we could *hope* to do.'

It is apparent that the problem with which CI is attempting to deal, is some sort of failure with regard to the work situation. Another staff member remarked:

> 'If you can get good time-keeping, reporting sickness, like in outside industry, then the rest follows by itself. Initially, you're not pushing, you're giving as much support as they need. They get to the point where they've got the confidence, and then they don't want your support, so they can fit into a work situation a lot better because they want to work on their own, and they know then that they've got a time limit you know, the Company's making a profit. Not only that, I mean, they're wanting to make money. They're not happy on £12.00 per week, they want to do bonus work, they want to do overtime, they want to be coming out with £20.00—£30.00 a week. By the time they've worked long enough with us, they're getting to a state where they're doing a good day's work.'

Thus we may see the 'problem' as expressed in 'the hoped for' outcome; additionally, some *parts* of the 'problem', failure to keep good time, failure to report sickness, failure to maintain output, failure to do 'a good day's work', are seen as arising from a 'lack of confidence'. It is also interesting to note in the above quotation certain values which are perceived as being related to an economically active work life; desire for money, bonuses, overtime. Various sorts of deficiencies in terms of being able to get a job in the first place are seen as constituting other parts of the 'problem'; this may again be illustrated in terms of desirable outcomes:

> ASM: 'Whereas now, having been subjected to interviews in CI, having been subjected to management and being able to cope with management in CI, they can go and sit through an interview which they wouldn't have done. So therefore jobs asking for letters of application and the willingness to go and sit for 10 minutes to be interviewed, I think they are now ready for that, which a lot of them weren't . . . If they've got the confidence to knock on the door and say "Excuse me, I'm here for an interview at 10.00 a.m." that to me is what we are trying to do rather than teach them to paint or be a joiner.'

It would thus seem then that another part of the 'problem' as perceived by CI staff is located in the inability of the young people to deal with interviews and the procedures associated with obtaining a job.

One important underlying assumption of area staff's ideology which is taken as axiomatic, to the extent that it is never mentioned let alone questioned, is that these young people should have a job and that it should be a permanent job. Given that axiom, the fact that the young people do not get or keep jobs, unemployment is seen as presenting a 'problem', with the reasons for this being a 'problem' appearing not to be generally examined; it seems to be a taken-for-granted fact'. There is a repository of 'conventional wisdom' concerning 'poor environment' and 'poor home background', but these notions are not connected in specified ways with the 'effective causes' of not getting or not keeping jobs. These 'effective causes' as we have seen are conceived as deficiencies in the individual young person: these deficiencies are seen as producing ineffective performance in industrial situations, in interviews and interactions with superiors. Discussions with CI personnel suggest that it is these individual deficiences which are construed as being the primary object for action, that is, as the 'problem' with which CI is attempting to deal. There is some vague awareness of the importance of the way in which the young employee relates to other agencies: the schools, the police, the Youth Employment Service, industry. These relationships are sometimes seen as diminishing the young person's options or as being unjust. Alternatively, they are seen as resulting in a failure to 'bring out the potential' of the young people. Both aspects are condensed into a phrase which was sometimes used: 'A lot of these kids have never had a chance to show what they can do'. For example, a scheme consultant said:

> 'When we get these boys, we get the impression from certain departments that they're no use to anybody. I mean, they must be some use. You've only got to look round you at what they've done here. There must be some use in them somewhere. There must be some good to bring out.'

It is perhaps useful at this point to pick up another thread of staff ideology. This is the notion of 'helping the young people'. The staff and scheme consultants are sincerely concerned to help the YEs on a personal basis by giving fatherly advice, support with court cases or help in obtaining jobs, and this certainly seems to take place. The following discussion should not, therefore, be taken as denigrating this good work. That would be a hasty and oversimplified conclusion; rather it should be taken as a tentative indication of some ways in which staff belief systems may place limits on the ways in which 'helping' is perceived:

> ASM: 'You build up a relationship whereby the youngster learns to accept, not just authority, but responsible authority; authority that he can see a reason why it exists for a start. If he can learn to accept that, he will learn to accept that no matter where he goes, he is going to be told to do a job, and how to do it . . . that's half the battle; if they can accept that, not all authority is bad and against them. Then we've established something else. If they can accept that people are interested in them and want to help them because from many of their home backgrounds they've never had this feeling before or genuine interest and caring, then that's something else we've established, and if they can actually get these factors, plus the fact of getting a job and the stability that a job gives them. If they can have all those things together, then it may, you never can tell, it may do them some good for when they leave us, because they in their turn, might change that vicious circle slightly . . . We are trying to incorporate every aspect of what the average citizen in society has, and we are trying to be able to give some degree of that to the kids who are at the bottom of the ladder.'

The nature of the 'problem' and its causes are thus conceived in a fragmentary way. It may be that the staff do not, as a result of their backgrounds, and previous experiences, have a form of cognitive organization which allows them to conceive of the situation in any other way. It is also possible that the CI's operational set with its orientation towards 'industry' does not allow for the possibility of seeing the 'problem' in terms other than those of individualized deficiencies arising within, and related to, the work situation.

Several important elements of the staff belief system are present in the following exchange which took place at a Staff Association Meeting during which discussion turned to appropriate salary scales for scheme consultants. Some compared their pay with that of tradesmen. It was pointed out that this was not valid because scheme consultants might be asked to do projects not related to their trade skill, though in practice this seemed not to happen:

ASM: 'A scheme consultant basically can take 8 young people and get them to work.'

SC: 'And teach them something.'

ASM: 'Not necessarily. If you can teach them to come out to work and to want to work in that respect. But nobody's asking you to teach them any trade or anything.'

SC: 'No, no. I agree.'

ASM: 'All we're trying to do is put into them some confidence that they'll want to go to work. You're not going to teach them all that much in a year, apart from coming to work, wanting to work.'

The scheme consultants, who are mainly tradesmen, find it difficult not to think of themselves as such and the emphasis on work reinforces this. But the main points which should be noted from the above, are the implied passivity of the young people, the implicit statement of the problem in terms of the person and his attitudes towards work, the emphasis on socialization to work roles, and the complete absence of references to other methods which could be adopted as part of the social/community education function of CI. A further constraint also arises from the concept of 'a proper job' and it was said that 'local values' were such that CI would not be accepted unless it was seen to be doing real work. However, the staff perceptions of what constitutes 'real work' also seem to be relevant here. This is suggested by the following dicussion of more 'unusual' projects; perhaps significantly this focused on provision for girls where experimentation may be less threatening for values related to beliefs about 'real work'.

ASM: '. . . the right type of female consultant has been very difficult to get . . . the more creative. We're getting one . . . who we hope will add a new dimension . . . She's got a new approach altogether from us with the girls. In one way, it's much more disciplined. She shows them how to use make-up. She gives them sex education. She took a team round . . . the schools. Well, bully for her if she can do this. I'm all for it.'

RO: 'You're not quite sure it'll work?'

ASM: 'Well, when one doesn't have any talent in that direction; it would be impossible for me to try it . . . for me it's . . . at the opposite end of the scale for me. It's foreign to my whole background, but I think it's terrific, and I'm really looking forward to it.'

RO: 'You think there's been a lack there?'

ASM: 'Oh, I think it's an area we haven't done enough in. We have been too conventional in a lot of things we've tackled. I'm very keen to get consultants who have a flair for something different.'

Here we see very clearly the effect of staff experience on the type of project carried out and ways of doing things with the YEs; it would seem that innovation and change depend on the presence of people with different backgrounds and skills. It follows that the lack of any clearly developed ideas or applications relating to social/community education might be located in the backgrounds of the staff and scheme consultants. This results in the selection of certain sorts of projects which do not readily accommodate the notion of social education:

RO: 'Would you say you did anything on the lines of what might be referred to as "social education"?'

ASM: 'No. That's one we haven't got.'

RO: 'What do you take it to mean?'

ASM: 'Well, I would presume getting them altogether and getting the consultants and young people to mix. Either setting aside one day for a film or something, or a football match . . . getting the scheme consultants and young people to mix socially and away from a work set-up . . .'

RO: 'These are social activities, but social *education* might be a bit wider?'

ASM: 'Social education? Oh yes, that covers a lot. What that means, I haven't a clue.'

RO: 'Are you happy with that area as it is?'

ASM: 'I don't think we're missing out on anything. Honest I don't. I don't think they're being worked that hard during the day that they're going to miss out on anything as such.'

It could be said that the above exchange points to the ambiguity of the term 'social education' which leads to difficulties in operationalizing it. Some confirmation for this point may be aduced from comments made at a staff meeting:

ASM: 'I would appreicate guidance on 'social education', and how it's conducted in other areas and how they could plan and run it. This is an area that we haven't really — well we've touched on it indirectly, and are probably touching on it within the teams every day. But we haven't as a committee sat down and had any brain waves. I would like to discuss with other areas any possible ways of introducing forms of social education and any advance we can get from other areas.'

There is thus a suggestion that the term 'social education' does not have much meaning for the staff; it is assumed that 'it', whatever 'it' might be, already happens in the work situation. This is not surprising in view of the fact that the scheme consultants' past experiences are unlikely to have resulted in the development of skills expected of an 'educationalist' in terms of presenting opportunities for active participation of the young people in their development.

Since the SCs are hired as skilled manual workers, the 'sympathetic foreman' role is probably the only quasi-therapeutic role that they could at best be expected to adopt to achieve 'social educational' ends. A small on-site incident illustrates this point. Members of a team were levelling a path by distributing hard limestone and after a while several of the YEs began to show an interest in the stones, particularly those streaked with calcite. Eventaully the SC intervened with a good-natured 'Come on lads — stop messing about . . . let's get on with the work!' In discussing this and similar interventions the SC responded:

'Well the main interests of their work here is to get on with the job we are set to do . . . we do most of our things not appertaining to the work on rainy days . . . if they were interested in fossils that would be when we would do it . . . we do have a fairly strict time schedule . . . we have seen rabbits and looked for trout in the river for a few minutes but this sort of thing, you must not let it get out of hand . . . we could have spent all afternoon with the boys edging up to you . . .'

Further discussion with the SC developed about the general educational possibilities associated with the task. The SC, whose fault might be described as an *over* concern for the problems of some of his YEs, finally declared where his priorities lay:

> 'One of my rulings with these lads you see is to teach them a 40 hour week . . . to be in work at regular hours . . . to advance themselves in the best way possible . . . we got lads who came in Monday and Tuesday . . . and that's it . . . no will to work . . . putting nature studies aside . . . the first thing to do is to get them to realize that they are part of society and society does expect some work in return . . . once you can get a YE up to these standards I do agree all work and no play does make a dull boy . . . I would like to see an afternoon of sport, they have it in the army.'

Similarly the AM estimated that the current local CI emphases were:

> '. . . probably 80 per cent industrial, 15 per cent social and 5 per cent on education, and what I'd like to see is 60-70 per cent on industrial, the rest equally divided with the aim always to push down the industrial until there is more of an equilibrium . . .'

Even with such an industrial emphasis there is a genuine concern for the development of the YEs and attempts are made to use the work situation as a means to an end. This may be illustrated as follows:

RO: 'Do the lads have any dealings with the alcoholics?' (in a centre which they were decorating for use by 'down and outs')

SC: 'Some of the boys are a little bit inclined to be a bit frightened of them you know. But the longer they have worked here, the more they have come to accept them, and realize. I explained to the boys how drink can affect people. They are beginning to accept that these men are ill. Plus the fact of how to deal with them. You know, they can be cheeky these men, and if they see they are getting cheeky just to get away out of the road and not start being cheeky back. But at the same time, if they see an old crippled chap trying to get down the stairs, to give him a hand down the stairs, you know. Which can be asking quite a lot, because some of these men are absolutely crawling.'

The point which needs to be made, however, is that because of the backgrounds of the staff and the organization of beliefs associated with these, reinforced by the work-oriented CI structure, there are many lost opportunities for developing 'social/community education'. The major caveat here relates to the girls who find themselves in situations where social/community education can to some extent occur directly as part of the project, as in visiting housebound people:

RO: 'Do they (the girls) get in a position where they can ring up social security and know who to ask for?'

ASM: 'Oh yes. The girls will come in and say "Can I use the 'phone? I want to 'phone the electricity board for Mrs So and So. They've left a card and they haven't come and read the meter yet". Oh yes, I must admit they've really been very good that way and they've caught on very quickly. They're not frightened about going and 'phoning up somebody.'

Thus the development of wider skills on the part of the girls may be a special case with certain kinds of social/community education arising because of the nature of the projects involved.

We have stressed the role played by the industrial backgrounds of CI staff in terms of the way in which this structures their beliefs and how these are brought to play in their relationship with the young people. However, this emphasis tends to neglect the wider organizational structure of CI which exerts pressure in an industrial direction even where staff's background and belief are not consonant with it. It is of some interest that the overall impression gained of the operation of CI in an area where there was a strong youth/community work emphasis in the backgrounds and connections of the area staff was similar, in terms of both methods and operations, to that of the other CI areas observed. It is perhaps in such an area where conditions seem ideal for the development of the social/community aspects of CI, that the effects of wider organizational constraints on these activities are most apparent.

The orientation of the organization and in particular the absence of procedures for handling 'social educational' aspects is reflected in the formal requirements governing the relaying of information to CI HQ. Only 2 of 45 official forms refer to 'educational matters' and these merely deal with recommendations to the National Training Officer that a YE should attend FE classes (C47) or non-vocational courses (C48), and, as far as can be ascertained, no great use had been made of these by area personnel. Similarly the quarterly narrative report does not contain a specific request for information on educational activities. Most of the feedback required is about finance, numbers of people and projects. The formalization of these requests is likely to convey certain meanings to the staff about the organization's priorities; that is they are a source of information on what their job is really about. This is reflected in area staff statements about a matter which is specifically mentioned in the CI Handbook as being a suitable 'non-vocational' element — literacy:

ASM: 'I'd like some sort of literacy course. This is something we've been talking about and got no further than talking about. Because with any squad there are probably a couple of kids who can't read or write or find it very difficult . . .'

RO: 'Why haven't you been able to do that?'

ASM: 'Mainly it's just really the time and the energy of sitting down and thrashing it out. You see, this is the thing, there are so many things flung at you, and although individuals may have time to spare each week, it's the sort of thing which almost all of us are interested in.'

The reasons for the delay in setting up the course seem to be related to a lack of time and the absence of a formal structure for dealing with the matter. 'Lack of time' may be seen as an indirect reference to organizational priorities with other activities being seen as more important and hence given more staff time and energy. There are, of course, some activities which come under the broad 'social education' heading. A few 'outings' may be organized for YEs, some simply visits to beauty spots, others more directly educational such as visits to a forest where the YEs were shown forestry techniques from planting to felling. The organization of such activities seemed, however, to be *ad hoc* and to occur without reference to an overall plan or systematic framework. The activities which are emphasized on a day-do-day basis are those associated with the work group:

SC: 'I will say to them "I want those tools spotless clean when they go up there tonight". They clean them. They do everything they are told. They do it right. And if they have done a job and I don't think it is right, I say to them "Listen, take that down. I won't have it" . . . If you put them all in the one place there is nothing being done and a lot of talking. But if you put two (*i.e.* together) it gives them a sort of competitive idea of life and the one is racing the other on the same type of job, you see. And you get the work done.'

There are other values and slightly different ideologies concerning 'social education' available to CI staff, but these seem not to be so readily articulated within the CI structure. Some of the constraints have already been mentioned in connection with the literacy classes; however there are others, for example:

ASM: '. . . two of the scheme consultants had taken kids for day trips . . . we got them to talk about this (at the SC meeting) and . . . (the AM) asked would anyone else like to organize something like this . . . And they were leaping up and saying "Isn't there anywhere inside we could have for wet days? Because I think my kids could do with some basic arithmetic". You know they were quite interested and keen on doing it themselves — having access to a blackboard and dealing with some of the finer points of the job.'

The quotation reveals the lack of facilities for these kinds of activities and, as pointed out in the concluding phrase, staff find it difficult to see the wider educational potential of projects, tending rather to see them in terms of teaching their own skills.

The following extract from an area staff meeting reinforces the view that occasions for 'social education' are fortuitous, as there is no structure specifically designed to deal with it:

ASM1: 'Is there anything else about projects we haven't talked about?'
ASM2: 'Yes. Schools project. It's going to be half term in a fortnight. We've got four days because the Monday is a Bank Holiday.'
ASM3: 'I'll try to get them into day nurseries again, unless anyone has any objections.'
ASM2: 'I really don't think it's satisfactory to put them in day nurseries.'
ASM1: 'What I personally would like to see us doing is to try to — we've got an opportunity to try to provide some social education.'
ASMs 2 & 3: 'Yes.'
ASM1: 'What days are they?'
ASM2: 'Tuesday, Wednesday, Thursday, Friday. I think we should set up some sort of training programme.'
ASM1: 'Yes, I do. Could you and I sort of pick the bones out of it and basically think of something?'
ASM2: 'Yes, can we set a time to talk about it?'
ASM1: 'Yes, let's make it 3.15 on Monday . . . How many girls are involved in total?'
ASM4: 'Five or six.'
ASM 2: 'I've got seven.'
ASM1: 'That's twelve or thirteen altogether. I'm thinking in terms of transportation. If there's no more than thirteen we can use a minibus.'

Thus, even though the staff in this case are particularly concerned about social education and are at least as well placed in terms of skill and outside contacts and resources as any area visited, they are constrained to running 'one-off' outings and uncoordinated fragments of courses.

There are, of course, additional constraints associated with involving non-CI members at local level. The structure and function of local support groups (SG) has been outlined in Chapter 1 but relevant to our present consideration is the fact that in some of the early meetings of such groups, representatives from local voluntary associations supported a concept of CI which created an ideological division among members:

> 'There were two distinct points of view within the SG. The first saw CI as just a way of getting jobs done and incidentally providing training in skills appreciation for young people. The second saw in CI the creation of an alternative society, and tended not to see any need for work discipline or overall organization. An attempt by members of the . . . (local activist voluntary organization) staff to dictate policy was adequately handled by the AM. In time, these people who did not see CI developing the way they would have wished, did not attend support group meetings. It is now a group consisting of a very capable and realistic chairman, the PCOs of . . . and . . . and representatives of participating LAs.'

The recollections of one of the aforementioned voluntary activists reflects his view of CI as being incapable of containing a critical dialogue:

> 'If I made critical comments I felt very much alone and became "fixed" as the lone voice who made comments . . . I never got the feeling that these could become part of a dialogue . . . at the moment it's just a question of a report about projects that have started, their present stage of development and then you all go away feeling "Ah . . . things are still ticking on" . . . there's no discussion about fundamentals . . . policy, training, aims and objectives, the development of the organization . . . you see I wouldn't think that CI HQ would really want that . . . but I think the local support group should have the authority to say "We want to be this kind of a body . . .", one that can discuss and recommend policy as much as one that just receives reports . . . if it is just the latter then I'm not interested in serving on it . . . I'm still there as a kind of loyalty after being there at the start . . .'

Individuals in the local Careers Service also tend to hold fairly definite views about CI. In answer to a question about the meaning of Community Industry, one CO commented:

'. . . I don't think one should attempt to look for purely social jobs from the point of view of helping old people or sick people, handicapped children . . . because I don't think very many of the youngsters who would benefit from CI are suitable for that kind of work anyway . . .'

A further reply related to the notion of social *education:*

'I think of the sort of boys involved and wonder how far you can take it . . . I would hope that they would develop in their contacts with each other a need to find suitable companionship and activities . . . you see CI boys are not the sort of boys that you would see at a youth club . . . or attached to scout groups . . . they don't organize their leisure normally . . . this community awareness . . . I think it shouldn't be overstressed . . . there's some sentimental thing in this one.'

RO: 'But is it stressed at all?'

CI: 'I think they've got it about right in . . . (area) now . . . I think they were overstressing it initially . . . they allowed the YEs to carry on in all kinds of unacceptable ways . . . they just disappeared from the jobs . . . they didn't want to work so they broke up the wheelbarrow.'

The presentation of our qualitative data so far suggests that the day-to-day actions of organizational members provide little opportunity for the practice of what is described in the formal charter of CI as 'an important part of CI's activities and one which requires thorough consideration'. We may probe the operational set of CI a little further, still within an action frame of reference, by considering the perceptions of members about the nature of their jobs and the tasks they undertake.

Division of labour and organizational tasks

As pointed out in chapter one the division of labour is embodied in the titles of the CI staff: Area Manager; Area Personnel Officer; Area Projects Officer; Area Office Manager and Scheme Consultant. The perceived differences in area staff functions are succinctly portrayed by a scheme consultant:

'As far as I am concerned . . . (AM) is the top man . . . (Pr O) next to him and then the personnel. And each have their own departments to run, and I take any problems to the department responsible. Wages go to . . . (the OM)'.

The division of labour which gave rise to the SC's perception of distinct 'departments' certainly appeared to exist from other points of view as well; the evolution of distinctive job areas being apparent in the recollections of an area PO:

'When the three of us started, we worked as a team. We had disagreements of course, but to start with we worked as a team but we gradually split up. Initially I went round sites with . . . (Pr O). But I said I want to do some of my own, I don't want to go round sites all the time with . . . So it ended up that I just did the personnel side of it; the interviews and that. I just seemed to take it on. It just seemed to fall that way. And . . . did projects. That was before it ever came out that we needed a projects officer and a personnel officer.'

The AM's role, being mainly concerned with control and liaison, is much less easily conceptualized by the staff. He is concerned mainly with the maintenance of relationships with the local authority, communicating CI HQ instructions and with the initial stages of dealing with sponsors and potential sponsors.

ASM: 'Well, the AM writes reports. Any of us find projects initially and then pass it on to him and he'll go and see it . . . the initial contact is made and then he'll go and see the sponsor and get it fixed up from there.'

The AM's job involves a considerable amount of 'public relations' work; keeping in touch with the local authority, with sponsors, dealing with enquiries about CI from other agencies, liaising with social services and probation departments. He is also concerned with overall policy decisions and with co-ordinating the activities of the staff. This activitiy is generally sustained by means of visits and by dealing with enquiries and complaints both in person and on the telephone. The AM summarized some aspects of his job as follows:

'I would tend to go to sponsors and say "How's the job going?" . . . I'm very conscious of the importance of the local authority and I want to keep that one right . . . Personally, I see the scheme consultants as my scene . . . When dealing with complaints from sponsors, from outsiders and things like this, generally try to keep the atmosphere sweet . . . Try to create a good working atmosphere.'

The initial negotiations of projects with sponsors, which is also undertaken by the AM, should also be included here in that it seems mainly to be concerned with establishing a relationship with the sponsors; the actual details of the work to be carried out on the project being dealt with by the Pr O and the SC involved.

The following edited sequence of questions and answers with an AM indicates that the lack of 'fit' at local level between CI and its Authority may adversely affect the overall planning aspect of his job. The AM in question tended to use a nearby CI area as a model

'It would really be better if we had been given a sum of money like other areas and left to spend it . . . it's this "cap in hand" attitude . . .'

RO: 'Did you put forward a list of your needs?' (to the LA with respect to budgeting for CI during the coming year).

AM: 'Well, in the past no-one's taken any notice . . . we've had bits from one and bits from another department and one day I happened to say to someone "This is ridiculous, tell us how much it's costing us" and they must have said "We don't really know" and they said £500 or £800 for 1974-5 . . . it was the only invoice they had . . .'

RO: 'Were you consulted in any way about the estimates for the coming financial year?'

AM: 'Not at all . . . it would be nice for someone to come along and ask "What do you think you'll need?" . . . I heard . . . (clerk) mention two or three thousand pounds in one "off the cuff" remark "Oh yes, I think you've got . . ." '

RO: 'But didn't you order specific items and lay down your requirements?'

AM: 'It's very difficult to try and plan what type of tools we may be using . . . I made the point last year about how CI was saving money for the LA but that was to a different chap than . . . (clerk) anyway . . . the question is do I make the moves or CI HQ . . . I was led to believe that the financial side was not for us but for CI HQ to deal with.'

There had been a meeting, early in 1973, between CI, the local authorities in the area and a representative of CI HQ. The LA promised continued support and assuming that this would be forthcoming, the AM sent a general statement of his requirements to the liaison clerk. This did not produce any immediate response and a changeover of clerks responsible for the financial aid previously referred to compounded the delay. The AM had thus tried the formal channels and, in the absence of a support group, seemed unable to lobby further. He was not prepared personally to use the media to 'stir things up' and was hesitant about involving a contact in the council too overtly ' . . . because then it becomes political . . .'. This particular AM was thus caught up in arrangements which served to emphasize his lack of political support at the local government level.

Apart from talking to the YEs on occasional site visits, the AM tends not to deal with them directly other than formally dismissing them when necessary. This action is said to be taken only after discussion with other staff members, unless this is precluded by the need for immediate action. The POs do not implement the dismissal because, as one AM remarked, 'the "senior" PO felt it would interfere with her relations if the kids knew that she could sack, and it's just grown from that'. In general the POs are concerned with 'counselling' young employees, allocating them to projects, dealing with disciplinary matters that are not handled by the SCs, moving young people between teams, dealing with certain 'educational ' matters and giving practical help with certain of the YEs' personal problems. In addition to these internal tasks POs are also responsible for recruitment and placement. Most of these areas of concern are more closely related to the conception of 'personnel work' as it applies in ordinary industrial settings rather than to the 'counselling' orientation described in official comments on the PO's role as contained in the CI Handbook. Concern with maintaining 'the work force', as a major aspect of the PO's role, is illustrated by the fact that as much as one day per week may be given to interviewing YEs, writing letters of appointment, and working out the allocation of the YEs to projects with a further half day spent on organizing the 'new starters' and sending them to sites. A PO described his job in the following matter-of-fact way:

> 'I interview kids, start kids and generally keep a check on them. I mean, I don't want to expand it any more than that. You know, I could tell you that I go out and we have long serious chats; however, to me you look after the kids in the sense that you're the only contact with the administration. You employed them so you're the only face they know. And if they've got anything to say they'll say it to you or the scheme consultant.'

This view was somewhat unexpected in that it does not invoke values about 'caring' and 'support' which are customarily the descriptions given by long serving CI staff about their jobs. Certainly the ironic remark about 'long serious chats' with the young peole appears to allude to prevalent conceptions about the PO's 'supportive' role which he seems to feel are at variance with reality. It was difficult to assess whether the tone of the remarks reflected unencumbered realism or cynicism. Certainly the meaningfulness of the PO's contact with the YEs on site is open to question; a scheme consultant remarks:

> 'They come onto a site "How's the job going?", they're here for a few minutes and off they go . . . I don't think this is right . . . they come and go . . . everything's OK so that's it . . .'

The POs are also concerned with 'administration' in the sense of 'organizing and controlling the work force'. This is illustrated by the following remarks in response to a question about how young employees obtain a job:

RO: 'It wasn't through anybody here?'
PO: 'I don't think so. You could ask . . . (the SC). That's what we're finding all the time — I think I'm going to have to institute a definite scheme consultant's report on the kids because they have far more information than we have. Personnel staff are just not in a position to get to know the kids that well really.'

The PO does, of course, constitute a source of alternative help for the young people:

PO: ' . . . any probation officer or social worker who refers a kid to me must accept that I'm going to use them to help our kids as well . . . if I see that a kid is in trouble . . . they must expect that they'll get a 'phone call from me and they'd better jolly well sort it out. So far as I'm concerned it's a two way thing.'

The POs help the YEs directly where possible, for example by helping the young people to deal with problems about income tax by writing letters and by discussing it with them. There is also assistance with court appearances:

PO: 'It seems to go in phases. Some weeks there's kids popping in and out of court all the time. I suppose on average there's at least one of our kids in court every week.'
RO: 'Do you go with them?'
PO: 'It depends on the kid . . . If I go down and speak on behalf of *every* kid that works for us, what I say perhaps doesn't have any particular value. So I generally restrict it to people who've worked for us for some time, who I can genuinely say "This kid is a very good boy as far as we're concerned he's been no bother and we'd be sorry to lose him as an employee". The only exception being, particularly with the girls, when I know that the parents aren't going to bother to go down with them; then I will go down. Or if the kid asks me to go down.'

In areas which employ two POs one may devote a considerable amount of time to this particular activity.

RO: 'You seem to do a lot of things involving the police and courts — is that a significant part of your job?'

PO: 'Yes. It's a significant part, yes . . . I haven't had much of it recently. You've been unfortunate this week, there's been two! There hasn't been an awful lot of it.'

Though there had not been 'an awful lot' of this sort of activity, its significance rests in reasons other than sheer amount of work involved; thus a scheme consultant when asked 'What does the Personnel's job consist of?' said:

'Well, I would say their job consists of — anything like the boys getting into trouble. Past records and going to visit the police or children's panel. If they are to go to court for a case that came up before they actually came to work here they would represent them from work. And they come and see us and ask what sort of boy he is first of all you know.'

If disciplinary action is to be taken at a higher level than the SC then it may be taken by the PO who acts as liaison with the law enforcement agencies:

RO: 'What's a typical problem for a personnel officer in . . . (area) to deal with?'

PO: 'Oh just the general problems, you know. Somebody misbehaving on site. A consultant may send them in. Fighting. I don't think there is a typical one. Time keeping may be. The thing is if someone's been sent in here, they've either been sent in for suspension or to be dismissed.'

The PO may see himself as having a personnel role in relation to the SCs and be active in the promotion of 'sessions' for them. One PO remarked:

'I like to be quietly looking from the wings, and yet being in the front and visible at the same time . . . give them the support I can . . . occasionally they're wrong and I tell them . . . if two of them have words I bring them together and ask them to re-tell their stories . . .'

Another PO, when asked about her job, was clear that:

' . . . it's possibly 70 per cent with the SCs and 30 per cent with the kids . . . the SCs may think we're just selling them down the river and just shoving the kids back to them . . . they don't always see the whole problem . . . just their little bit of it . . . when the problems come up you go out and have a little chat, and they learn and perhaps not go that way next time.'

She defined 'problems' by citing an example of a SC who wanted to sack a particular YE; in this context the role of the PO was to try and prevent this by putting the case within a wider framework. Such problems were to be solved by talking rather than by way of implementing formal structural arrangements.

While the personnel officers engage in these rather diffuse and wide ranging activities, the Pr O is almost exclusively concerned with projects planning and materials supply. A scheme consultant saw this in industrial terms with the personnel side being an appendage to the central concerns:

SC: '. . . (AM) to me is the boss, . . . (Pr O) is a "travelling foreman" and we are the "charge hands". And that's the scale I work on.'

He went on to say:

> 'Personnel, as far as I'm concerned, are there to do a personnel's job. Not to run jobs.'

Thus defining the role of the Pr O also involves making a statement about the primacy of 'work' as the central plank in staff perceptions of their job. An edited sequence of questions and answers reveals that the AM is frequently the link between CI and particular sponsoring agencies, but that once this has been formalized the Pr O has a crucial part to play in the process of creating and maintaining the 'work situation'. The following interchange brings out the relative importance of the 'work' and 'educational' emphasis in CI:

RO: 'What is the role of the Pr O?'

Pr O: '. . . to keep everything turning over . . . supply people with the materials which they require and, when the AM has sorted out a project, to go in and start working out the details . . .'

RO: 'What are these details?' (In connection with a conversation about a proposed project involving excavation of an old furnace site.)

Pr O: '. . . tools for a start . . . site offices . . . toilets, water, somewhere to wash . . . all their needs and requirements . . . and liaise with authorities if we need heavier equipment than the Archaeological Society can afford . . .'

RO: 'What about the historical significance of the work?'

Pr O: 'We shall use local recruits (YEs) educating them in the area in which they live . . . the museum will send an expert to us to explain the project before we start . . . we'll have somebody coming up at set periods to take photographic evidence and also instruct the boys on any other finds . . . we'll have a pictorial record (after a second prompt concerning more

> permanent CI based educational initiatives) and a written one because it's good for future reference . . . but at the moment we have only other people's cameras . . . we need a CI camera . . . as I'm on sites more than most and I'm connected with the physical side of the work I should have a camera for anything of interest . . . from the work point of view or a local one . . .'

A Pr O may occasionally be involved in obtaining a project, one remarked:

> 'Officially it's not my job to find them . . . but I was the only one who seemed to round them up so I got left with the job.'

He continues:

> 'I'm responsible for the quality and quantity of work . . . I have to know when a job is being deliberately held up because of a training aspect or because the SC is not keeping the kids working, and to know when a job is a high enough standard for CI.'

He wished to emphasize the need for job appreciation courses but felt that 'our SCs aren't really of a high enough standard to engender an enthusiasm for such things among our YEs'.

An interesting alternative definition of 'projects' is available from a local 'Project Centre', one of whose chief officers was influential in attracting CI to the area; he was also a CI support group member. A member of his staff, a local councillor originally employed by CI as a Pr O, defined 'projects' as having to do with more than 'wheelbarrows and cement'. He felt that there was a need to obtain commitment and interest among local people:

> 'We are more of a resource centre . . . information, skills and advice . . . neighbourhood groups . . . to effect policy along with local services, schools, local government and industry . . .'

This is a rather different emphasis from the CI Pr O who summarized his position as follows:

> 'What we've got to aim for is that CI is just a work area which is doing identical to what outside firms are doing but we are not making a profit . . . it is for the benefit of the youngsters . . .'

As a deviation from the general pattern a 'second PO' may be involved in work which is usually associated with the Pr O. This is illustrated in he following remarks:

RO: 'Could you describe what you do?'

PO: 'Well, there are two sorts of routine things that must be done. First, I do the travelling expenses and secondly, I do the statistical return which we send off every month to London. This covers the number of employees who have been interviewed, the number we've taken on, the number who have left for various reasons, why they've left and fitting them into jobs in the various age categories and so on . . . since I joined 6 months ago now, I've been doing a bit of everything to tell you the truth. I see my job as being half projects and half personnel at the moment, because although I'm classified as a Personnel Officer, although I do personnel work, I've been also involved to the extent of going out and trying to get work which is usually the job of the projects officer. The . . . project (house decoration) which started about 4 months ago now, that started up, and the PO asked me if I would look after the project side of it as well because I had been there from the outset.'

This dual responsibility is the exception rather than the rule with the division of labour giving rise to a dualistic perception of the organization in terms of activities relating to 'personnel' and 'project'. Thus in a discussion of 'social educational' activities for the young people, an area staff member (ASM) said:

'In terms of doing our "normal job": personnel officers being concerned with personnel . . . being concerned with projects, you always seem to be operating at such a pressure that you've got one hell of a job, or at least I have, of even mentally letting into your mind the possibility of deviating from it (*i.e.* the division of responsibilities) and saying "Let's stop that and do so and so" '.

The 'projects' or 'industry' side of CI receives considerable emphasis in all areas; this was pointed up by an ASM who, when referring to educational activities, said:

'I would guess that to some extent there are certainly things here that we should be doing but the pressures are all on the daily job; . . . I would rather fail on that aspect (social educational) rather than anything which seriously undermines the job concept . . . The original idea of the work situation as a means of developing the young people still seems sound. But perhaps it's not possible in practice. Maybe it'll always slip over into concentrating on the job, even though one constantly tries to maintain the balance. This is the inherent conflict between "industry" and "the caring role".'

The scheme consultant is mainly concerned with getting his work group to do a job which is acceptable to the sponsor, the Pr O and the AM. He is also concerned with making the young people behave on site in ways which are perceived as appropriate to the work situation, and with regard to this he is accountable to the PO and the AM. While the consultants exercise authority within the work group on matters perceived as directly and indirectly related to the work situation, their powers in this respect are not unlimited and management staff reserve the right to overrule a SC's decisions. In practice this seldom occurs as area staff are conscious of the fact that this tends to undermine the SC's authority with the young people. The PO often acts informally to iron out problems as described previously but may advise the AM on those occasions when he feels that a SC's decision should be overruled; the final decision then resides with the area manager. The usual procedure, however, is for area staff to draw the SC's attention to what they consider is going wrong on a particular site or to informally indicate that the SC is not handling problems in ways that they feel appropriate. Thus with respect to the work on one site, the POs told the SCs that they were being too lenient. They thought that the YEs had had enough time, three weeks, to 'settle down' and that the SCs should now start to enforce rules more strictly. This occurred after there had been some thefts on the site.

The scheme consultants are not generally involved in decision making on an individual basis outside the bounds of the projects which are allocated to them:

RO: 'To what extent are the scheme consultants involved in decision making?'

ASM: 'Well, the scheme consultants don't decide about much other than about the projects. A project is allocated to him. He'll go and estimate it, get materials and whatever. He'll decide where he's going to start, which bits he's going to do. It's a matter of saying to the kids "This is what we're going to do. This is what's to be cut. You put that up there" or whatever.'

RO: 'So he decides what's to be done, which kids are going to do what, the order in which things will be done?'

ASM: 'Yes, yes. He takes the full responsibility of running his project. If he's willing to do that, then it's all left to him. Whether it be even meeting the sponsor one day a week to decide on the progress of it. He can do that, if he's willing to do it.'

RO: 'And are they?'

ASM: 'On the whole, yes. There's only been one or two of them need support . . . they're quite happy to leave it to the staff to go to the sponsor and arrange things.'

Thus, it seems, that the scheme consultants are autonomous within the bounds of their own projects but on a wider front there are certain sorts of policy decisions which consultants are not involved in.

RO:	'What about decisions about expansion: "it's time we had a project in such and such a place?"'
ASM:	'No, that comes from amongst ourselves.'
RO:	'Do they say which projects they'd like to do?'
ASM:	'No. They're told they're to go and do that one and that's it.'

The consultant representatives are, however, consulted in terms of projected activities through a staff/consultants committee. Three scheme consultants are elected by their colleagues as their representatives on the committee and monthly meetings are held at which they and the staff discuss matters affecting area personnel as a whole. Compare, for example, the following extract from a discussion involving the scheme consultants' representatives with the remarks just quoted:

RO:	'When the staff are making decisions and trying to develop policy about where to start new teams and what kind of projects to go for next and this sort of thing, are you involved in this?'
SC1:	'We act as a sort of sounding board representing the scheme consultants.'
SC3:	'He's still the manager as such, but not a manager as known in outside industry.'
SC2:	'He's not the sort of manager who's a dictator.'
RO:	'He doesn't just walk in and *tell* you "We're going to do this"?'
SC1:	'No, no.'
SC1:	'Rather than get to the stage where it can be thrown back at him again, as I say, he uses us as a sort of sounding board.'

In this way the representatives committee is a forum for decision making. It also allows the staff to discover fairly early on in the decision making process whether their thinking is likely to be accepted or whether they'll have to modify their intended approach. Conflicts of viewpoint are thus reduced because only a few people are involved and the decisions have the support of the scheme consultants' elected representatives. The following conversation with SCs' representatives suggests that direct contributions from the mass of scheme consultants to decision making are infrequent and their influence is exercised in an indirect fashion:

RO: 'How do you relate back to the other consultants? Do you see them?'

SC2: 'Well, as far as if there's a particular issue brought up. They have given us the right as spokesmen so we do carry a certain amount of authority where we can say "OK . . . (AM) this is fine. You can go ahead with this. We accept it." But if it comes to a point of issue and we think this could be objected to, then . . . (AM) has given us the right to call in the other scheme consultants, say on a Thursday night, and have a meeting.'

To illustrate this process in action we may refer to a meeting which was called in response to differences between the staff and some scheme consultants about discipline. These appear to have revolved around the limits of the scheme consultants' disciplinary powers and authority and brought to the fore the relationship between staff and scheme consultants in handling disciplinary procedures. The following quotation indicates a staff member's point of view:

ASM: '. . . there's some of them (SCs) . . . well, you know, they're just not capable of deciding what's a big problem and what's a small problem . . . this was one of the big things: with some of them, if you tell them about something they'll give it to you all the time. Maybe a few things have happened on a site; then it happens again, and this time they send them in to me and say "You suspend them". I say "What for? That's the first time it's happened". Then they say "No, it's happened on a previous occasion". So I say "I don't know anything about it. I can't take that sort of action on somebody for a first time thing". So then they think "Right, we've got to tell everything!" So you get everything then! Some of them can't strike a happy medium. I'm still trying to battle that one out.'

This 'ironing out' was done by the scheme consultants' representatives committee with the staff. The scheme consultant's position was put in these terms:

SC: 'We had to iron out with personnel just where the scheme consultant's authority lay about sending a boy home, say, for a misdemeanour. What was happening to the boy was, he was maybe told "Don't be a naughty boy and go back to your site", making the consultant look a fool.'

The outcome of the discussions at the committee was essentially bureaucratic: a paper being issued outlining procedures to be followed by new scheme consultants on handling disciplinary matters thus removing the ambiguity at the centre of the conflict. The suggested procedure involved joint action between the PO and scheme consultant for serious cases of misconduct; two members of staff having to jointly agree that the suspension of a YE was the appropriate action to take. If agreement is not reached then the AM's opinion is sought. The document was introduced to the committee in the following terms:

ASM: 'One point that has been at issue since our last meeting was the point of disciplinary procedure . . . We agreed that we'd draw up some form for new consultants particularly during expansion when there's not going to be the same close liaison . . . It's a draft copy of the procedure — I haven't finalized anything. You can have a read through. I think it's what we discussed. If there are any points or comments you wish to make . . . the gist of it is that where a consultant feels he's got to take action during the course of the day, be it quarter to nine or three o'clock, there's two ways of doing it: if he wants to send them home and leave it at that, then he would send them home, notify the office for the purposes of information and for records, and the boys would return to the site the following morning. If, on the other hand, he felt it was more serious, and he wanted to involve personnel in the detail of it and take joint action, then he'd notify personnel immediately it happened and the two of them would then discuss what course of action should be taken . . . I think that's what we agreed . . . it means the new consultants coming in can get it.'

Thus in terms of the sanctions available to the scheme consultants, they can send YEs away from the site. This amounts to being able to suspend young people for up to a day. The scheme consultants can also report lateness on the time sheet and money is automatically stopped from the YE's pay. These are effectively the scheme consultant's only formal sanctions: they cannot suspend YEs for long periods nor can they dismiss them. On the other hand, the staff (PO) may suspend YEs for longer periods with three days being the maximum; if further action is necessary, after appropriate warnings, dismissal is the likely procedure.

One reason that 'industry', or the project *per se,* gains such emphasis is because of the kinds of backgrounds most of the SCs have. They see themselves to some extent as 'foremen', since this is a role congruent with their previous work experiences; modifications do, however, occur so that the foreman role is played in a benign way, with more patience and restraint than a typical foreman in open employment might be expected to show. They also see themselves as teachers of work skills; again, a form of self-presentation which is readily assimilated within a framework developed by past industrial experiences. This may be pointed up by extracts from a conversation with a SC:

SC: 'I like to work with the lads like I used to in other jobs. You know, you tell them what to do and then you let them get on with it.'

RO: 'How would you say you are different from a foreman?'

SC: 'Well, a foreman on the job, taking house building or anything, he's got an office or something like that. He sees that they are on time . . . he is the man in charge of that job . . . he says "Fetch that man off that job, you do that job, I want that doing". Well that man has got to go and do it. Now with the lads it's different. They are not grown men are they? If I say to a lad "I want that floor mopping" he will say "I'm not doing that, it's a mug's job". This is what they say "I haven't done that, I did not make that mess". They have not had experience of being on a job before and anyone telling them what to do. If a man said to the foreman "I did not use that mixer, get the one who dirtied it to clean it" he would get the sack. Now we are not like that. We can suspend him yes. If they turn round and say "You are a fool" and "I'm not doing this or that", throwing things down, you know, he is refusing to work, we can say "Right if you don't want to do it you can go home" or otherwise "Right then, I'll get somebody else to do it; you can do so and so". We are being more lenient.'

RO: 'What are you trying to do for the lads?'

SC: '. . . trying to teach them something so that they will go away and have knowledge of different jobs. It isn't just one job like painting or joinery. It's getting them to be capable themselves to accept something, you know, something that they don't know how to do and they have a go at it, like . . . we showed them how to lay flags or lay a path.'

Observation of work group interaction, dealt with more fully in chapter four, suggests that the SCs perform the task of teaching skills to the young people with considerable patience and forbearance. A number of YEs were mentally retarded and had to be shown how to do very simple jobs; for example, a scheme consultant showed two boys how to scrape flaking paint off a wall.

One boy's attention appeared to wander continually, but the SC repeatedly drew his attention back to the task and continued to explain it without any sign of irritation while the lad made intermittent remarks which were unconnected with the job in hand. The level of intrinsic job satisfaction among the scheme consultants appeared to be uniformally high but occasionally the need for greater staff-YE contact was emphasized. Thus one SC acknowledged the inaccesssibility of the non-work areas of the YEs' lives but felt that:

> '. . . you can develop them a lot . . . give them a sense of responsibility and let them know what they're really doing . . . it's no good them coming here and just painting . . . they have to know what it's all about . . . if you gain their confidence it does help . . .'

This particular SC was considering the feasibility of a day trip which might spark off other 'social aspects'.

Superficially the only differentiation which appears to exist amongst the scheme consultants is that occasionally one scheme consultant may act in the capacity of a 'storeman/driver':

RO: 'X (SC) does all the driving. Have you any other "specialist" scheme consultants?'

ASM: 'No, he's the only one. And the stores — he does the stores too. He's the storeman driver and if a consultant has to leave a job, he'll stand in whilst the consultant is away. If someone's away for a week, then he goes in. He hasn't got a team of his own. Well, he's put down under the "Nurseries" project. If figures had to be given he'd have all the girls in the nurseries and the playgroups.'

However, observation of area activities indicate that there is further specialization with the scheme consultants tending to specialize in those projects or aspects of projects which are related to their own skills.

SC: 'Take W (SC) for example. He's a joiner so his team deal with that kind of work. Y (SC) is a painter, so his team do painting and decorating.'

Teams whose SCs were painters or joiners tended to be referred to by the staff in such terms as 'Jim's painters', 'the joinery squad', 'the painting team'. There was also a subtle distinction within the category of 'painters' between teams which specialized in house decoration and teams which specialized in painting and decorating halls or community centres.

Further Education Provision

At the time of the research many area staff claimed that they had not received advice 'on day release and other FE needs and facilities available' nor assistance with negotiations 'with FE authorities for the introduction of suitable courses for young employees' (CI Handbook, C7) from CI HQ. Observation suggested that the organizational emphases of CI are such that activities in the field of further education do not form an integral part of the staff's routine activities. As may be seen in the following remarks, the staff perceive themselves as having insufficient 'time and energy' to organize further education activities:

ASM: 'Mainly, it's just really the time and energy of sitting down and thrashing it out . . . there are so many things flung at you . . . (the OM) was off for three or four weeks, which overlapped with AM on sick leave which was sheer chaos . . . there's all that sort of thing. You just don't have sufficient time you know sometimes to start new work.'

There is also the problem of allocating facilities which are under considerable pressure and the motivation of YEs. As an illustration the head of General Studies at a local FE college and a member of his staff visited two teams, a boys' printing squad and a girls' sewing workshop, and talked to the young people about courses they might like to do. The response of the boys was described by the member of the General Studies staff:

FE Teacher: 'We said if they came to college what kinds of things would they be interested in doing, and they said first of all "We don't want to come to college", and then after that "Well, we wouldn't mind things like making our own fibre glass canoes, or if that was impossible, football would do". But apart from one lad who expressed an interest in geography of all things, that was it. And some of them had been on Industrial Apprenticeship courses (pre-CI) at this college . . . and they hadn't liked that very much.'

The outcome of this discussion was:

FE Teacher: 'Well, we came back and we talked about the lads and we didn't really think there was a great deal we could offer them. But we went round the various workshops and the technical teachers and said "What could you do?" and they threw their hands up in horror and said "Have you any idea how many people want to use these rooms?" . . . the workshops were hardly ever empty . . . and that really did put a damper on it because we hoped we could fit them in unobtrusively on one afternoon a week, say, as a sample to see what happened. There just wasn't going to be an afternoon.'

The problem of pressure on facilities was also related to the needs of such a special group of young people. In the lecturer's terms:

'. . . bringing into a college, where discipline is very strictly enforced, a group of people who would want to treat it in quite a different manner; we'd probably have to keep them quite separate, which would be an artificial experience.'

The college staff gave considerable thought to how a course for the boys might be arranged; the FE teacher quoted above thought that a setting in which the boys could improve their verbal communication skills would be helpful. Such a setting might occur within the work group with a lecturer working alongside a particular group; a lecturer previously employed in the painting and decorating department and now in general studies at the college was mentioned as being eminently suitable for this type of informal educational activity. The reality of organizational demands, however, were seen as militating against this:

FE Teacher: 'It's being thought about yes. But it's purely a matter of time-tabling and "Thou shalt do thirty hours a week on the premises" kind of thing as far as the staff are concerned."

The visit to the sewing workshop was, however, more successful:

FE Teacher: 'So then I went to see some of the girls who were doing sewing and tried to find out what they'd like, and they fancied cookery, which they could do. So the upshot of that was that for four weeks in June they should come into college, experimentally for four weeks; just four afternoons really and try and do some basic cookery and dressmaking. Talk about fashion, appearance, accent and behaviour and all that sort of thing although without obviously trying to preach to them.'

Further probing indicated that there were several aims in this experimental course. Firstly, it was hoped to allay any anxieties the girls might have about going to college and to stimulate their interest; secondly, to develop the girls' social and communication skills and to emphasize the importance of personal grooming and care; thirdly it was hoped that the course would generate ideas and information so that a longer course, full day release for ten weeks, might be organized. The FE teacher appeared very enthusiastic about this course and had suggestions to make about the form that a more extended course might ultimately take in terms of an extension of the work environment. With the right kind of staff support it was considered practicable to have FE teachers placed with the young people for one day per week in their work situation. This idea reflected a concern for using the work situation as a context for learning construed in a very general sense and points up the paradox that whereas college staff have the educational skills to realize these ideas they are constrained by lack of space, staffing, and time-tabling problems in terms of their implementation. Within CI the time and the procedures are officially available, but the staff tend not to have an 'educational orientation' nor the inter-personal skills necessary to realize the potential of the work situation. Thus in terms of on-site informal education in one particular area the YEs repaired to the site-hut with the SC when it rained and if this continued for more than 5 minutes the latter talked about the work situation and future development. In this talk there were references to the building industry and the vital need to cost materials, be on time, and other related issues. When this ran 'dry' the SC fell back on recounting his experiences as a painter and decorator and days spent in the Merchant Navy and Army. It seemed natural for the YEs to talk about their experiences too and the SC's tales were often punctuated by sequences from talkative members. The sequences revealed that the SC had an easy rapport with his group and was in a position to introduce a number of topics but in this respect he lacked knowledge and also the finer social skills required for involving the non-talkers.

Discussion with area staff suggested that the benefits assumed to be associated with further education provision would only be derived from courses specifically designed to meet CI's needs and by a relaxation of the bureauratic arrangements governing entry to the further education section. Thus in one area some problems arose during the first year of a course which were said to be caused by CI boys being disruptive, although some young employees who attended said that the teaching was not very well organized and they were sometimes left in a room for long periods because teachers were not available. The particular college in question subsequently established a selection interview which, according to the Deputy Principal, attempted to identify those young people competent to take the course and to filter out the potentially disruptive element. The boys were given a short test which essentially provides legitimation for rejecting young people rather than providing an indication of their ability.

DEP. PRIN.: 'It is not designed to test them, but simply to give us an opportunity of saying — this is sheltering behind paper, I know — of saying that you didn't make the grade, rather than saying we think that you aren't prepared to work on the course, etc.'

The CI staff tended to recruit for the course simply by asking for volunteers, with little persuasion being employed:

ASM: 'I can't see any point in persuading them. I'll tell them why they should go, how it'll help and all the rest of it. But there's no point in persuading them because they won't go every week then. I go round all the sites and ask if anyone is interested and leave it purely up to themselves to come and say "I'd quite like to go".'

Some boys who asked to go were 'cooled' out of the idea. Others are simply told they cannot go if they are thought likely to 'cause trouble'.

ASM: 'Like, our special school boys . . . they're dead keen to go, but it's no good for them . . . I would talk them out of it. You know, "It's not really a good idea. Look at all the travelling" or maybe tell them "There's no places just now, but I'll keep your name'. I'd rather not send a boy . . . on the whole they can't keep the pace . . . And they just don't understand. And quite honestly the teachers haven't got the time to spend on them.'

A major constraint on the variety of course content and the number of YEs who can attend is the shortage of teachers and rooms at colleges, the CI courses having to be fitted into a complex timetable. However, the provision of courses is also related to wider considerations reflecting particular educational ideologies:

DEP. PRIN.: 'I think "general studies" or as we call it "liberal studies" is useful but I don't think that's the kind of group (CI YEs) to start it with . . . I don't think if you're going to start an experiment along those lines you'd begin with that group, it'd probably be the most difficult to make a success with.'

A further problem which is perhaps easily overlooked is the difficulty of teaching the kinds of young people employed by CI:

DEP. PRIN.: 'A problem is that these kids who work for CI really need the best teachers, the ones with most skill and ability. And to be quite honest, we haven't got many really good teachers. We have some, but the majority are just reasonable teachers, who can do their job very well as long as the youngsters are fairly bright . .... the really good teachers that these boys need, well, there aren't many of them around.'

The Further Education needs of the young people do not seem to have been very clearly thought out. According to a CI staff member, some of the boys get frustrated because they do more complex and detailed tasks at work than they do at college. The rationale for the course is often stated in very general terms; e.g. to communicate the idea that college isn't like school; to enable the YEs to mix with other types of people; to improve their trade skills. Nobody seems able to say whether there has been any changes in the young people as a result of going to college. Certainly, there did not appear to be any follow-up courses, nor did YEs go on to take other courses at college. The provision of such courses does, however, serve to break the routine and may often be an enjoyable and instructive experience:

RO: 'What did you get out of it?'

YE: 'Oh you learn a lot. I know a lot that I didn't know before: about building materials, how to order things, different sizes of nails and that. A lot of things I didn't know.'

RO: 'Did you enjoy it?'

YE: 'Yes, it is very interesting.'

In addition the FE College provides the opportunity for contact with a number of adults who have links with employers particularly in building and construction firms. The area staff mention the chance of getting a job as a result of attending college as an incentive to motivate YEs to enrol for the courses. Thus the FE course may function not so much as a means of training but rather as an avenue to jobs and apprenticeships for CI boys and to structure expectations in a particular way. This is referred to explicitly by an area staff member:

ASM: 'The value of the course itself was probably questionable. But certainly what is not questionable is the end result of how employers view the fact that a youngster has been attending a course. I mean, it doesn't change the youngster but it changes the attitude of the employer to the youngster, albeit it was an unacademic course. Similarly . . . the college, the teachers at college, have a lot of good contacts, so if they find a boy who's very good they'll push him in somewhere. That's why I like to hold on to college on the boys' side of it, because really it can come out quite well for them.'

Quantitative analysis of adult perceptions

The preceding qualitative analysis has hopefully provided the reader with insights into the day-to-day operations of CI. The quantitative analysis[1] which follows is meant to complement this description by presenting material at a more general and abstract level. Though it draws on statistical analysis of questionnaire information, we will provide, in keeping with the non-technical nature of the book, only the simplest tables and restrict our presentation of statistics so that they inform rather than distract.

A number of items were developed for use in an adult questionnaire by extracting statements from transcribed discussions with CI staff representatives about 'the aims of CI'. These discussions were angled towards the interrelated though conceptually distinct issues of 'work' and 'social education' which, as we have seen, provide a distinctive philosophy for organizational functioning. The final version of the questionnaire drew on this item pool and provided staff with the opportunity of indicating the extent to which they thought CI should be concerned with activities relating to both work and education in their day-to-day functioning. The resulting responses were first intercorrelated and then subjected to a components analysis to establish the dimensionality of the underlying response structure. The first two rotated components were readily identifiable as referring to social and work orientations. Items 32 and 40 had the highest loadings on the first component and reveal its essential meaning; it was termed 'social facilitation'.

(32) Build up the young people's confidence.
(40) Develop the young person's sense of initiative.

Items 53 and 55 load highest on the second component which was termed 'work facilitation'.

(53) Help the young people develop habits of good time keeping.
(55) Show the young people that adults can be friendly people with a genuine desire to help.

The items most descriptive of these two dimensions were subjected to a scaling procedure which maximizes internal consistency[2] (Baker, 1970) and which provided two scores for each staff member: high scores indicating a desired emphasis on both social and work facilitation. Two further scores relating to the purposes of CI were obtained using a rather more indirect method. This involved assessing the relative emphasis placed by CI staff on the leadership behaviour of the ideal scheme consultant. Two measures, termed 'task orientation' and 'consideration', were derived from an Ideal Leadership Questionnaire which has been widely used in social psychological investigation (Halpin and Winer, 1957); the two measures are scored positively, high scores indicating high 'task orientation' and 'consideration'. The four scales together with their maximized reliability coefficients are tabulated below:

Table 1: *Scales relating to the goals of CI as perceived by adult staff.*

Scales	*Maximized Internal Consistency*
Social facilitation	.89
Work facilitation	.88
Task orientation	.88
Consideration	.80

In order to examine the extent to which there is a shared belief about the purposes of CI at the staff level, scheme consultants were compared with office staff[3] using the four measures described above. The results (F, 0.41, NS) show no significant difference between the groups. This finding suggests the prevalance of a homogeneous set of beliefs about the purposes of CI. Thus even though the two adult groups have different functions — scheme consultants dealing directly with the young employees and possessing some specialist trade skill, office staff acting in an administrative/advisory capacity — it seems that they form a relatively tight group in terms of their outlook on the structure and purposes of CI. However, in spite of this broad consensus between staff levels, differences may still occur between both scheme consultants and staff in the different areas in which CI operates. Certainly comments received by the research team from outside observers with regard to the orientation of CI suggested that there were considerable differences between geographical areas both with regard to the work-related behaviour of area staff and their beliefs about the function and purposes of the organization. The four scales described in the previous table, together with four additional scales relating to the perception of organization structure which are described later, were used to test for differences between areas; all area office staff and scheme consultants were included in this analysis. However, at this level the generally held view of substantial differences between geographical areas was not supported. (F 1.31, NS).

The relatively small number of area staff and their established nature, coupled with the induction processes associated with joining the organization, have probably helped to bring about a homogeneity of view concerning the purposes of CI and perception of its organizational structure. This homogeneous ideology has no doubt been reinforced by the periodic meetings which have been convened for area staff, the visits made by CI HQ staff to the areas, and the flow of material from headquarters.

The transcribed discussions previously referred to revealed certain recurring themes which were seen as influencing the performance of area staff's work. Eleven such 'influencing factors' were listed on the adult version of the questionnaire and respondents were asked to indicate their degree of felt satisfaction with each factor on a five point scale: very satisfied to very dissatisfied. Space was provided for an open ended response explaining the reason for the degree of felt satisfaction/dissatisfaction. These work-related influences were initially ranked for the total staff sample in terms of the mean response category score. In

Table 2: *Adult staff's expressed degree of dissatisfaction with work-related influences.*

Work-related influences	*Mean item scores*
Pay and conditions of service of adult employees	3.82
*Stress on 'throughput'	2.62
Facilities and/or equipment	2.61
Public 'Image' associated with CI	2.63
*Feedback with regard to job performance	2.41
Backing from the Local Authority	2.36
*General paper work which is required	2.34
Number of meetings which are scheduled	2.29
Ratio of staff to young people	2.17
Interest shown by sponsors	2.04
*Projects of the right type	1.83

* Significant differences between scheme consultants and office staff for these items.

addition a x^2 analysis was run to test for differences between scheme consultants and office staff on each 'influence'. For four of the work-related influences significant differences were found between these groups at better than the .05 confidence level. The results of this analysis and ranking procedure are presented in table 2; high mean item scores represent dissatisfaction.

To a certain extent the division of labour as reflected in organizational tasks may account for the significant differences between scheme consultants and area office staff which are asterisked. On 'projects of the right type' there are significantly more scheme consultants than office staff who are very satisfied, though both groups are satisfied to some extent with this aspect. This is understandable when we consider that scheme consultants are, by and large, employed for their skill at a particular trade which accords with a particular type of project. The area staff, on the other hand, strive to achieve variety in the range of their projects and may not succeed in this respect. The second work-related influence which shows differences between the staff groups is that of 'Throughput', that is, the policy whereby the young employees are encouraged to leave CI for other employment after a maximum of twelve months in the scheme. Again scheme consultants are generally satisfied with the stress laid on 'Throughput', whereas the office staff express a degree of concern and dissatisfaction. From comments made by office staff, it appears that they see this policy as a challenge to their managerial autonomy: 'diagnosis' and length of 'treatment' being seen as their perogative.

The issue of 'general paper-work required' also shows the office staff somewhat more dissatisfied than scheme consultants. Again, comments made by the office staff indicate that they are doubtful about the usefulness of much of the material they receive or supply. They also see it as taking up time that they could otherwise use to visit and maintain a close contact with their young employees. The fourth item which differentiates the scheme consultants from office staff is 'feedback' with regard to job performance. Scheme consultants are significantly more satisfied as a group than the office staff who are more or less evenly divided on this issue. This fits with a picture of close contact and co-operation between scheme consultants and office staff at a formal and informal level. Thus the scheme consultants have direct contact with their 'superiors' which provides direct feedback for them and in addition they have visible evidence of their team's progress on a particular project. In contrast, achievement for the office staff is less well defined, and feedback from CI HQ is most likely to come in the form of monthly circulars. The general trend of these differences between area office staff and scheme consultants reflects the greater dissatisfaction expressed by the former group on the four items mentioned. Possibly the fact that the scheme consultants are in a more well-defined role and removed somewhat from decision making protects them to some degree from situations where anxiety is common and dissatisfaction normal.

Leaving aside these differences it is apparent that the four major areas of staff dissatisfaction are: (1) Pay and conditions of service; (2) Stress on throughput; (3) Facilities and equipment; (4) Public image associated with CI. Greatest dissatisfaction is expressed with regard to 'Pay and conditions', whilst in general the staff are most satisfied with the projects they obtain. In this respect special mention is made of the lack of job security and there is also a feeling that wage rates have fallen below that which they might expect in comparable employment elsewhere. The following remarks are not untypical of the open ended comments accompanying the rating of this effect:

'I am getting about £1,000 pa less than I could earn outside the scheme.'
'Unsatisfactory conditions and wages for the responsibility assumed.'
'Not enough security for the long term.'
'Absolutely scandalous — taking advantage of good people particularly field staff.'
'Employees have accepted CI terms because the job is better paid in satisfaction than in cash.'
'Lack of guarantee of employment and no inbuilt promotion scheme to encourage long term commitment.'

Negative comments on *throughput* included the following:

'I feel it happens naturally for most, should not be enforced.'
'Very unfair to pressure YEs to give up CI and go back on the dole. Leave it to area staff.'
'Inhibits our work as the job seems insecure. We are in the best position to assess individual needs.'

Positive comments included:

'It is necessary to encourage young people to obtain jobs in open employment.'

'It is a good thing because it takes any suggestion of "play" out of work.'
'No stress here; gives young employees a definite aim.'

In terms of facilities and equipment, references were made to 'inadequate temporary premises' and equipment was often seen as being 'poor and inadequate' though many individuals acknowledged that things were 'getting better as we develop'. Typical statements were:

'Very little new equipment in 21 months, steps are dangerous, brushes worn out, no dust sheets.'
'CI and local authorities must realize the importance of workshop facilities.'
'I have to use my own tools far too often.'
'Young people's lives and limbs could be at stake through lack of proper facilities and equipment.'
'One hammer between 10 boys.'

The public image of CI was seen as being adversely affected by the connection with NAYC: a need for greater publicity was also expressed in order to make an impact on prospective employers:

'Don't like youth club image; doesn't help in obtaining sponsors.'
'Not enough people know about CI; those who do think we are to do with "youth work".'
'People get a wrong impression of CI; we are not youth workers.'
'Has not got a reputation reflecting what it does; this effects attitude of other local bodies.'
'Inadequate advertising and public relations give a vague public image. We have nothing to do with youth clubs.'
'Some misunderstandings about the purposes of CI: NAYC on sign and notepaper does not help.'

The eleven work-related influences listed in Table 2 were treated as variables for a between-area analysis in order to establish whether difficulties were being experienced by particular areas, and if so, what were the major sources of anxiety. Results of this analysis indicate that there are indeed significant differences between areas (F 2.68, $P<.001$). Examination of the descriptive statistics accompanying the analysis indicate that two dimensions are largely responsible for the difference between areas; the first and most salient is characterized by high loadings on variables 6 and 8 with low to moderate loadings on variables 5 and 7; variable 9 is common to both dimensions. This dimension clearly describes differences in *local support* given to CI in terms of local authority backing (6), the provision of facilities and equipment (8), interest shown by sponsors (7), and the public image of CI (5). Inspection of the table of means for these four variables indicates which areas are most and which least satisfied with 'local support'. As an aid to interpretation the areas were ranked from high to low using the means of these four variables then ordered in terms of their average rank computed over the four measures. The results of this procedure is illustrated in Table 3 over.

It is apparent from this table that areas A, E and D are most dissatisfied with the degree of 'local support' for CI whereas C, F and B are most satisfied. In terms of the specific aspects of 'local support', H is most dissatisfied with the 'public image' of CI whereas E is more satisfied with this aspect than its overall rank might suggest.

To continue with our analysis we may note that the second dimension of difference has its main contribution from variables 1, Projects of the right type; variable 4, Number of meetings scheduled; and variable 10, Ratio of staff to young people. This dimension would thus seem to refer to differences in the internal administrative arrangements of CI from area to area. Judging from the mean scores of these variables the pattern of satisfaction/dissatisfaction among the areas on this dimension is similar to that evidenced with regard to local support.

This form of analysis has served to provide a picture of the overall pattern and dimensionality of responses to questions of organizational functioning which would have been difficult to obtain by other means. Its disadvantage lies in the fact that it can say nothing about the processes involved in such functioning and hence points up the value of the qualitative material previously presented.

Theoretical overview

In Chapter One we briefly touched on the issues of organizational goals and environmental adaptation. In this chapter we have considered these notions more fully by employing both quantitative and qualitative methods of analysis. The former is used to describe the overall pattern of organizational purposes as perceived by adult members of CI and the latter enables us to examine actual operational commitments as revealed in staff ideologies and the

Table 3: *Area dissatisfaction with 'local support' for C I*

Areas	* *Index of dissatisfaction with 'local support'*	*Rank order on variables contributing to 'local support'*			
		Public 5. Image	*LA 6. Backing*	*Sponsors 7. Interest*	*Facilities/ 8. Equipment*
A	2.0	2	1	3	2
E	2.2	4	2	2	1
D	2.5	3	3	1	3
H	3.5	1	4	5	4
G	5.2	5	5	4	7
C	6.2	6	8	6	5
F	6.5	7	6	7	6
B	7.7	8	7	8	8

* Low index represent dissatisfaction

division of labour. This points up the fact that whether we talk of 'goals' or 'commitments' various levels of conceptual analysis are involved. Perrow (1961) distinguishes between 'official' and 'operative' goals; the latter tells us what the organization is trying to do, which may or may not coincide with the major organizational concerns as expressed in the official goals. Gross (1969) terms goals which are ranked high as an intention but low as an activity as 'utopian' and those ranked low on intention but greatly evident in activities as 'unstated goals'. Similarly the dynamic nature of organizational goals reflecting environmental pressures has been referred to by Thompson and McEwen (1968) and their precariousness in marginal situations by Clarke (1956). The quantitative analysis which has been presented at the staff level is conceptually limited to an empirically derived set of generalized goals which may be thought to represent the 'symbolic' or 'utopian' commitments of CI, with the qualitative aspect of the research providing insights into its actual operational set. Similarly environmental adaptation is dealt with both in terms of a quantitative analysis of perceived influences on work activities and a qualitative analysis intended to point up how this is reflected in the division of labour and provision of further education.

Inseparable from and indeed implied in the phrase 'division of labour' are theoretically interesting questions relating to processes of leadership and group formation. Despite the enormous interdisciplinary literature on these topics there is still a great deal of ambiguity in defining these terms at both conceptual and operational levels, and much of the empirical work is inconclusive (Stogdill, 1974). A recent commentator has remarked:

> 'Most leadership theories make the assumption that the leader has a great deal of unilateral control; if the leader only used the appropriate style, the group would be more productive; if the leader understood group processes, the group would be more cohesive, creative and effective. Understanding how non-leader variables influence such outcomes would help both researchers and leaders by providing a more realistic perspective on just what the leader can and cannot hope to achieve.' (McCall Jr., 1976, p.48).

In general this book describes the contribution of both situational factors and personal attributes to questions of leadership, but in this chapter we have focused particularly on the role of the scheme consultants for they constitute the 'cutting edge' of the organization and as such are central to realization of organizational purposes. As we have seen, and indeed this will be a recurring theme throughout subsequent chapters, a consideration of the individual attributes and background expectancies of such men and women cannot be fully understood without reference to the larger forces which created and which re-create their 'new settings'. We will be exploring this issue more fully in chapter four, but relevant here is Sarason's (1972) discussion of the problems arising from the creation of such settings. In particular the movement of adults from an established setting, typically an industrial one focusing on an end product, to a looser more educational environment may pose considerable problems of adjustment for the individual concerned. In the face of anxieties and unfamiliar demands he may attempt to 'cope' with this new situation by cognitively substituting his 'old setting' for the new one; by doing so he fails to confront the substantive issues which the new organization has generated. It is, of course, true that leaders, in the face of political and other pressures, 'choose' leaders but by embracing the myth of unlimited human resources they may prejudice outcomes from the start; there are relatively few adults who, without an infrastructure of prolonged supportive training, can undertake the leadership tasks required in innovatory settings like those to be found in CI. As Sarason says 'if those who choose do so without real understanding of the dynamics and ramifications of the context out of which the new setting has emerged, it is no wonder that wrong choices are made' (p. 49).

Notes

1. In terms of the statistical procedure associated with comparisons of scale scores referred to in this and subsequent chapters, the underlying conviction is that it is best treated as a whole rather than as an isolated series of tests relating to particular scales; consequently, multivariate analysis is considered appropriate. A detailed description of this form of analysis would not be appropriate here; we may remark, however, that the well-used factorial analysis of variance design is 'unilaterally multivariate' in that it is only multi-dimensional in its form of classification with several effects being examined in relation to one dependent variable. When the analysis is extended to include more than one dependent variable the design may be termed 'bilaterally multivariate'. Multivariate analysis is thus concerned with analysis in terms of multiple measurements which are considered in combination, the multi-dependent variables being taken as a 'team' rather than singly as in the univariate case.

   The general form of the analysis employed for the various comparisons made with regard to the quantitative aspect of the research thus takes into account not only differences between levels of the independent variable but also the covariation between dependent variables represented by scores on the attitude scales. Our interest thus shifts from the univariate concern of whether our populations (groups) are centred at different points on the particular dependent measure being considered to whether the populations are differentially located within a multi-dimensional measurement space spanned by the dependent vector variable; thus, in contrast to the factorial analysis of variance which is multi-level in the independent measure the distinguishing feature of m.a.n.o.v.a. is that dependent variables are considered as a team.

The complex system of variances and covariances involved in this form of analysis is handled by a programme known as GUMMA which has been developed at the University of London (Baughan, 1973), and which is sufficiently flexible to allow for the statistical control of related variables by introducing them into the model as covariates. As the canonical analysis used to maximize group differences is essentially performed on the SS's of cross products the resulting vectors, which are usually given as a series of canonical coefficients, are not directly interpretable because they are influenced by the different scales of the original variables; when these coefficients are expressed as 'canonical loadings' they are similar to 'factor loadings' in that they represent the correlations between the standardized original variables and canonical variates and consequently allow interpretation in terms of their relative sizes. These canonical loadings associated with the analysis are a valuable descriptive aid which we turn to when the overall multivariate test is significant. For an excellent discussion of the advantages and pitfalls associated with this form of analysis the interested reader is referred to Kerlinger and Pedhazur (1973).

2. In addition to examining the answers given to each individual question there are advantages to be gained from aggregating responses to those questions which have a 'common content'. Before such advantages accrue, however, it is necessary to demonstrate that such a 'common content' exists; thus the questions or items should be positively correlated. Clearly, if the items are uncorrelated then adding responses over items serves no useful purpose since they share nothing in common. Consistency in responding to items is thus a minimum condition for the definition of 'scales' which allow individuals to be ordered with regard to their assumed content. Scaling by the method of

Distribution of scheme consultants and office staff by age and sex.* (Ns in brackets)

	Scheme Consultants				*Office Staff*			
	Age 20-29	30-39	40+	*Totals*	*Age* 20-29	30-39	40+	*Totals*
Males	17	25	58	100	41	32	28	100
	(12)	(18)	(41)	(71)	(9)	(7)	(6)	(22)
Females	31	23	46	100	58	17	25	100
	(4)	(3)	(6)	(13)	(7)	(1)	(3)	(12)

*There are 13 missing observations: 7 for scheme consultants and 6 for office staff.

reciprocal averages is briefly described in Murray (1978), and the reliability coefficients presented in the text are indications of the internal consistency of scale responses.

3. The distribution of the CI staff sample at the time of the research as described by function, age and sex, may be observed in the table on p.92:
It is apparent from this that the ratio of male to female scheme consultants is of the order of 5 to 1 and in fact the great majority of female consultants (69 per cent) are employed in two areas. This pattern reflects both the emphasis on male recruitment to CI and the type of projects operating in the areas. Whereas the majority of office staff are under 30 years of age, most scheme consultants are over 40; this age difference reflects both the emphasis placed on experience in recruiting adults who will have direct contact with the young people and the availability of this age group for such work in areas of high adult unemployment.

References

BAKER, F.B. (1970). Quantifying qualitative variables by the method of reciprocal averages. *Occasional Paper No. 7.* Laboratory of Experimental Design. University of Wisconsin.

BAUGHAN, B. (1973). *Program GUMMA: The Universal Multivariate Analysis Mark II.* University of London.

CLARKE, B.R. (1956). Organizational adaptation and precarious values: a case study. *American Sociological Review.* 21. 854-866.

GROSS, E. (1969). The definition of organizational goals. *British Journal of Sociology.* 20. 277-294.

HALPIN, A.W. and WINER, B.J. (1957). A factorial study of the Leader Behaviour Description Questionnaire. In Stogdill, R.M. and Coons, A.E. (eds.) *Leader Behaviour: Its Descriptions and Management.* Bureau of Business Research, Ohio State University. 39-51.

KERLINGER, F.N. and PEDHAZUR, E.J. (1973). *Multiple regression in behavioural research.* London: Holt, Rinehard and Winston Inc.

McCALL Jr., M.W. (1976). Leadership research: choosing gods and devils on the run. *Journal of Occupational Psychology.* 49. 139-153.

MURRAY, C. (1978). Methods and measures. In Murray, C. (ed.) *Youth in Contemporary Society.* Windsor: NFER Publishing Company.

PERROW, C. (1961). The analysis of goals in complex organizations. *American Sociological Review.* 26. 854-866.

SARASON, S.B. (1972). *The creation of settings and the future societies.* London: Jossey-Bass.

STOGDILL, R.M. (1974). *Handbook of Leadership.* New York: Free Press.

THOMPSON, J.D. and McEWEN, W.J. (1968). Organizational goals and environment. *American Sociological Review.* 23. 23-31.

Chapter 3

The Young People

Their careers and characteristics

The term 'career' is used throughout our discussion of CI in a wider sense than the usual one of a movement through the occupational structure of an industry or profession. It is used to refer to the process whereby an individual comes to be identified by others and by himself as a particular kind of person. In this sense the notion of 'career' may be used to discuss not only how a person becomes a consultant surgeon but also how a person becomes a 'down and out', tradesman, one of the long-term unemployed, a thief, a labourer or scheme consultant. This interpretation of 'career' thus incorporates the idea of movement through a sequence of contingent events, choices and pressures, where with the adoption of a particular course of action certain options become closed, others are opened and the range and type of possible future events, choices and pressures is changed. Inseparable from factors affecting both employment and educational opportunities is the expectations and beliefs of adults about different 'types' of young people and the various categories of behaviour assumed to be associated with such types. We will explore some of these processes in the following section of this chapter.

Careers and contingencies

It will be apparent from our discussion so far that the kind of work experience which the young people have had prior to CI, that is those who had been in employment, are in general those involving unskilled manual jobs. For instance, many of the boys have worked as van-boys, market porters, general labourers. The girls tend to have had experience of work in shops or on production lines, or doing routine tasks of a simple kind in factories. The young people may have lost their pre-CI jobs through their own fault, or by their own decision, but this is considerably less prevalent than is generally thought. Those who have been dismissed tend to be those who have been bad timekeepers or have a history of work absenteeism. However, a number of the young people lose their jobs through no fault of their own:

> CO:'I don't always blame the youngsters, because I think some of the employers are very unfair, although we tend possibly to think the girls are dodging, but in fact I think there are some pretty awful employers. So you might get a youngster who's off sick for half a day and I've even had cases where the youngsters are producing a certificate and they've been dismissed. Sometimes the employer has to do it because he can't do without staff.'

It is thus necessary to emphasize that the characteristics and attitudes of the young people who may be generally termed 'alienated' do not by themselves provide a sufficient explanation of their being unemployed.

The staff and careers officers pointed out on a number of occasions that the young people were not always at fault in terms of their failure to obtain and hold down regular jobs. Many of the jobs they had experienced were boring and repetitive and some employers use the young people as cheap labour and are prepared to dismiss them when they are old enough to come on to a 'man's wage'. The job aspirations of the young people and the nature of the local labour market also play a part in the careers of the young people. Thus high value may be placed on 'having a trade' and hence boys may not want to do unskilled work such as 'van-boy' or warehouse assistant. However, there may not be enough local vacancies for skilled jobs or apprenticeships and these are the kinds of opportunities that many boys want:

> CO:'We've got more unskilled vacancies than we've got boys willing to do unskilled work.'

The situation also arises where boys who have done unskilled work on building sites have received unusually high wages and are not then prepared to take other unskilled jobs where the pay is lower. The 'normal' problem with some girls was summarized by a CO as follows:

> CO:'. . . there's the girls wanting "social work" types of jobs, wanting to look after people and look after children, and not being able to . . . There's

quite a few girls actually who are now regretting having left school. I think there's about 17 who have had one dead-end job after the other and are now regretting it . . . That's a problem we don't really solve. I hear . . . (local hospital) has a psychiatric wing (a special unit for adolescent girls) full of them, you know, full of these types of girls.'

Further discussion with this careers officer helped to clarify the context in which young people become unemployed and supplements the descriptions given by CI staff about the kinds of employment difficulties that the young people have had before joining CI. The kinds of jobs available, employer expectations and the maintenance of the CO's credibility are involved as well as the characteristics of the young people. In terms of deciding whether to send a young person for a job the CO remarked:

'The employer might say he wants such and such CSE's and he might say he wants somebody smart, and if we think they fit the bill we send them for the job. We flick through the vacancies; we say we've got one, perhaps they want a sales assistant and this person wants to be a sales assistant and they say "No long hair" and he's got long hair, then we just wouldn't mention that vacancy . . . that's one of the advantages of not having a self-selection system . . . because you might say to them "You aren't quite suitable" but they insist on going for the job, so the employer would get that person and say "Oh, this careers service is hopeless, sending me the wrong type of people".'

RO: 'You have to be careful about sending the right kind of people?'

CO: 'Well there are some employers, well we find great big notes on the vacancy card and it'll say 'BE SELECTIVE' so you make sure that they've got nice manners and they look nice, and that they've got the right qualifications, the right amount of intelligence . . . but you could always ring the employer up and say "Look, I'm sending so-and-so, I know she looks a bit scruffy, but really she's very bright and I'm sure she would be able to do the job." You could always do that.'

The reasons suggested by area staff and Careers Officers for young people not being able to obtain jobs before they come to CI are varied. However, their appearance and self-presentation were often cited. A member of the Careers Service described the importance of self presentation for securing employment in the following terms:

CO: 'There are kids who are just socially inadequate — who just don't fare well at interviews. Kids who I've sent for interview after interview and they go to the employer and their mouths hang open and they just don't make a good impression. They generally get depressed and the more depressed they get, the less able they are to cope with an interview.'

It appears from discussion with the Careers Service and with area staff that a large proportion of the young people who come to work with CI do not appreciate the importance of the interview situation, and do not have the skills to present themselves to their best advantage. They do not dress tidily for interviews, and they say very little to the interviewer. It seems reasonable to suppose that the formal interview is not a form of social relationship which occurs naturally in the day-to-day lives of the young people. Therefore their immediate experience does not provide, and does not need to provide, the skills relevant to handling this sort of relationship. They enter into the interview situation in much the same way as they enter situations in their day-to-day lives. The situational demands which require the young people to verbalize about themselves, and about their work, places them in a highly unfamiliar and alien setting. Not suprisingly, they are not generally successful in dealing with it. Their approach to the interview and their lack of ability in handling the relationships it embraces may be perceived by potential employers, not for what they are, but as signs that the person is stupid or unlikely to make a good employee. Clearly this is not necessarily the case, but the impressions gained do serve to keep young people out of employment. The young people may be perceived as having nothing 'to sell' to a potential employer. If they fail to dress tidily, and speak up for themselves, and are also small of stature and not very bright, then it is highly unlikely that an employer will offer them work:

CO: 'They might not even be capable of much, these kids. Almost illiterate, if not completely illiterate. And they just can't give a good account of themselves. They've got nothing to sell the employer and they've got to have something to sell, whether it's muscle or brain powers, and a lot of kids have neither, and they don't even have a good appearance to sell. These are the ones who form the 'hard core' of unemployed — or part of the hard core; the real hard core are the ones who just don't want to work, and have got really ridiculous criminal records — some people wouldn't even send them to CI because they know that as soon as they got in amongst a crowd of guys they'd start a gang, or they would start a fight. These people I don't feel it's my — even if it was my job — I wouldn't have time to deal with them. These are jobs for the psychiatrist I think, more than anything else, or child psychologist.'

The problem of basic literacy is also related to obtaining and keeping jobs:

Youth Worker: 'One of the reasons kids can't get other jobs is because they can't fill in the forms. So you can give him as much work experience as you like (*i.e.* in CI) but if they can't get another job because they can't read and write, it's hopeless!'

ASM: 'I had a group of lads in when there was some apprenticeships going at the corporation . . . the Careers people sent the forms and I got all the lads together . . . and one lad sort of looked through it and said "Well I can't apply" and was just about to walk through the door and I said "Why not?" and he said "Well, it says there what CSEs have you got? and I never took CSEs" so I said "Just because they ask on the form it doesn't mean to say they want you to have CSEs . . ." In fact it wasn't a job that required CSEs. The corporation has a standard form.'

The Careers Service was said not to be used much by the kind of young people who work for or are eligible for CI:

ASM: 'Whether they like it or not, they've (the COs) got a bad name with our sort of kids . . . the entire upstairs waiting room and all the offices off it are now being made into a further education advice centre, with three COs doing this full time, sitting up there in lonely splendour. I imagine they'll be busy from "A" level results time 'till University starts . . . but that's the slant of things — the more qualifications you've got the more interested they are in you . . . as a result, kids like ours, who are always on the border line of having a job and not having a job and who probably need the Youth Employment Service most — or have done in the past — have by and large got very bad experiences of it . . . you really have to persuade a kid to use them.'

Most of the young people entering CI have not achieved a great deal, in academic terms, at school. There were one or two young people with 'O' levels, but in the main they were unqualified and indeed a number had been to special schools for the educationally subnormal. While it is known that children are sent to special schools for many reasons other than a low level of mental ability, all the teams contacted and, according to the staff, the other teams too had at least two and sometimes three or four young employees who were ESN. Additionally, some young people have physical handicaps or physical attributes which might cause them difficulty in obtaining work. These ranged from being deaf and dumb, through epilepsy, dermatitis, slight spasticity or poor eyesight to obesity, poor motor co-ordination, small physical size and immature appearance. A general impression gained from observation of the young employees was that they were 'young for their age' in that there appeard to be an 'immature' element in their behaviour. A scheme consultant remarks:

> 'The kids are a bit cagey at first. It takes a while to get to know some of them. But you begin to find out things and they tell you things. It comes out in different situations, like, say, when you stop them half an hour and they say "I can't afford to have half an hour stopped" and you find out his dad belts him if he doesn't have his pay there. For instance, I had a lad who didn't get any excess fares one week. He burst into tears when he didn't get his right money because he would be in trouble with his mother. She expected his money every week — the set amount of pay and the set amount of excess fares. He was so upset I finished up giving it him out of my own pocket. It was only a matter of twenty pence.'

The young people consistently expressed the view that they didn't like to be 'on the dole' because of there being nothing to do, not enough money and an awareness of the ease with which they might become involved with the police. These points came up in discussions with the young people:

YE: 'Working here is better than being on the dole.'
RO: 'Why, for the money?'
YE: 'Well, and you don't get trouble. Just like you know, work. Better than being on the dole because when you're on the dole you have all day to yourself, you start doing daft things. Breaking and entering and things like that, because well, for a bit of excitement and the dole money isn't all that good! When you are working here you don't get time to do daft things like that. Keeps your mind occupied.'

This last remark draws attention to the fact that a number of young people, though not the majority, have been 'in trouble with the police'. The offences sometimes involve breaking and entering and shop lifting, but often they are offences such as 'conduct likely to cause a breach of the peace', 'drunk and disorderly behaviour' and 'under-age drinking'. These are minor offences, often involving ambiguous situations where police discretion may be exercised. Thus a group of lads acting in a rowdy manner may attract the attention of a policeman; the lads answer him back when told to move on and may then be arrested for 'conduct likely'. High levels of police surveillance also play a part in the development of delinquent records. The following long quotation will be allowed to speak for itself and describes an incident involving CI, the police and a young employee:

ASM: 'We had one classic one yesterday. One of the boys who was working in . . . on the decorating; they finished this ceiling you see, and they were told "Once you've finished, just go" because neither of them could paper and some of the other boys were going to paper today. So there's this emulsion left. Not a full can, half a can. And he was told "just take it home with you and bring it to the office in the morning". That was fine. The boy took the can and went away. He was standing at the bus stop, when two policemen on the beat came up to him and said:

P: 'Where are you going?'

YE: 'I'm going home.'

P: 'What are you doing with the can?'

YE: 'I'm taking it home.'

P: 'Who gave it to you?'

YE: '. . .' (name of SC)

P: 'What have you got it for?'

YE: 'I'm taking it home! I've to bring it in tomorrow.'

P: 'Come with us.'

YE: 'Where have I to go?'

P: 'To the office.'

YE: 'Well, our office is down that way.'

P: 'No, to the police office.'

YE: 'I'm not going to the police office. You can't charge me with anything. I've not done anything.'

P: 'Come to the police —'

YE: 'No.'

ASM: 'So they took him to the police office and 'phoned here. . . . (the AM) took the call and they said:

'Charge him with stealing paint.' The AM replied 'I'll not charge him. Just send the boy up to us.'

'The PC was quite indignant about it, that we wouldn't charge the boy. So the boy came in yesterday afternoon. So when he came in and I said "What happened?" he was wild, he really was. He was quite indignant about the whole thing. I said to him "Will you take the paint home?" He said "No! Me taking it?! That's me finished! I'm not taking anything home." He said "I've got all the papering tables to bring back the next day but I'm not touching anything else. You wonder why we don't like the police, and you ask us why we're not so nice to them! You're just standing waiting for a bus and . . ." which is quite right you know, I mean I was angry, and as I say the policeman was quite indignant because we wouldn't charge him with the theft! . . .'

This particular situation did not result in a charge being made because of the intervention of the CI staff. It seems likely, however, that the level of police surveillance with regard to such young people plays a part in the development and maintenance of their delinquent records quite apart from the actual commitment of offences. Staff, scheme consultants and Careers Officers all mentioned the fact that some of the kinds of young people employed by CI are likely to be approached by the police merely because of their age, appearance and manner. Several cases of this happening during work-time were instanced by scheme consultants who had prevented the situations from escalating by explaining to police officers that boys were working with them. When responsible adults are not available to give such explanations, a young person may well respond to the police in ways which result in his being arrested.

As has been previously pointed out, it is perhaps significant that most of the offences which contribute to the sort of record which a young person may develop, involve an element of ambiguity as to whether an offence has actually been committed; breach of the peace, loitering, drunk and disorderly are examples of such offences. Other kinds of offences are certainly committed, but these more ambiguous types predominate.

RO: 'What other kind of offences are there?'

ASM: 'Car thefts and house breaking — well it's classified as house breaking, but it's shops. Offensive weapons.'

RO: 'How many of those kind of things?'

ASM: 'Offensive weapons we haven't had many of. House breaking we've had quite a few. House breaking and car thefts are the main ones of the "offences" in that sense. Most of the boys with police records I'd say, it's breach of the peace. For example, there's a boy starting on Monday. Unemployed since December 1973. Four convictions for breach of the peace. Spent a week in . . . (young offenders prison) because of being drunk and disorderly. Due at court on . . . (date) for disorderly behaviour. Age 17 and spent a week in . . .! A guy 17 spending a week up there — I mean, you can't really expect them to be any better coming out of that place, really.'

The following extract from a discussion on a site hints at the essential 'non-criminal' nature of these sort of offences in the eyes of the young people; they seem to be committed for excitement and as a means of obtaining things which are considered desirable, but which they can only obtain by illicit means:

YE1: 'I was put away, like.'

RO: 'What for?'

YE1: 'Pinching cars.'

RO: 'Where did you go?'

YE1: 'A detention centre. But I've learned my lesson now, like. My younger brother has just been put away for pinching a tractor.'

RO: 'What did he want with a tractor?'

YE1: 'Well, he wasn't pinching it. He had a go on it and got scared and jumped off. It ran into a ditch. He did a couple of hundred pounds worth of damage.'

RO: 'Why do people pinch cars? To sell them?'

YE2: 'No! for a ride.'

YE1: 'For a bit of fun.'

YE2: 'And to see what is in them.'

YE1: 'I got an eight-track cassette of "Zeplin". A great band aren't they?'.

The long-term consequences of a 'guilty' plea are not often realized by the young person:

ASM: : 'In many cases the kids are quite prepared to plead guilty in order to get it over and done with — "It's a fine, so what?" But what they're doing is adding to their criminal record and they don't realize that. You know, they're just concerned with immediate problems: don't drag it on, don't go into too much cost. If it's a fine they'll pay it and that's that.'

The chances that poor working class adolescent boys from poor areas in a big city will at some time be arrested, are high. In addition to personal attributes, the fact of being unemployed and the range of opportunities for being arrested, perhaps resulting from having a 'record', increase the probability of further appearances before the court.

RO: 'What happens when you're on the dole?'

YE1: 'Well, you've nothing to do.'

YE2: 'You stand on corners and get caught for loitering.'

YE1: 'You try to explain to your parents you can't get a job, it's not that easy to get one. But they won't listen to you.'

YE2: 'Then you have no money to go to a film — so you go and thieve it, along with your mates and that.'

As has been previously pointed out according to CI and careers staff it is almost impossible to obtain work if it is known to the potential employer that the person has been in 'trouble with the police'. It follows from this that Careers Officers are reluctant to send people with criminal records for interview:

CO: 'These people come out of Borstal or detention centres and there's very little can be done with them. There's not many employers who are prepared to take an ex-Borstal boy. But if they can come out of there and come straight into CI even for a few months they get into the way of working — I think it's tremendous what it can do. There's no rehabilitation scheme for these lads: there might be for adults, but certainly not for youngsters. And they just come back. They've got a record so they're avoided on the work scene: we don't tend to submit them to places. They're existing on a fiver a week, so they've got to get more money, so they go and steal again, and they're back inside. Even if they don't steal again, they're back inside because the police know them, they pick them up if a crime takes place within 500 yards of their homes. That's the way it goes on. So I think CI's a good thing for these people.'

Thus the possession of a 'delinquent record' makes it difficult for the young person to obtain employment for, as is pointed out, employers tend not to take people who have been convicted of an offence. A dilemma confronts such a young person; if he tells the truth when the employer asks at the interview if he has been in trouble with the police he is unlikely to be hired and if he lies he is likely to be dismissed if the employer finds out the truth. Similarly, an employee who has to have time off to go to court may lose his job. The young person may resolve the dilemma by 'opting out' which increases the probability of association with others who are in the same position and the development of particular ways of dealing with boredom, lack of money and the negative attitudes of other people towards him; some of these adaptive tendencies may bring the individual into further conflicts with the police, which in turn make it less likely that employers will take him on.

To round off our presentation of qualitative material we may present a brief pen portrait of the members of one particular CI work group and four individual cases who are not untypical of the young people employed by CI.

'A' classed as ESN, was the only member of the work group with a special school background:

ASM: : 'He left his first job (filling shelves in a supermarket) because the boss kept sending him to the Post Office and he got a bit fed-up . . . they tended to use him as the message boy which must have been all they felt he was capable of doing . . .'

'B' in complete contrast was lively, witty and had no difficulty in obtaining jobs because of her good performance at interviews:

ASM: : 'You can see why she's wandered from job to job . . . very much a girl who needs to make her presence felt and this might not always be looked upon kindly . . .'

This kind of nomadism was also associated with 'C'; it was thought by the CO that CI would 'never keep her' particularly in view of her lengthy period of unemployment. Apparently this was because 'C' didn't want to do anything and the CO 'in desperation stopped her dole because she just didn't want to work . . .'

One of the difficulties involved in any understanding of the causes of this nomadism is associated with the lack of objective information and hence reliance on reported statements. For example, it was said that 'D' 'had always wanted to be a painter and decorator but couldn't get this job and was pushed into a clerk's job because he had some CSEs . . .' 'E' reported that her first and longest job was in a laundry, which she left because she 'didn't like it', the second was in a fibre-glass factory where she contracted a rash. In the third and fourth jobs she had been declared redundant, whilst she left the fifth 'for a better job' filling shelves. The young people may be referred to on site in terms of a classification which shows disparity between SC and CO; for example, in discussing 'F' the CO said:

> 'You mention a job to him and you can bet he's got an excuse . . . he sounds aggressive . . . we haven't noticed any stutter.' (The latter phrase being elicited by the researcher).

The SC noted:

> 'He gets excited and then he tends to stammer a bit . . . he accepts jobs given to him . . .'

and totally rejected the 'aggressive' label.

Categories of handicapped, job-rejection and the like as applied to YEs were often partially re-expressed on site in terms of social labels; YEs being seen as belonging to the aggressive/initiators of horse-play, the clowns, followers/spectators, the objects of horse-play or relative loners. The nature of interaction in the work group is discussed elsewhere, but we may remark here that in some cases members' 'handicaps' tend to re-inforce these labels; one of the 'clowns' was subject to regular epileptic attacks whilst the 'loners' included a homosexual, an ESN and a very fat boy. This work group mix determined to a large extent the kinds of interaction that ensued. Thus 'G' was a very aggressive individual and during the period of the research he was sacked for the second time from CI. The SC had made him 'leading hand' during his initial period of employment and he was considered a good hard worker and enjoyed physical labour. Punctuating his immersion into work, however, were pieces of horse-play often involving the young person prone to epileptic attacks. The careers staff and the SC were apt to explain these behavioural episodes in terms of his home life in a 'well-known' local family. Allegedly 'G' was regularly beaten by his father and 'swearing and fighting are part of his normal life' (CO). His older brothers drank a lot as did 'G'. He had been in trouble with the police whilst at school and fined for rowdyism, stealing and crashing a van, drunken behaviour and grievous bodily harm on a policeman. The local CO who was a former Education Welfare Officer, had dealt with G's family on a number of occasions; his 'rough and ready' view was:

> 'What he needs is if he comes up against his equals or betters where fighting is concerned . . . somebody who can control him like that . . . then he might settle down.'

By way of contrast 'H' was from quite a good home and had not been involved in any major delinquent acts which had had to be dealt with at official level. His mother had died a few years previously but all his working class sibling group of 6 had permanent employment. He had left school for an apprenticeship at a local engineering works and left voluntarily after one month. He then worked for a building firm for a period of four months, was dismissed and became a trainee baker for one day. Subsequently, for a 3 month period, he became a trainee steward in the Merchant Navy which had involved a short period of training and one world trip. He told the RO that he had left the navy because his girl friend had become less faithful whilst he was away whereas the CO concluded that '. . . he just can't hold a job'. After another short spell as a trainee butcher he joined CI. On site he worked well, seemed pleasant and intelligent and kept regular hours. When someone like 'G' initiated a sequence of horse-play, 'H' was inclined to stop work, spectate and then follow suit 'his trouble may be that he lives too near one or two bad families . . . he lives near "G" and the . . .' (CO).

Of the four individual cases previously referred to 'I' was one of 8 children many of whom, including him, were ESN. The home was dirty and untidy and the labourer father was not very 'involved' with his children, except in so far as it was reported that he thrashed 'I' periodically. From the time of infant school 'I' had been irregular in attendance, and although the mother was from a 'good local family' there seems to have been little parental guidance. These problems were compounded by 'I' having been involved in deviant sexual activity; the CI staff and the work group members felt he was a homosexual, whereas the psychiatrist's report had pronounced him 'normal'. His recent experiences had included spells at a special school and a stay in hospital. At the time of the research he had lived away from home with brother-in-law and elder sister and had been irregular in attendance at CI. There were some domestic difficulties and the husband had clashed verbally and physically with 'I'. There were few suggestions as to what CI could do to help such a YE:

CO: '. . . regular employment might have helped . . . his longest job before CI only lasted 3 months . . . being in hospital last year seemed to do him a power of good, but as soon as he got back home he lapsed into the old familiar ways . . . may be some kind of short-stay residential accommodation would be better . . .?'

'J' aged 17 had had five jobs since leaving school; butcher, apprentice chef, apprentice motor mechanic, apprentice engraver, apprentice lens surfacer. His time in these jobs varied from a few days to a maximum of about 2 months. Some of these movements were described by a CO:

CO: '. . . a month on a training course to be a chef, got paid off that because he kept taking time off for being sick. About a week or a fortnight later got a job as apprentice motor mechanic and stayed there for about 6 weeks. Then out of work for about a month. Did 4 days as an apprentice engraver, paid off after being on the sick.'

RO: 'Four days; paid off for being on the sick?'

CO: 'Well, it's a poor firm anyway, but what probably happened was he wasn't sick anyway, he just sort of didn't like it because the old fellow who runs it gets on their backs a bit . . . Out of work for a week, then back in as an apprentice lens surfacer for two months. Left that willy-nilly, then out of work for a couple of months before getting CI. Not a bad record really; he hasn't been out of work for really considerable periods. He's chopped and changed and he hasn't stuck things but he's been there (CI) since October so this is the best so far.'

'K's' school report showed low grades and referred to 'frequent absences'; he did, however, get a C in woodwork and had a good grade in religion. He obtained a job almost immediately he left school as a van boy which he did for about four months and was then paid off, being made redundant. A four-month period of unemployment followed before he got a job as a packer which he worked at for six months. He was paid off from that job also and after five weeks of unemployment obtained a position as a porter, moving furniture; he did this job for eight months before being dismissed: 'He assured me for "no real reason"' (ASM).' He was then out of work for four months before joining CI and, according to a staff member, 'seemed to do alright'. However, he obtained another job almost immediately at a tea distributors and was due to start on a Monday when:

ASM: '. . . he got himself into trouble that week-end — either he was drunk or he stole some spraying equipment from a shop and there was a dramatic police chase and various other things. Thus he was at court on Monday morning and lost his chance of another job. He was remanded into custody and then he came back here. He got fined £81. That was in March, so he'll still be paying that off.'

This particular young person is therefore officially recorded as being employed by CI for a second time.

The final case to which we briefly refer is also that of a boy who worked for CI twice, but for different reasons. 'L' left school at fifteen and worked as an apprentice painter for five months before being made redundant. He was unemployed from November until the following May then went to work for CI where he stayed for about seven months; during this period he appeared in court charged with breaking and entering and was fined. He left CI voluntarily when a fellow YE decided to leave and was then out of work for six months:

CO: 'He came here in November. These were all the jobs he was sent to (the unit shows a list of about 20 jobs). No, no, no, etc., then Community Industry!'

RO: 'Does that mean he didn't get those jobs?'

CO: 'Yes he didn't get those (pointing to the unit). These mean that the firm sent a card back to say that they hadn't accepted him for one reason or another. Where there's a blank it means that the firm haven't sent the card back. We don't check up on every single interview, so it could be that he didn't go. It says there "did not go". He probably said he didn't go. He certainly came in regularly enought looking for work.

(Quotes from unit):
14″2: Negative attitude to work. Small surly character. Obviously not making an effort. Very poor candidate for jobs at the moment. Very

> down. Will probably become worse if no work forthcoming. Looks almost in tears. Very sorry for himself. Still down and out. If this is the attitude (*i.e.* impression) interviewers have, don't wonder he's out of work. Does not really know what he wants to do. Very vague. Same as ever. A 'no hoper' at present. Unsuitable choices. Wants to go back to CI. Definitely needs a job to boost his confidence.'

Community Industry had in fact been suggested to him a month after he had first left but at that time he was not interested in going back. The quotations from his record provide some hint, even though written from a certain institutional perspective, of the effects of unemployment on a young person. Towards the end of the observational period this same young person obtained a job, as an apprentice painter; the same sort of job he had obtained on first leaving school.

Recruitment and selection

A critical aspect of the CI experience is the entry phase. This is the first point at which the range of potential experiences and events to which the young person might be exposed changes. In terms of the model with which we conclude this chapter this refers to a change in the individual's position but such change is not simply a matter of the individual's actions for these relate in a complex way to the actions and beliefs of others involved in the selection process. We will attempt to point up some of the subtle processes involved in the rather disarming phrases 'change in position' by considering the process by which young people are recruited for CI.

The Careers Officers (COs) are in a key position in relation to the young people obtaining jobs in CI and in open employment. As has been pointed out in chapter 1 the COs are generally seen as playing a central role in CI selection. But what do COs see as their main job?

CO: 'We ourselves are out normally. We're in this week because the schools are closed. But normally we're out almost all week.'

This suggests that work in schools forms the major part of the COs' work. It seems likely that the kinds of people who go to CI, the youngsters who cannot obtain or keep jobs and who have been out of work for long periods, are apportioned only a small amount of the CO's time.[1] What are the nature and results of such young people's interactions with the COs? This question is difficult to answer but CI staff seem aware of some aspects of these relationships:

ASM: 'A social worker had asked the boy to go to the Careers Office to see them so that they could send him down to us. But, as usual, we know that the Careers (Officers) aren't in during the week . . . if a young person goes in during the week for an interview, they *cannot* see a Careers Officer . . . I think the Careers Officers are *not* interested in our type of young person. It causes too many problems for them. They can't place them. They're more interested in people at school: someone with a string of 'O' levels or Highers, who knows exactly what he wants to do and they can place him . . . but our lot: they're quite happy for you to take them and that's it. There's the odd one or two COs I've come across who are really genuinely interested. But on the whole, no . . . (the young people) have to make an appointment to see a CO! These kids are not the kids who are going to do that.'

These remarks, though perhaps somewhat partisan, do call attention to perspectives; the young people who are the major concern for one organization (CI) may be only of marginal interest for another, the Youth Employment Service (YES). This is not to say, that members of the YES are unconcerned about the young unemployed, but that organizationally speaking these youngsters do not obtain a major part of the 'resource time' of the organization. There were some hints that processes within the YES may particularly affect the young people who are difficult to place: when COs remarked on the sort of young people dealt with by particular colleagues there was some indication that status within the organization may be related to the academic qualifications of the clients. Thus senior COs tend to deal with young people who have 'higher qualifications' and are potential university candidates, or candidates for professional/technical courses. There was also a suggestion that dealing with the long-term unemployed and job-changers might be a 'low-status' job in the YES. This was first indicated by a remark made in passing by a CO who said of a colleague who liaised with CI:

'He worked in the City Careers Office before he came to this office a few months ago as the senior so he was dealing with the academic people and had no contact with Community Industry.'

A member of Community Industry staff who had been a Careers Officer gave further details:

'. . . the more intelligent the kind of kid you're dealing with the better your status, this has always been within the Careers Service, if you become a senior Careers Officer you're either dealing with handicapped, and that means usually physically or ESN, or you're dealing with the more academic and able kids.'

This status hierarchy was sketched in more detail by a senior Careers Officer:

'I don't think it applies to "regular customers" I think it probably works with school leavers. I mean the people that have been here, what, about six months, they had to deal with the Easter leavers — this is the Careers Officers — they had to get the Easter leavers jobs and they're the non-academic. Now we two senior Careers Officers are dealing with CSE leavers and the area CO he's dealing with the 'O' level people, now that's within the ordinary careers work, but then we have a specialist officer for the 'A' level people and in our office that has greater status than the handicapped specialist, in most offices the specialist officer for the handicapped is on a higher grade than the further education specialist but it's not so in this office, that is because of the particular preferences of the Principal Careers Officer.'

O: 'Who does the PCO interview?'

CO: 'Well the PCO interviews at independent schools but is very much in favour of getting a good further education service going. I think that's why the FE specialist has got such a high grade. The Principal Careers Officer interviews girls and boys at independent schools but in the office if we're short staffed the PCO interviews anybody, you know, which is quite exceptional.'

The COs' responsibility to 'employers' may be an additional influence on the development of the young peoples careers in that the COs have jobs to offer only in so far as employers notify them of vacancies. In recommending individuals for such vacancies they must necessarily take into account the employers' possible attitudes and prejudices. This institutional constraint becomes particularly apparent in the case of individuals with a criminal record:

CO: (re. YEs coming out of Borstal or detention centres) 'These people come out and there's very little can be done with them. There's not many employers who are prepared to take an ex-Borstal boy . . . They've got a record so they're avoided on the work scene: we don't tend to submit them for places.'

Careers Officers take criminal records into account in this way and tend not to submit people with a 'record' to employers in the belief, no doubt borne out by experience, that they won't be accepted. It is also conceivable that they might also pre-empt an employer's refusal of a job on the basis of other beliefs associated with an individual's prior experiences. A CI staff view would tend to support this point:

ASM: 'Just because a report has maybe said "Bad home background. So many in the family", that to start with puts them (the COs) off. Maybe not very tidily dressed. They're not willing to work on that person. We've got a girl . . . doing typing. Now she's always been dead keen to do typing. The Careers said to me when I had this vacancy and I was going to put her there, they said "No. She's not suitable for typing. The school report said she'd never be able to do it." Well she's doing fine. Granted she's slow, but she'll get there eventually. But nobody was willing to give her the chance before . . . So the school report says "Not suitable" and it's just getting handed down 'till the person's labelled "unemployable" . . . they could have gone into a factory, they could have gone into other things. But either because of their dress or because they've been in that bit of trouble the Careers people feel they should always be honest: they will not recommend anyone to a factory who has a record.'

It must be stressed that the quotation is offered as tentative support for the particular point being made; however, it would be a gross over-simplification to view the COs as non-responsive with regard to these particular clients. The following remarks may offer a corrective to a possible unbalanced view of the CI staff's opinion of the role of the COs in relation to the young unemployed:

ASM: 'Some of them (COs) are really first class with them. Some will go and get them out of bed for a job. There's one in particular like that. He's so dedicated. And he knows them like the back of his hand. He'll go out and look for them.'

It seems reasonable to suggest, however, that the kinds of young people which CI employs are a problem for the COs and that CI is sometimes used as a means of solving this problem. After mentioning some categories of people who would be referred to CI, a CO said:

CO: 'There's also quite a few individuals who just stick out in my mind for a variety of reasons. I must admit that quite often I'm tempted to send them to CI just to get them off my back for a few weeks. I can think of one in particular who lasted a few weeks in CI and then he was back home again.'

An interview with another CO brought this point to the fore:

RO: 'Is CI of use to the Y E S?'

CO: 'I suppose if you wanted to look at it cynically they get some of the kids off our hands who, most of the time, we just couldn't do much about, whereas CI can give them this chance with the sort of supervision they have. They could do more with them than we could as we don't have the time to spend with the unemployed or we don't have the vacancies to suit the amount.'

These remarks by COs provide some hints about the real basis which is involved in their selection of young people for CI. However, insights into the selection processes may also be gained by looking at the kinds of young people the CO would not send to CI. These include individuals who are considered to have a reasonable chance of finding open employment and hence points to the perceived therapeutic role of CI; in addition youngsters who constitute the low grade mentally or physically handicapped and who are the real hard core of the young unemployed. The ones who just don't want to work and have very bad criminal records would not be referred. In addition to these youngsters there are others who may be considered 'appropriate' recruits but who for one reason or another are thought unlikely to accept the offer of a chance to work for CI. It is not clear whether COs offer these youngsters the chance of working for CI or whether they simply refrain from suggesting this possibility to the youngsters because of their predicted likely response:

CO: 'A lot of them for instance in the centre of the city are living in flats. They're people who have dropped out, left home. Flats take a lot of money; their social security benefits are roughly as much as CI are prepared to pay them, so they're obviously not going to bother about it. The money wouldn't be enough, and there's a fair number of characters who are just so "bolshy" they just wouldn't even consider such a thing. The basis they'd turn it down is that it was doing the community some good and undoing all their good vandalism!'

In terms of the official two stage selection procedure for CI several points may be made. Not all CI recruits came through the Careers Service because some young people refuse to have anything to do with it. Sometimes the CI staff are approached directly by social workers and more rarely by probation officers. For example, a social worker 'phoned up while the researcher was present. A staff member later explained:

ASM: 'He (prospective employee) hasn't signed on at the local Youth Employment Office. He's only been out of the detention centre for a fortnight so he hasn't signed on. So the Careers Office know nothing about him . . . So it was just a matter of me 'phoning up the Careers and simply saying "I've had the boy, he'll probably come in and see you. I'll see him for interview next week." So they will say "That's fine. We'll send him along to you . . ."'

RO: 'Do you sometimes take people and just let them know?'

ASM: 'Yes. You know I've started a person and had them in for interview and just 'phoned up the Careers and said "Look, so and so is starting with us Monday", and they say "Fine, we'll mark it on the unit," And that's all . . .'

Other sources of such direct referal are teachers at approved schools who feel that their young people have to get jobs as soon as possible to keep them from getting into trouble. It seems likely that the Careers Service are happy to let CI take people directly under these kinds of circumstances as long as they are informed because of the difficulty they have in placing people with police records. This kind of relationship between the careers service and CI occurs where both sides have worked at building a close liaison and have agreed to share information:

The importance of external forces influencing the number and type of young people recruited for CI should not be underestimated. This point is illustrated by the recollection of a CO who describes the recruitment process as it used to operate:

> '. . . when we had lots unemployed in fact I would suggest some people, they would interview them and then we would get our heads together and see which were the best bet, bearing in mind all sorts of considerations.'

This quotation underlines the fact that under the impact of the raised school leaving age and an improved employment situation, before the three day week, the recruitment process changed. Whereas initially the COs provided more people than CI had places for and therefore some sort of selection was necessary, at the time of the research almost all the young people put forward by the COs were taken. Thus CI's interviews can hardly constitute a selection process at all for young people are rarely turned down. The CI staff accept that their interviews are not really selection interviews:

ASM: 'I've only refused two. The selection has been done before they come in to interview. So really, the ones that we get to interview are all eligible for

CI . . . As I say, there's only been an odd one or two that I've ever turned down. One boy it was because he was *so* retarded really, and at the time there was *nothing* we could offer him.'

There is a realization that the 'judicious mixture' of young people mentioned in official documents is not being achieved:

CO: 'Now we tend to be giving them more of the problem kids with both employment and social problems, because we haven't got the long term unemployed as a result of ROSLA. This time two years ago we had about 60-70 boys and girls signing on. This year, before the three day week, we were down to single figures . . . we've been obliged to talk with CI about putting up youngsters who are a bit more difficult to cope with.'

A CI staff member supported this point of view:

'. . . with the improved employment situation and a smaller range to select from, the majority of a team are now ESN or disabled or have very difficult problems at home.'

Thus external factors influence the pool of youngsters available for CI with positions becoming available for the most difficult cases when the open employment situation is buoyant. This changed emphasis in recruitment may have implications for 'locating' CI in the perceptions of other young people:

ASM: 'It's difficult enough now because kids think that CI is a place for duffers, just a place for thickies . . . you have to show them that there are a variety of people working here.'

Without direct observation of peer groups outside CI this remains a statement of the staff member's opinion. However, it does point up a plausible additional explanation for the difficulty in recruitment. The ASM adds:

'. . . the employment situation has forced it (the image) upon us; the sort of kids who are eligible to come and work for us are either very backward or highly delinquent.'

The types of jobs available in CI and the number of jobs in a particular category may also affect the sort of young people the COs select in response to area staff's requests:

CO: 'The sort of kids who get referred are those who come in week after week and aren't getting fixed up, and the kids who looked obviously difficult and looked as though they were going to be difficult to place. But normally you think "Oh well, there is a chance for this kid getting a job" (in open employment). There's a shortage of labouring jobs developing now: I think probably we *are* mentioning it more to boys, because a vacancy is there in a box you see under "Labouring" and you say "Oh God there's nothing — ah! Community Industry, right!" Whereas if there are six labouring jobs, you flick over Community Industry.'

RO: 'It's filed under "Labouring" is it?'

CO: 'Yes, and for the girls it's filed under "Factory".'

This quotation indicates a further external influence on the referal of young people to CI: the shortage of jobs in a particular category. In the example given it is not the attributes of the young person that are presented as a reason for referal to CI, but a particular state of job availability. There may, of course, be an implicit consideration of attributes of the young person; he may be perceived in terms of someone who could only do a labouring job. Even so, the quotation as a whole suggests a mixture of criteria involving the needs and attributes of the person 'kids that looked obviously difficult', institutional demands on the CO, 'kids that looked as though they were going to be difficult to place', and the state of the job market 'a vacancy is there in the box . . . under "Labouring".'

Given that external and other factors to a certain extent pre-determine selection for CI, what function do the 'selection interviews' conducted by area staff serve? Discussion with CI staff members and observation of such interviews indicates that at a rudimentary level they act as a mechanism for establishing contact between staff and young persons and hence ease the transition for both parties:

ASM: 'It's much better if I can go in that morning (YE's first day with CI) and say "Hello . . ." or whoever it is.'

Additionally they are seen as having an educational value in that whereas for the young person job interviews have been previously synonymous with failures they are here equated with success, the first hazardous step towards establishing a successful career:

ASM: 'They've probably been to so many jobs and they've been turned down for all of them. Now they've come for one interview and they've been accepted.'

In addition to these purposes the interviews do also serve to some extent as a check. The staff have turned down a person on interview because he was too mentally handicapped to be given a job. In another case, a boy with bad eyesight was turned down because he refused to wear glasses, and would therefore have been a safety hazard on a site. The staff also check that the young person really wants a job: people who come to interviews sometimes say that they don't actually want the job or refuse it when it is offered. Thus it seems that if a person is physically and mentally able to do *some* job that CI can offer, and is at least minimally willing to try a job, then he is offered a job with CI.

Characteristics and attitudes

In this section we will employ a quantitative analysis to describe the opinions and attitudes of young people in varying environmental circumstances in order to throw in broad relief the characteristics and beliefs of young people who are eligible for or employed by CI. To this end a number of comparison groups were chosen for the research, the major group being sampled from apprentices on day or block release courses offered by Colleges of Further Education. The requirements borne in mind in obtaining this group were that its members should have as nearly as possible the same age and sex distribution as the CI employees and should also show regional variations compatible with the geographical distribution of CI areas; in addition they should be engaged in 'manual labour'. Consequently young builders and engineers employed 'on the tools side' appeared to be appropriate in this respect and liaison officers in eight Colleges of Further Education in each CI area were asked to choose appropriate samples of young workers attending their college.[2]

The foundation for the distinctions which have been drawn between those teenagers who will enter stable employment and those who are considered to be 'At Odds' can be seen at the school level and are perhaps most evident in the final year of school. It was therefore considered desirable, both in terms of identifying more closely the characteristics of young people considered to be 'at risk' and in examining the effectiveness of CI, to include a sample of school leavers in the research design. Two groups of school leavers were chosen from selected secondary modern schools or their equivalent in each of the eight geographical areas in which CI operated. An attempt was made to choose schools which had been attended by CI employees and the pupils within them were chosen so as to fall into two groups, those who might be predicted to be 'At Odds' youngsters, and a second group of average youngsters who were predicted as likely to enter stable employment on leaving school.[3]

The sample size of the four adolescent groups chosen for comparative purposes is illustrated in Table 4.

Table 4: *Sample sizes of the four adolescent groups* after the exclusion of cases with missing observations on sex of respondent.*

Sex	*Workers*		*School Leavers*		*Totals for Sex*
	CI Employees	*Apprentices*	*'Unstable'*	*'Stable'*	
Male	424	667	219	227	1,537
Female	204	56	76	73	409
Group Totals	628	723	295	300	1,946

* The two school leaver samples are matched on age both averaging approximately 15 years 4 months. The CI employees tend to be somewhat younger than the apprentices, the average ages being respectively 17 years and 17 years 4 months.

The young people in the samples described above expressed their views and provided information about themselves by means of a questionnaire[4] which, as with the adult sample, provided a number of measures or scale scores for each individual. The items making up these measures were chosen on an *a priori* basis with regard to their theoretical meaningfulness but to a greater or lesser degree the scales are perhaps best regarded as being exploratory in nature, adequate for our intended purpose but requiring further development before more general use. This work thus constitutes merely the first step in the development of a number of interesting and potentially useful measures in an area not renowned for the sensitivity of its instruments. The theoretical areas covered by the scales which were constructed or modified specifically for the research are as follows:

(a) Motivation and commitment to work.
(b) Alienation and estrangement.
(c) Organizational structure and process.
(d) Personality and cognitive functioning.

We will briefly describe the scales[5] related to these four areas before outlining their application at both school and employment levels.

The 42 item pool covering 'motivation to work' was reduced to 3 scales involving 13, 11 and 8 items respectively. For the first of these scales the label 'work cynicism' was eventually settled upon. In a sense disagreement with these items would seem to represent a strong conventional 'idealism' about 'equal opportunities' and 'each man doing the job he is best suited for'. One may speculate that the CI employees in particular will have experienced the cynicism that is expressed by agreement with many of these items. It may well be that such an attitude, associated with their position in the economic and social structure, is in fact a 'realistic' one and indeed examination of responses to individual items, to be considered later, offers support for this view. However, the term 'work cynicism' was retained since it covered the item content and the theoretical issues underlying it. The two items numbered as they appeared in the questionnaire, which are most descriptive of this scale, are:

(25) Many firms would be better off if they let the workers run them.

(34) It's best to take whatever job you can get, and not be too choosey.

The items on the second scale are clearly related to the concept of the meaning to the individual of the work he performs as well as the meaning of work in general. The label 'work meaning' was chosen for this scale. The elements which are tapped by this scale cover 'work as a place solely to earn money', 'work as a place for self-realization', and 'work as a purpose in itself'. The two most descriptive items are:

(9) I would feel lost if I were to be unemployed for any length of time.

(18) Work's a place where you make real friends.

The content of the two items most descriptive of the final scale in this area suggests that an individual who scored high on it would show a high degree of commitment to both his own job and to the idea of working in general; they are:

(35) The only way to get noticed at work is to work hard.

(19) When you start work people begin treating you as a grown up person.

This scale relates to the conceptual basis of the work area but may not be consequential on work cynicism or on work meaning. An individual may be committed to his work because he agrees with the conventional ideas of work ('that it is a good way of life') or because work has meaning for him ('he finds self-fulfilment at work'), or both, or neither. Commitment to work may be a phenomenon associated with socialization in a particular kind of society, and it may be that this commitment is only questioned when it is not rewarded or is positively frustrated. This third scale was termed, therefore, 'work commitment'. The direction of scores on each of these scales is:

(i) *Work Cynicism:* Contrary to the normal convention, higher scores on this scale indicate lesser not greater cynicism, and therefore a high score will indicate a 'positive' attitude to the contemporary work situation.

(ii) *Work Meaning:* Higher scores indicate lack of meaning for the individual in the work he does. Lack of meaning is not necessarily a 'negative' disposition towards the modern work environment.

(iii) *Work Commitment:* High scores indicate high commitment and are thus 'positive' in relation to work attitudes.

The alienation pool of 28 items represented three clusters of questions, one of ten and two of nine items. Inspection of the items which figure most prominently in each cluster in conjunction with a regard for the theoretical foundation for choice of items provided the labels of powerlessness, moral righteousness and self-doubt for these scales.

The powerlessness scale by and large fits the original conceptualization of this aspect of alienation in terms of a perceived inability to influence events which have implications for the individual. Thus the individual feels that his own behaviour cannot determine the occurrence of the outcomes or reinforcements he seeks. The two most characteristic items are:

(167) People are always trying to stop me from doing what I want to do.

(158) No matter what I say or do, things seem to go against me.

The scale 'moral righteousness', used in the sense of 'conventional contemporary mores', contains items referring to the closeness of parental ties as well as straightforward moral items. The two most characteristic items are:

(149) Shop-lifting is a serious crime and should be severely punished.

(165) I think it's better to admit my mistakes than to try to cover them up.

The cluster of items labelled self-doubt was originally referred to as 'self-confidence' as the most descriptive items appeared to fit this description:

(147) I find it difficult to believe in my abilities sometimes.

(148) If I decide to so something then I always succeed.

However, as a result of the scaling procedure the new weights assigned to each item of the self-confidence scale were found to be U-shaped across the response categories with the extreme responses (Strongly Agree and Strongly Disagree) receiving the largest weights, and the Undecided category receiving the smallest weight. Thus an individual receives a high score if he strongly agrees or strongly disagrees with every item, and a low score if he is undecided on each item. Thus the scale is, in effect, measuring how extreme his responses are, or how assured he is of his self image; low scores appear to indicate uncertainty about self. In terms of the latter interpretation the scale still measures some form of self-confidence but not in the sense indicated by agreement or disagreement with the content of the items. Any interpretations of differences associated with this sub-scale must remark this point and consequently it was labelled 'self-doubt'. The direction of scoring for these scales are:

(i) *Powerlessness:* High scores indicate stronger feelings of powerlessness.

(ii) *Moral Righteousness:* High scores indicate righteousness.

(iii) *Self-doubt:* High scores indicate self-assurance, either positive or negative self image; low scores indicate uncertainty about one's own opinions of self.

The items chosen to tap the perception of organizational structure reflect a particular view of an organization as a 'human' enterprise and have been previously described (Murray, 1978). Analysis of the 58 questions chosen to represent this theoretical area produced four scales which appeared to be a reasonable fit to the model employed. The first scale is referred to as 'Supervisory Satisfaction' and reflects the employee's perceived satisfaction with his immediate superior. The most characteristic items are those directly associated with this label:

(60) All in all are you satisfied with the person who is in charge of you?

(47) Is the person in charge of you a friendly person who you feel able to talk to about things?

The second scale is termed 'Organizational Consideration' and refers to the employee's view of his organization as being 'caring' and supportive; the most characteristic items are:

(81) Does your organization care whether the people who work for it are happy or not?

(75) Does your organization try to give people good working conditions?

The third scale is termed 'Work Group Support' and reflects peer group processes of an informal kind within the work group. It essentially taps the individual's perceived rapport with work mates in terms of the satisfaction of affiliative needs; characteristic items are:

(68) Are the others in your work group friendly people who you can talk to about things?

(78) Are the others in your work group willing to listen to your problems?

The final scale refers to processes which act to encourage job performance, particularly with regard to the perceived appropriateness of administrative arrangements; it is termed 'Task Accomplishment' and characteristic items are:

(84) Does the person in charge of you encourage those who are under him to work as a team?

(83) Are work activities sensibly organized in your organization?

These four scales appear to be a good fit to the description of CI as a 'caring organization'.

In terms of the possible outcomes of measurement it should be emphasized that CI is by definition a 'human organization' and part of its declared intention is to help youngsters settle in open employment by providing a realistic industrial environment. Thus we have a reversal of the criteria usually applied by organizational development programmes; the effectiveness of the organization being in part related to its success in orientating young employees to the 'less human' systems which characterize the open employment situation.

In choosing measures to tap the personality area we clearly cannot be comprehensive and hence have to limit ourselves to scales which seem appropriate for the target population and pertinent for present research purposes. Bynner (1969) employed a scale of 'self-image' for his research into 'The Young Smoker' which appeared to tap the three dimensions of 'educational success, toughness and precocity'. The first dimension appeared to be particularly well defined and ten of the most characteristic items on this dimension were used for our research. In terms of responding to this scale subjects were asked to rate themselves on a three-point scale each of which, as in the original form, consisted of two opposing attributes with a neutral category in between. The phrasing of the attributes was sufficiently general to allow this scale to be termed 'Self-Image' with high scores representing positive self-image in terms of a conventional stress on such attributes as neatness, obedience, modesty and hard work. The scale was presented in two forms on separate pages of the questionnaire; one form asked the respondent to rate himself as he actually is; the other as the kind of person he would like to be. This latter form of the scale is referred to as 'Ideal Self-Image'.

A scale of 'psychosomatic anxiety' was also used by Bynner and with the provision of an extra item was adopted in an unchanged form, high scores indicating high anxiety. This scale was chosen for our research as the physical component of personality seems to be particularly salient for such special groups as the CI youngsters; in addition anxiety is seen as the motivational base for the development of cognitive mechanisms which help shield the individual from pressures which might unsettle him. These cognitive processes are seen by some psychologists as giving rise to a general personality disposition underlying a whole series of social attitudes. This disposition has been given a variety of labels such as fascism, rigidity, dogmatism, authoritarianism, conservatism. A shortened and simplified form of the adult dogmatism scale has been developed (Murray, 1974) and after further item analysis to reduce its length still further was used in the research. High scores on this scale indicate high dogmatism which is perhaps best viewed as a cognitive shield necessary for coping with felt anxiety. The two measures of psychosomatic anxiety and dogmatism are seen as being related to the way in which individuals cope with day to day pressures and hence were included in our choice of scales for the personality domain.

A group test of general intelligence, suitable for use with the target population, was also included in the battery (Heim, 1970). Part I of the test has a verbal/numerical bias and Part II a diagrammatic bias. The scales together with their maximized reliabilities are given in Table 5.

These scales may be thought to be useful not only to the extent that they will serve as pointers for assessing the effectiveness of CI but also in that they may be used to described individuals who are thought to be at risk or, put more generally, who are considered 'alienated'. While feeling sympathetic towards colleagues who experience a sense of irritability at the mention of 'alienation' the position taken is that further refinement of this concept is preferable to abandoning it altogether. The battery of attitude scales developed for the research thus provides a means of describing in a systematic and objective way the extent and direction of differences between our samples.

In relation to the sample of school leavers chosen for the research two analyses are pertinent. The independent variables used for both

Table 5: *Scales used for the young people sample together with maximized internal reliability co-efficients.**

Related Theoretical Area	*Scales*	*Maximized Internal Reliability Co-efficients (Hoyt)* *CI Young Employees* (N = 106)	*Apprentices (N = 96)*	*School Leavers* (N = 80)	*Average* r's
Motivation/ Commitment to work	Work cynicism	.71	.76	.73	.73
	Work meaning	.84	.66	.76	.75
	Work commitment	.74	.67	.56	.65
Alienation	Powerlessness	.84	.69	.65	.73
	Moral righteousness	.62	.63	.67	.64
	Self confidence	.75	.70	.76	.74
Personality	Actual self-image	.72	.66	.74	.71
	Ideal self-image	.85	.84	.76	.82
	Dogmastism	.74	.70	.74	.73
	Psychosomatic anxiety	.79	.75	.78	.77
Organizations	Supervisory satisfaction	.75	.84		.79
	Organizational care	.79	.80		.79
	Work group support	.74	.81		.77
	Task accomplishment	.79	.75		.77
Cognitive	Verbal IQ				
	Non-verbal IQ		Reported as .92		
	Total IQ**				

* The internal reliability co-efficients have a theoretical range from 0.00 to 1.00, no internal consistency to perfect consistency. They were calculated for a sample of CI young employees from one area chosen at random; coefficients also being computed for samples of apprentices and school leavers chosen from the same area.

** Though the abbreviation 'IQ' is used throughout the text, the intelligence test result is expressed as a raw score and hence is not a 'quotient'.

sets of analyses are group membership, for the sake of convenience referred to as 'alienated' and 'stable' school leavers, and 'sex' with statistical control being exercised over age by deploying it as a covariate. The first analysis uses the ten attitudinal measures previously described as the dependent variables and the second incorporates, in addition to these measures, total IQ and family size. The results for both analyses indicate that there are substantial differences between groups and between sexes for both the first (Groups: F=30.6, P<.001; sexes F=8.1, P<.001) and second set (Groups: F=34.2, P<.001; sexes 6.81) of variables.

In terms of this observed sex difference we may note that little additional information is afforded by including IQ and family size in the dependent variable set; the dependent variables of analyses 1 and 2 'explaining' respectively 12 per cent and 13 per cent of the systematic attitudinal variation between the sexes. Inspection of the loadings for analysis 1 indicate that the most powerful discriminator between boys and girls of this age and socio-economic level is psychosomatic anxiety (−.68) followed by moral righteousness (−.35); dogmatism (.32); ideal self-image (.31); powerlessness (.31) and work cynicism (−.29). The mean differences between boys and girls on these measures display the pattern illustrated in fig. 2.

Fig. 2: *Schematic presentation of attitude difference between male and female school leavers.**

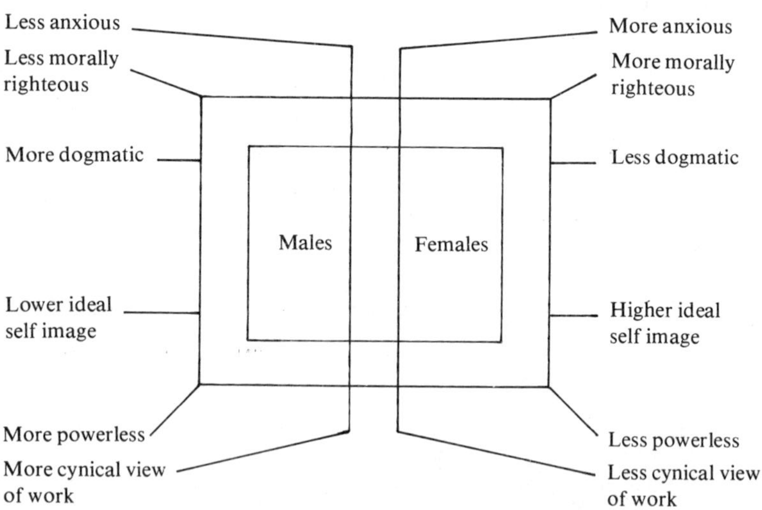

*These differences also apply at the employment level.

In terms of the between group differences we may observe that for the first analysis all variables with the exception of Work Meaning, Moral Righteousness and Self-Doubt make a contribution with the measures of Work Cynicism and Dogmatism providing the largest contribution. In all the ten variables account for a useful 34 per cent of the variance associated with differences between the groups and it is noteworthy that this percentage is increased to 43 per cent when we include family size and total IQ into the set of variables used for the second analysis. Indeed in this analysis inspection of the loadings suggests that total IQ is the major discriminator with the other variables making a similar relative contribution to that observed for analysis one. The contribution of family size to between-group separation for this analysis suggests that it is not such a useful predictor, at any rate at the school leaving level, as might previously have been supposed from an inspection of the literature (Wedge and Prosser, 1973): though it should be noted that we are sampling within a 'working class' population and are reducing variability associated with socio-economic level and hence family size. The relative contribution of these variables to between-group discrimination, using the loadings for the second analysis as descriptive aids, and the direction of group differences may be illustrated in graphic form as shown in fig. 3.

Fig. 3: ***Schematic presentation of the 'alienated' school leaver****

CI Employees		*Apprentices*
Lower IQ	.81	Higher IQ
Cynical view of work	.66	Less cynical view of
Dogmatic	.66	Less dogmatic
More powerless	.59	Less powerless
Less positive self-image	.55	Positive self-image
More commitment to work	.54	More commitment to work
Less positive ideal self	.48	More positive ideal self
Large family size	.36	Less large family size
More physical anxiety	.34	Less physical anxiety

Direction of 'alienation'
←

*Signs associated with the loadings omitted. Variables with loadings less than 3.0 omitted.

The figure illustrates, as expected, that the 'alienated' group fall well below their stable counterparts on IQ; indeed it would be rather perturbing if this were not the case as low achievement/ability at school was one of the criteria by which young people were assigned to groups. This group, however, also show a greater cynicism and less commitment towards work and exhibit a higher level of dogmatism and psychosomatic anxiety than their 'stable' school peers; these differences are also related to the greater sense of powerlessness exhibited in the figure. To a certain extent the lower scores of the 'alienated' group on self-image and ideal self-image are to be expected given the original criteria used in the classification of these individuals. The picture we obtain of such teenagers is essentially one of low ability and high physical anxiety associated with cognitive rigidity and a feeling of powerlessness; these differences are coupled with greater cynicism and less commitment to work and an overall lowering in self-worth.

The analysis described above for the school leaver sample was repeated in our comparison of CI employees and apprentices. The first analysis again involved a multivariate treatment of the set of ten attitude variables using group, CI *v.* Apprentices, and sex as the independent variables, with age as a covariate. This was extended in a second analysis by including family size, number of jobs held since leaving school, and total IQ score in the dependent variable set. As mentioned previously a comparison of the two analyses will indicate how well the attitude variables characterize the CI employees compared with the contributions made by the three additional characteristics of measured ability, family size and number of jobs held. The results of the analyses indicate that significant differences are evident between groups ($F = 20.8$, $P<0.001$) and between sexes ($F = 18.5$, $P<0.001$) for the first analysis. In terms of the difference between sexes, amounting to appoximately 14 per cent, we may note that, as for the school leaver samples, psychosomatic anxiety and moral righteousness are the important discriminators with powerlessness and work commitment playing a part. The direction of difference is as illustrated in figure 2.

Observation of the loadings relating to group differences for this analysis suggests that work cynicism is the major contributor. Other variables that contribute to this difference are dogmatism, work commitment, powerlessness and psychosmatic anxiety, with work meaning making a weaker contribution. Comparing this pattern with that previously discussed in relation to the school leavers we see that the two self-concept variables no longer make a contribution to between-group differences at this level and that work meaning now plays some part. The important discriminators remain the same, however, which implies that they have a general usefulness in discriminating between the alienated and the non-alienated teenager regardless of level. We may observe from the direction of mean differences that the CI employee is more cynical and less committed to work than his contemporary in stable employment; he is also more dogmatic, more anxious and feels a greater sense of powerlessness. There is also a suggestion that the CI employee feels that work is more meaningful than the typical apprentice.

It is worthy of note that the variance accounted for in this analysis, 13 per cent, is increased to over one-third when we extend the dependent variable set in the second analysis. Here we see that the emphasis has now shifted to the three additional variables introduced at this stage; the major contribution being made by the number of jobs that the individual has had since leaving school. Since this is a formal selection criterion for recruitment to CI and hence an *a priori* means of defining the levels of our independent variables we would expect this measure to be an effective discriminator between groups. Total IQ and family size both contribute to group separation and we see that the relative importance of the attitude variables has been somewhat diminished. Noting the mean differences on these variables it is seen that the CI employees are characterized by larger family size, lower IQ and greater number of jobs held since leaving school than is the case for the apprentices. In fig. 4 over, the between-groups comparison on the important discriminators is presented in schematic form.

In terms of the between-groups differences at the employment and school levels we might speculate that the differences on IQ and family size influence, in a complex manner, the development of the other differences which have been noted. A low level of verbal ability can be especially damaging in this respect since the inability to communication effectively with authority figures can often be mistaken for stubbornness or lack of motivation. It is worthy of note

Fig. 4: *Schematic presentation of the alienated young manual worker.**

CI Employees		*Apprentices*
Job changing	.80	Job stability
Lower IQ	.74	Higher IQ
Cynical view of work	.61	Less cynical view of work
Large family size	.48	Less large family size
Dogmatic	.41	Less Dogmatic
Less commitment to work	.36	More commitment to work
More physical anxiety	.30	Less physical anxiety

Direction of alienation
←

*Signs associated with the loadings omitted. Variables with loadings less than 3.0 omitted.

that the role of dogmatism and psychosomatic anxiety in contributing to group separation is the same as we move from the school to the employment level. Similarly there appears to be a consistent feeling of powerlessness among the 'At Odds' groups, with their cynicism and lack of commitment to work apparent even at the school leavers level. Drawing on the analysis at both the school and open employment levels we may present a schematic view of the 'alienated' young person in terms of the variables studied here in fig. 5.

Multivariate analysis is a powerful tool which has helped us to build up a picture of the alienated young person both in school and employment contexts. Not only has it provided a means for maximally discriminating between the various sample groups but also, in terms of the loadings associated with each scale, offered a systematic explanation of the role of each dependent variable. In our quest for further explanation we may usefully link this analysis with the qualitive aspect of the research by describing the differing responses of apprentices and CI employees to the individual items of the work and alienation scales. A simple x^2analysis using the group response frequencies for each item will serve our purpose

Fig. 5: *Schematic view of the 'alienated' young person at school and employment levels.*

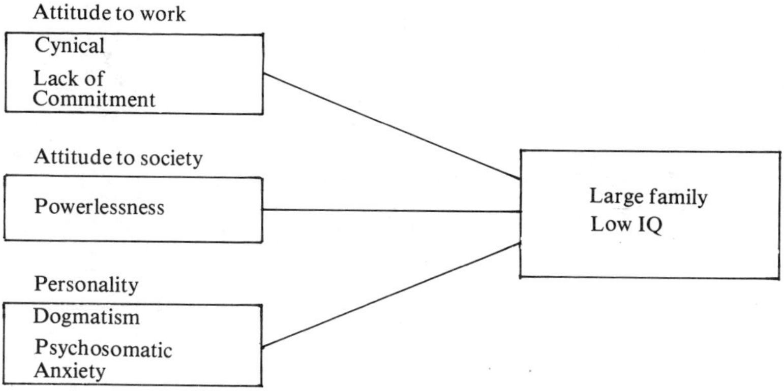

with those items having P values of <.001 being presented in graphic form to illustrate between-group differences.

The items depicted in fig. 6 provide a picture of the different emphasis given by the young people in the two groups to the desirability of being employed and their opinions about entry into the world of work. This is germane to our interest in that a considerable number of young people at or below craft level who have been unemployed for some time or have changed jobs frequently are often termed 'work shy' and thought to prefer social security payments rather than income from regular employment.

It will be seen from the distribution of responses to item 3 that two-thirds of the CI group and four-fifths of the apprentices express a definite dislike of unemployment. There is very little equivocation about this as indicated by the low proportion of uncertain responders. Approximately three-quarters of CI's young workers express concern about the prospect of being unemployed which, bearing in mind the recruitment policy previously discussed, is a surprisingly high figure. This view about the desirability of being employed is not solely a function of the need to obtain a livelihood, for both groups of young people see employment as being preferable to unemployment even if there was no financial compunction to work (item 16); surprisingly, there is slightly greater emphasis in this respect from the CI group. Perhaps their experiences of unemployment may act as a corrective to the often

Fig. 6: *CI and apprentices*: responses to items 3, 8, 16, 21, 31, 32, 34*

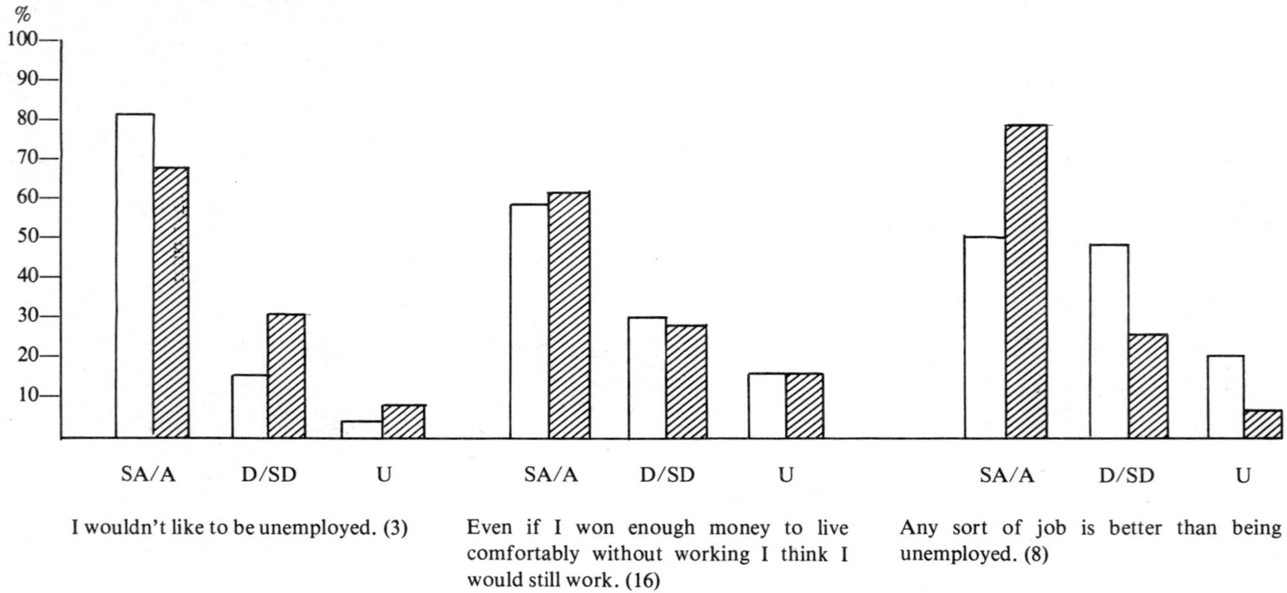

*In this and the following figures: ☐ Apprentices ▨ CI

The bars represent the percentages of each group responding to the given categories.

Fig. 6 continued.

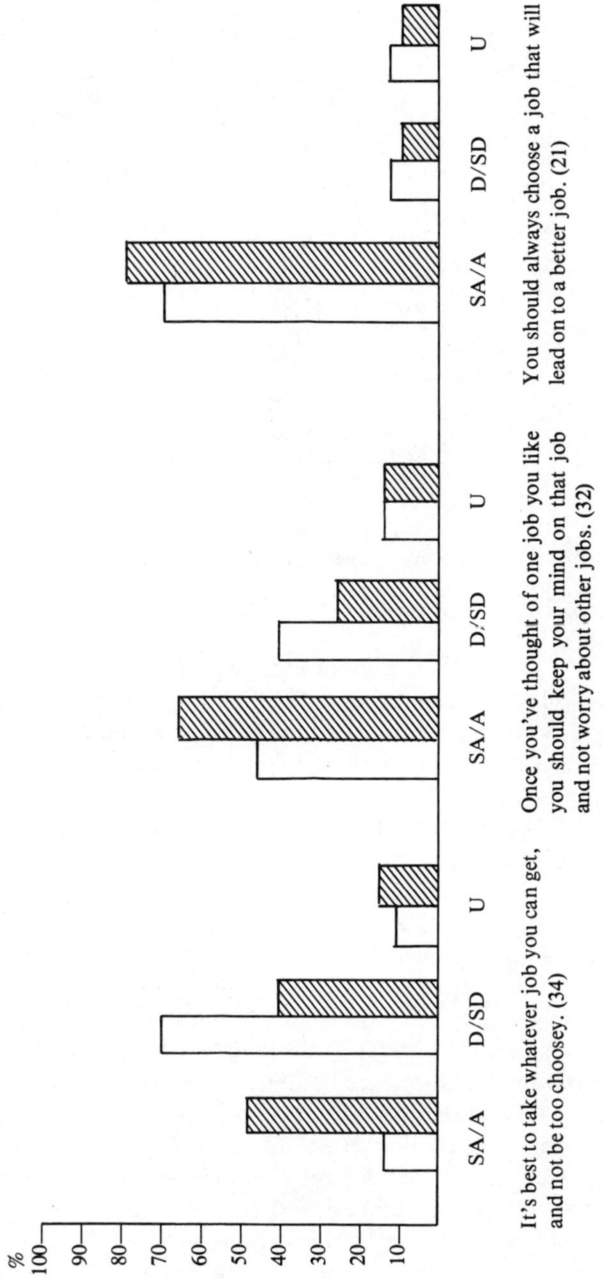

Fig. 6 continued.

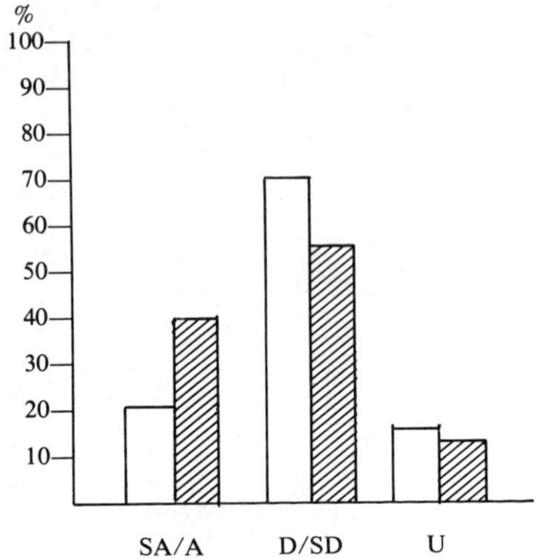

Getting a good job depends on luck more than anything else. (31)

expressed view of the benefits assumed to be associated with absence of occupation. The differential response between groups to item 8 illustrates rather well the qualifications necessary to the global picture presented; thus while over two-thirds of the CI group feel that 'any sort of job is better than being unemployed' the apprentices appear to be more or less equally divided on this issue. This response no doubt in part reflects the special position of the apprentices who as a 'privileged' group have not experienced the rigours associated with unemployment but it may also point up the socialization processes associated with obtaining a work and trade identity conferred by their work situation.[6]

Responses to item 34 refer to the degree of discrimination which is employed in choosing a particular type of job. Whereas a slight majority of CI workers feel that 'It's best to take whatever job you can get', nearly three-quarters of the apprentices feel that it is in their interests both to be selective in choice of occupation and also to keep the situation under review (item 32). An idealized response of the CI group in relation to this item in terms of 'all things being equal' might well fall in line with the apprentices' view and is borne out by group responses to item 21, but their prior experiences, both at school and in open employment, coupled with a lack of formal qualifications, no doubt contribute to a realistic assessment of their situation in that they cannot afford 'to be choosey' for, as has been pointed out in a previous section, they have nothing 'to sell' to an employer. The responses to item 31 fit this picture, for while both groups feel that luck plays a 'secondary' role in obtaining what is considered to be 'a good job' the CI group tend to place a much greater emphasis on the operation of chance factors in this respect that the apprentices; a difference which is strongly marked at the school level.

Fig. 7[7] presents in graphic form the opinions of the young people about the meaning and significance of work in their lives. Thus while a slight majority of CI's young people feel that in general work is 'dull and boring' over two-thirds of the apprentices feel it is 'interesting' (item 15). This finding is perhaps not unrelated to the fact that the apprentices show a greater interest in and have an enhanced opportunity for an appreciation of the total work process rather than its component parts (item 2). This picture is filled out a little more by an examination of responses to items 22 and 41; the apprentices are more ready, and we might add able, to meet challenging work situations (item 22) and less tolerant of self-imposed rest periods (item 41) than the CI group. There are other interesting differences between the groups with regard to the non-economic aspects of work: while there is a general consensus that the work situation is an important arena for making lasting friendships (item 18) the CI group tend to lay greater stress on this. They are also more gregarious than the apprentices in their job orientation showing a more pronounced preference for working in a group rather than individual context (item 1) and with age-related peers rather than older workers (item 42).

Turning to the economic aspects of employment, items 17, 33, it will be observed from the distribution of responses that the apprentices are less instrumental in their views of work than the CI group. Thus while both groups feel that in the final analysis the most important aspect of a job is the pay (item 33), with slightly greater emphasis placed on this by the CI group, a true reversal of opinion occurs with regard to opinions about the purpose of work (item 17); the apprentices, unlike the CI group, see more in work than merely financial return.

Fig. 7: *CI and apprentices: responses to items 1, 2, 5, 15, 17, 18, 19, 22, 33, 41, 42.*

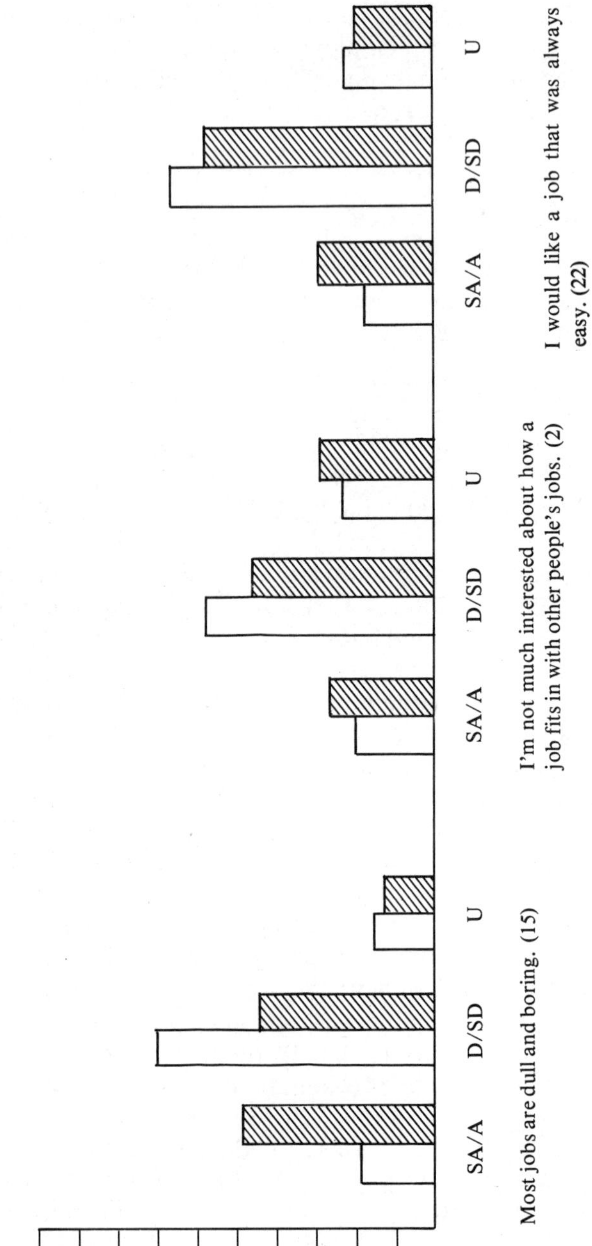

Fig. 7. continued.

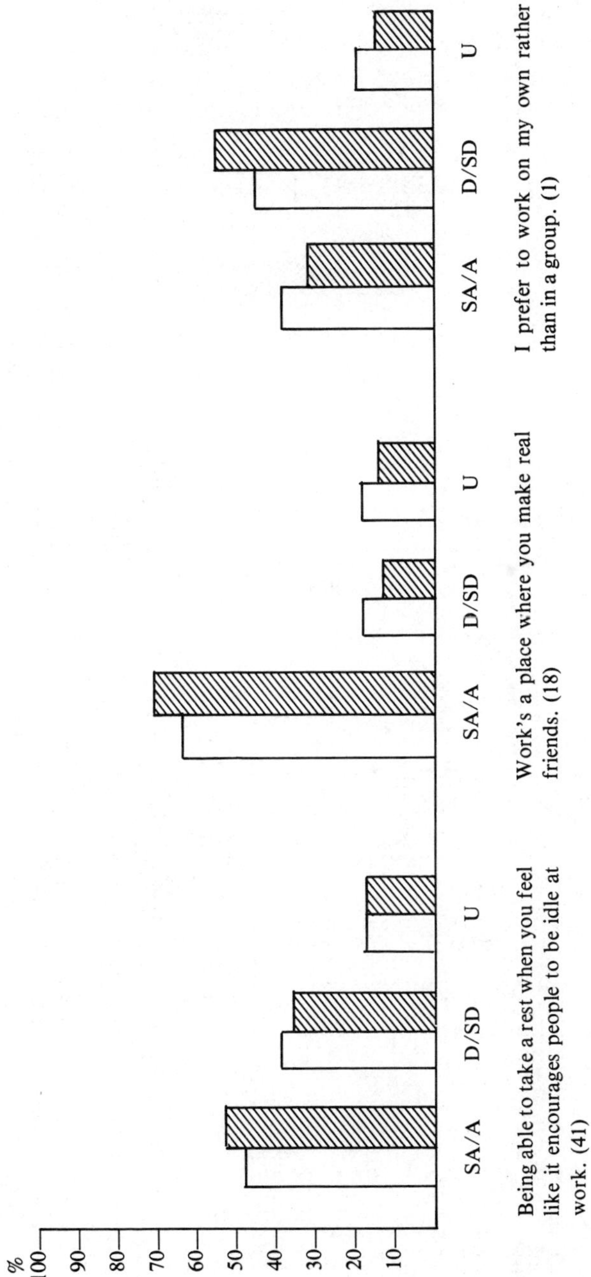

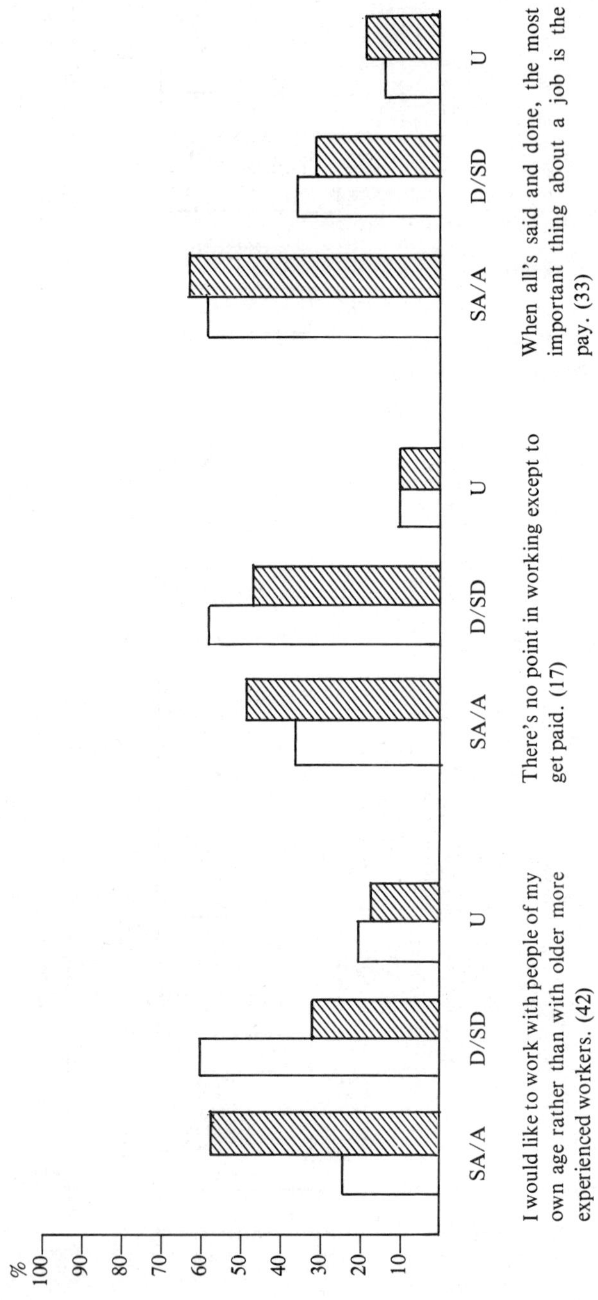

Fig. 7. continued.

In terms of job advancement, the type of work-related experiences provided in the secondary sector, where there is a lack of enterprise, specific training and ineffective unionization coupled with limited opportunities for advancement, no doubt contribute to the prevailing view among CI's young people that 'knowing the right people' doesn't contribute to getting on in a job (item 36, Fig. 8).[8] By way of contrast nearly two-thirds of the apprentices, who as individuals have access to craft trade unionsim with all that this means in terms of informal contacts which can enhance job prospects, feel that access to influential individuals is an important part of their job prospects. Related to this point is the differential group reponse to item 39; in this respect the majority of the CI group feel that not having a skilled trade acts as a considerable bar to self advancement in the work sphere wheras the apprentices take an opposite view. The latter may underestimate the importance attached to skill in the labour market for it is something they will acquire on termination of their apprenticeships and hence to a certain extent is taken for granted. It is worth emphasizing, however, that this skill is acquired in a particular social context and once entry to this context has been negotiated a form of sponsorship in terms of 'knowing the right people' may be more important to job advancement than possession of a skill *per se*. This 'negotiation' begins prior to the actual entry to employment.

The response to item 11 suggests that while both groups feel that a certain amount of conformity is necessary to advancement the CI group tend to place a much greater emphasis on this than the apprentices. In particular the latter are more uncertain than the CI group with regard to how far conformity contributes to self advancement and this may in part reflect their autonomous yet 'dependent' status. Similarly, while both groups are in broad agreement that pay rises have to be fought for (item 24) the CI group take rather a harder line than the apprentices on this issue. This view of employer/employee relationship may be associated in part with the greater degree of powerlessness experienced by such groups of young people which is associated with their position in the social and economic structure both at school and open employment levels. Following on this point we may remark that the involuntary removal of a young person from employment has considerably greater implication for those with some future prospects compared with those whose employment related experiences are predicated upon casual access to and departure

Fig. 8: *CI and apprentices: responses to items 11, 24, 30, 36, 39.*

Fig. 8. continued.

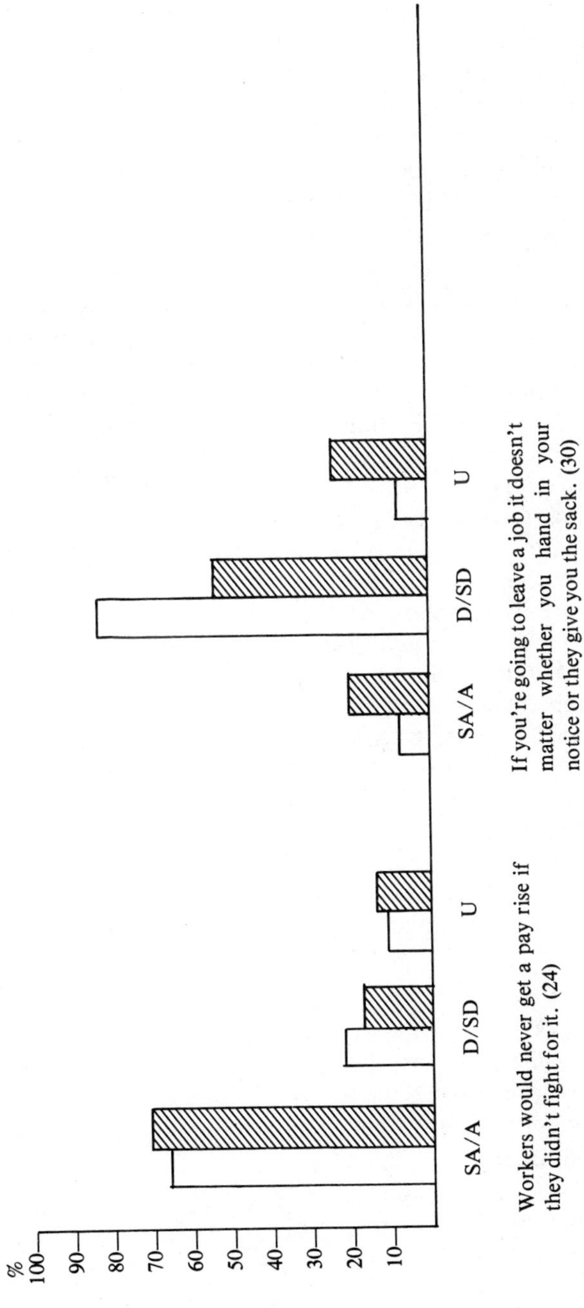

from jobs, these being the typical circumstances of many CI employees and 'unstable' school leavers. This view is rather dramatically pointed up by the differential response to item 30; whereas over four-fifths of the apprentices feel that involuntary termination of employment in terms of being sacked is damaging to the individual a substantial proportion of the CI group are either uncertain or feel that 'it doesn't matter'.

While both groups like to feel that they can be trusted with any new important job that arises in their work situation (item 6, Fig. 9), the apprentices are less confident and more uncertain in their ability to cope in this respect than the CI group and express far greater need of adult approval of their work (item 12).[9] In terms of the perception of authority relations in the work situation, both groups of young people, while being nearly unanimous in their wish to be left to get on with a job without over close supervision (item 38), feel that a certain measure of discipline is necessary from those who act in a supervisory role in order to ensure equality of treatment for workers in their charge (item 27). The apprentices, however, perhaps in part resulting from their lessened vulnerability in the work situation, place less emphasis on the relationship between supervisory discipline and equality of treatment than the CI group. Similarly, the apprentices as a group have less confidence in the job capabilities and skills of immediate supervisory personnel than the CI workers though in the eyes of both groups of young workers the 'foreman role' is relatively de-authoritized in this respect (item 26). This response does not appear to reflect an unfounded cynicism for the responses of both groups to a non-scale item (item 37) appear to reflct the acceptance of legitimate criticism on the basis of superior ability; the apprentices in fact show slightly greater acceptance of this than the CI group.

We may now extend our consideration of sample responses to individual items by considering the relative emphasis given by the young people in our two groups to questions drawn up to tap alienation. The same procedure was adopted as that previously described for choosing work-related items and the picture of perceived external constraints on the individual's course of action is presented graphically in figure 10:

Observation of the pattern of responses depicted in this figure[10] suggests that whereas the CI youngsters feel they have less control over those factors in their external environment which may

Fig. 9: *CI and apprentices: responses to items 6, 12, 26, 27, 37, 38.*

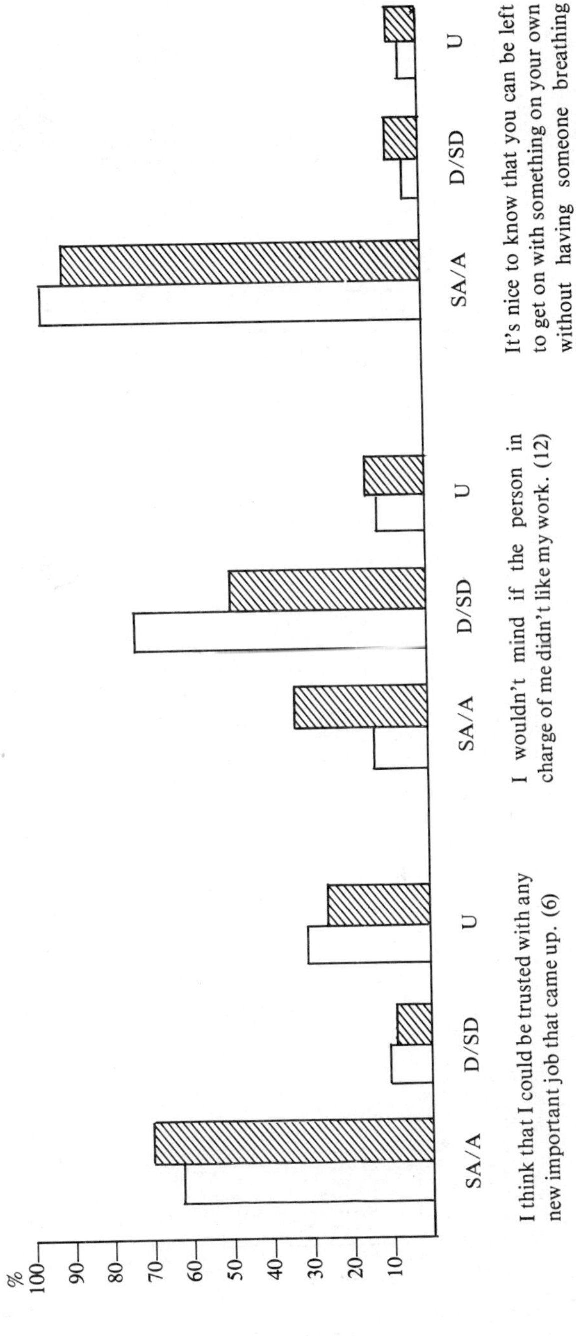

Fig. 9 continued.

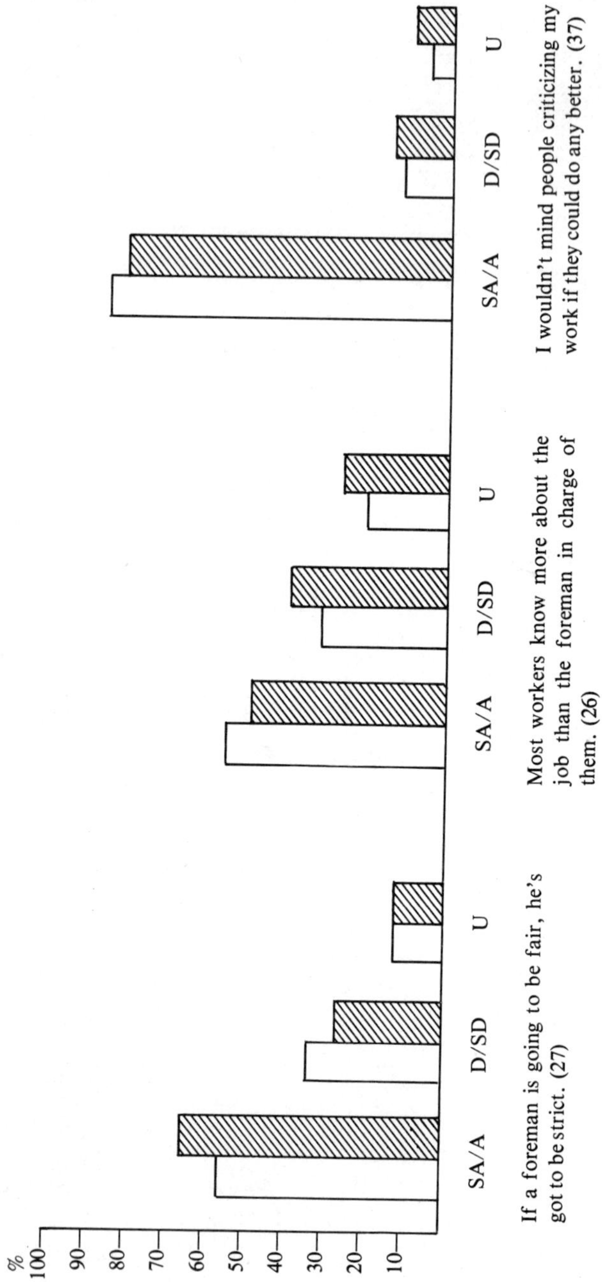

Fig. 10: *CI and apprentices: responses to items 147, 158, 167, 171.*

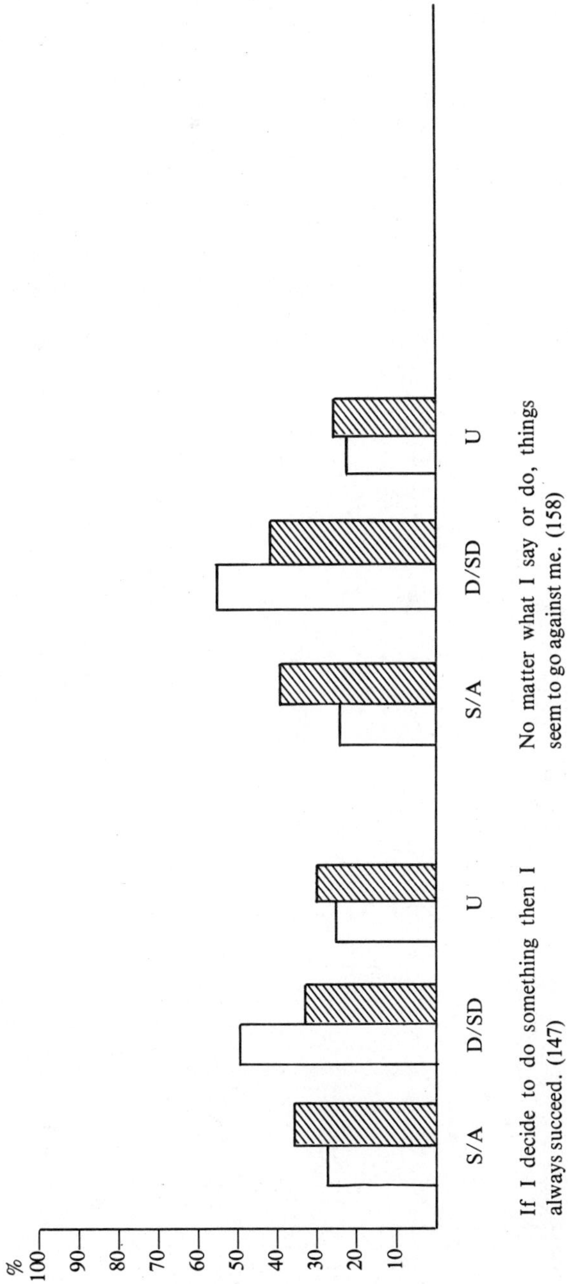

Fig. 10 continued.

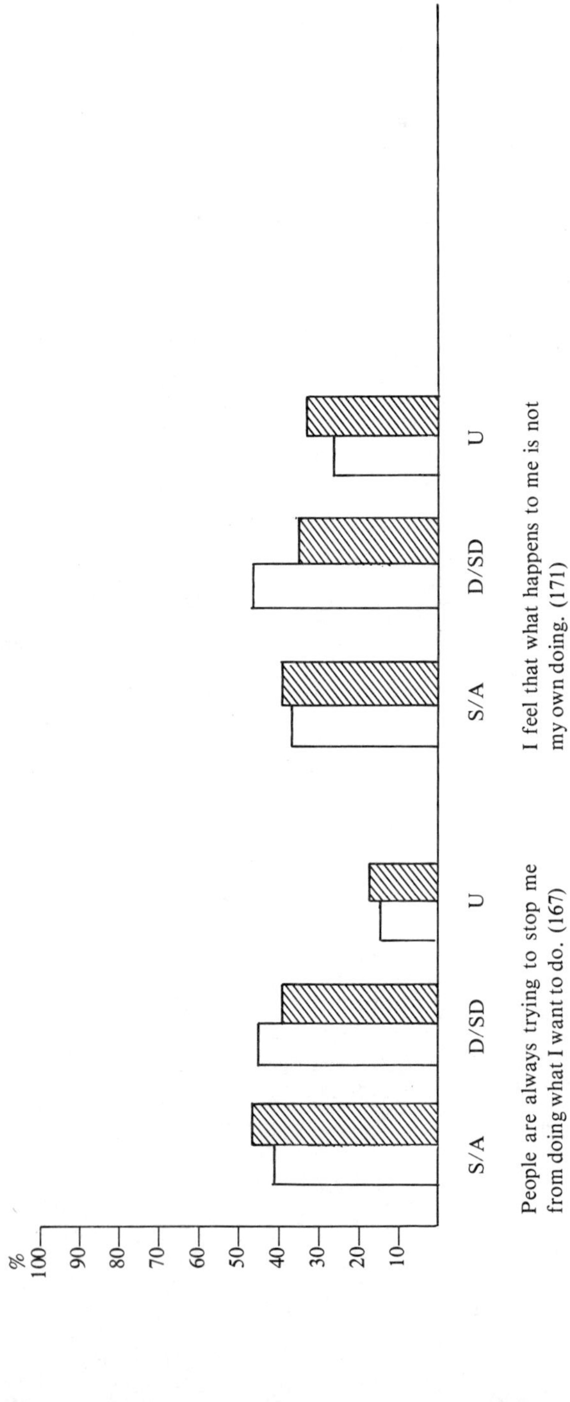

Fig. 11: *CI and apprentices: responses to items 155, 157, 162, 163, 169, 173.*

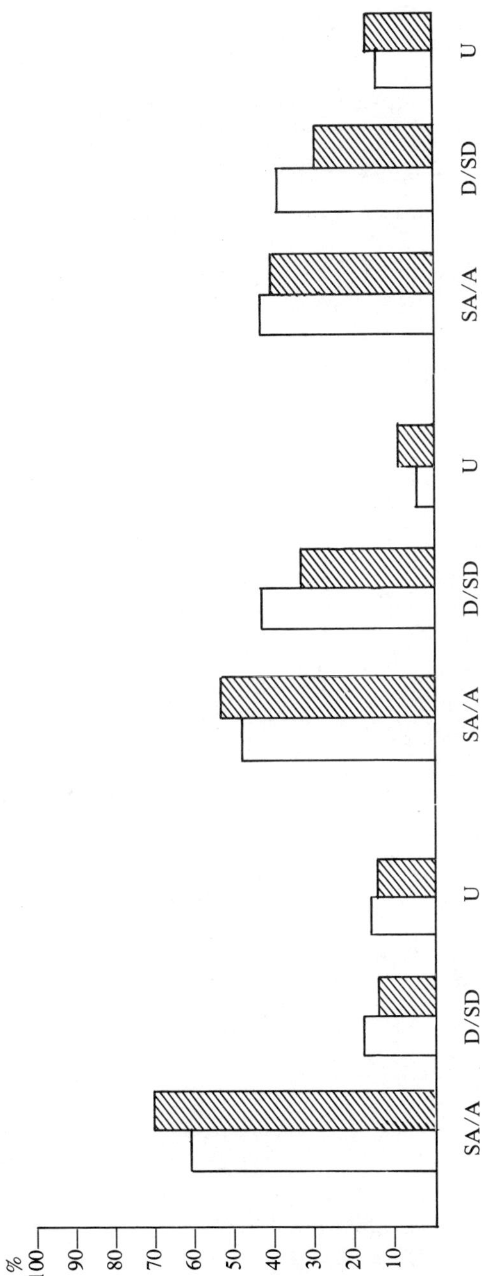

I've always felt close to my parents. (155)

If someone stole something of mine because I'd left it lying around, I would feel that it was my own fault. (157)

I stay out of other people's trouble because I know they won't stick their neck out for me. (162)

Fig. 11 continued

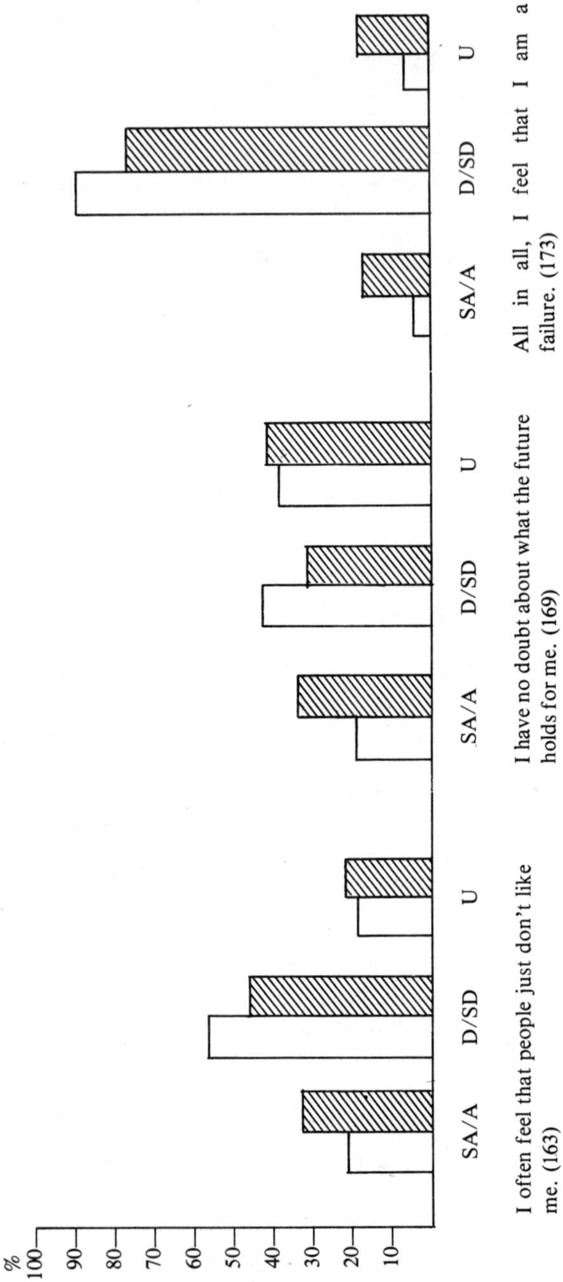

adversely influence them (158, 167) and exhibit a greater sense of passive determination (171), they report greater success in terms of the outcome of actions (item 147) than the apprentices. This pattern is not as contradictory as it may appear on first sight for the CI group may set their sights at rather a lower level than the apprentices and consequently enhance the chances of a successful outcome to particular courses of action. This interpretation, rather than one couched in terms of paranoia, is supported by observation of the responses depicted in figure 11.

Whereas we are encouraged to find that the great majority of both groups of young people do not consider themselves as being outright failures (item 173) there is both greater uncertainty and emphasis on this in the CI group. The groups' responses to the question about the future (item 169) fit the pattern so far observed with the CI group being more certain about their futures than the apprentices. In this respect we may note that given their experiences both during and after leaving school[11] the range and structure of opportunities for young people who find themselves in such schemes as CI will be seen as more closed with less room for changing direction than those undergoing further training. In terms of personal relationships it is apparent that the CI group have not shed the affective ties with parents to the same extent as the apprentices (item 155) and tend to lay greater stress on hostile perceptions of themselves by others (item 163). Perhaps not unrelated to this view is a greater reluctance on the part of the CI group to engage in mutually helpful relations with others who may be in difficulty (item 162) and a tendency towards an endorsement of petty thieving and shifting responsibility to self (item 157).

In conclusion we may present a group of items[12] which provide us with an insight into differential group interests and characteristic modes of action. (Fig. 12).

The CI group tend to see themselves as being more action orientated than the apprentices (item 174) and as having less interest in the mass media (item 161). Interestingly they show a greater tendency to prefer the more solitary and less socially demanding leisure situation afforded by the cinema when asked to choose between this and dancing (item 151).

Theoretical Overview

We are not short of models which attempt to explain the

Fig. 12: *CI and apprentices: responses to items 151, 161, 174.*

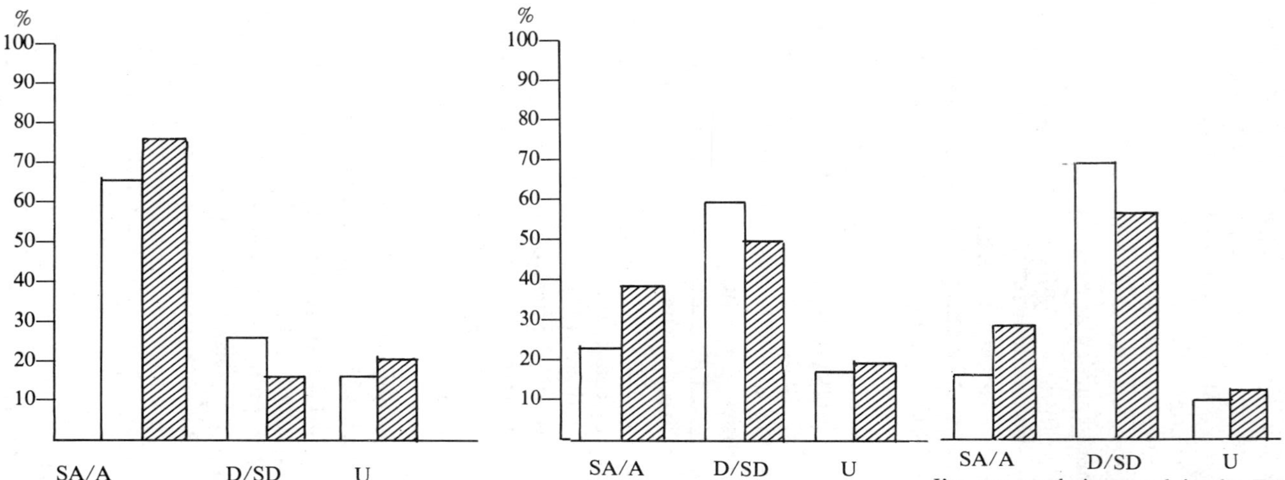

Instead of talking about life I just get on and live it. (174)

When I go out I prefer going to the cinema than to dances. (151)

I'm not much interested in the TV programmes, films and magazines that most people seem to like. (161)

vocational development of young people. These have been variously described as accident, rational, impulsive, need-reduction or situational, depending on the academic orientation of the particular theorist concerned (Osipow, 1968). The discrepancy between the conceptual and metholological work in this area has also been noted in the following terms (Crites, 1971):

> 'We have a fairly comprehensive conceptual framework of the stages through which an individual supposedly passes in arriving at a choice, but only a few of the objective details are filled in . . . The most striking conclusion which emerges from this review of theory and research on the stages in the choice process is that theory has far outstripped research.'

Paradoxically the vocational guidance movement has largely taken as its model the 'middle class' career and attention has thus been diverted from those groups who experience most difficulty in employment.

A useful model for pointing up some of the processes described in this chapter is that offered by Mansfield (1973). He suggests that an individual's 'career' results from three processes: the general adaptive process as encompassed in socialization, the choice by the individual of various alternatives open to him and changes in the individual's social environment. Changes in the social environment are seen as resulting either from the actions of the individual or from events which occur outside the individual's control. A schematic presentation of the elements involved in this conception of career is contained in Fig. 13.

Referring to the figure a change in position is assumed to change the individual's social environment, the individual then adapts to such changes by changing his subjective assessment of himself in relation to the changed environment. This subjective assessment of self corresponds to what is termed 'career sub-identity' (Hall, 1971) and Mansfield suggest that:

> 'The change in career sub-identity following upon a change in position, may be in the direction of conformity but it is not suggested that greater conformity always follows the change of status, rather it is suggested that the individual must in some way take account of the changes in his environment, he must integrate his perceptions of them into his sense of personal identity.' (p.110).

Thus the sub-identity really refers to the organization of the individual's beliefs, attitudes and values, and it is assumed that by

Fig. 13: *A schematic presentation of career development. (Adapted from Mansfield in Child, J.G. (ed.) Man and Organization, P. 109).*

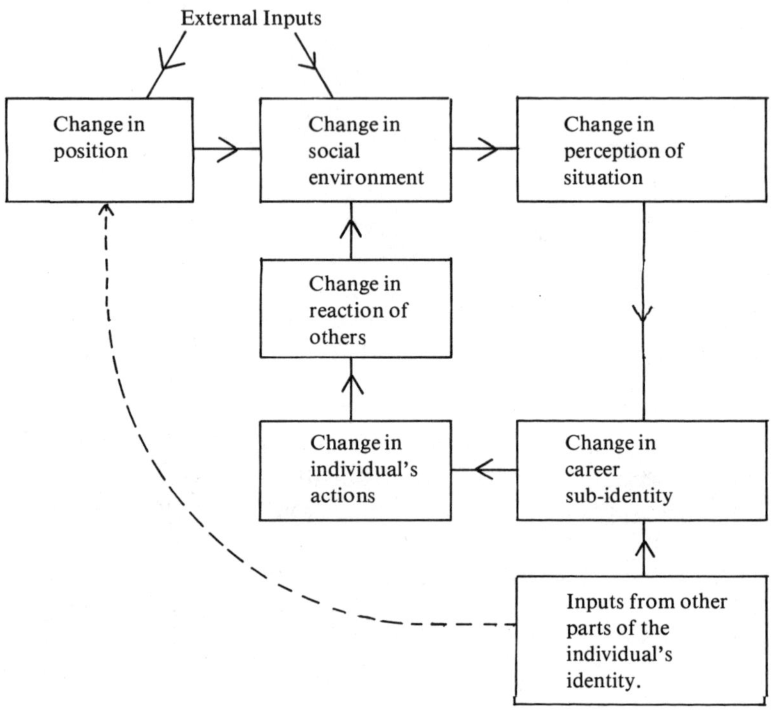

choosing particular courses of action rather than others the individual will re-structure the ways in which others react to him which, in turn, changes his social environment and completes the cycle; alternatively the individual may choose a different position thus completing the cycle in a different way. It follows from this that there are two kinds of career choices, one type refers to the individual making a choice yet staying in a given position, the other involves the individual changing his position in a particular way. The two arrows at the top of the figure indicate the way in which other factors in the individual's environment may directly impinge upon him and influence the cyclical process. This model is a useful device for illustrating the career phenomena associated with CI.

The characteristics and prior experiences of individuals are important constituent elements of the model and in interaction with 'external inputs' help determine particular career patterns. Thus our quantitative analysis of the opinions and attitudes of young people in varying environmental circumstances helps to pick out the characteristics and beliefs of the young people who are eligible for or employed by CI. In that these dispositions are related to the notion of alienation the interested reader is referred to some recent general texts on this topic which will be helpful to him in evaluating its theoretical status (Schacht, 1971; Johnson, 1973). This picture, however, is incomplete without an understanding of the various social contexts which mediate the effects of such personal attributes. The presentation of qualitative material, describing the work and delinquent experiences of some of the young people employed by CI and the external influences associated with that element of the model, termed 'positional change', helps fill out the picture by providing an insight into some of the processes involved.

Notes

1. This statement requires some qualification in that there is considerable variation between local authorities with regard to the amount of staff time given to such groups. It is worthy of note that some authorities are establishing special 'task forces' of COs whose sole remit is to help disadvantaged young people find employment.

2. It was pointed out that an 'ideal' sample would constitute 80 apprentices, all on the tools side in the building and engineering industries, distributed so as to provide 16 who were 16+ years of age, 48 17+ years and 16 18+ years. It was further pointed out that the responses of 20 female trainees in the 17+ range would constitute a desirable further sample. This suggested mix of young workers with regard to age, sex and trade represented an 'ideal' and was not followed exactly by any one college.

3. The assignment of individuals to groups and the administration of the questionnaire to these samples was carried out by members of staff of the schools involved; details of the characteristics which served as a basis for choosing an individual and placing him/her into one of the groups is given below:

   Group 1:
   15 boys and 5 girls of 'average' academic ability. Evidence of good attendance and punctuality at school, though not necessarily outstanding in this respect: on the whole co-operative and willing to learn. Likely to make a satisfactory adjustment to working life: boys suited to apprenticeship on the 'tools' side in the building and engineering trades, girls to routine clerical or factory work.

Group 2:

15 boys and 5 girls who are judged to be of 'poor' academic ability or of 'average' ability but who score consistently low in academic achievement. History of rebelliousness and poor attendance/punctuality at school but likely to be available for completion of the survey schedules within the time indicated. Perhaps from a disturbed home background: unlikely to make satisfactory adjustment to the demands of working life.

As a check on the accuracy of allocation of the young people to the potential 'at risk' group they were independently assigned to the two groups, again on the basis of the brief descriptions given above, by a member of staff not involved in the original assignment. The extent of agreement between the two teachers was recorded and any differences reconciled. In addition a brief thirteen line summary was prepared for each member by the teachers concerned. The summary indicated, where known, family background, school career and an indication of the individual's major difficulties.

4. The school leavers' questionnaire contained 112 questions and that for the young workers 174 questions; the discrepancy in numbers arises from the fact that certain questions relating to the young person's perception of organizational structure and processes were inapplicable to the school population and hence omitted from the questionnaire. These questions or items were constructed so that they could be answered by simply checking one of a number of response categories. The degree of endorsement of an item being indicated by assigning a numerical value to the particular response category chosen. Thus the question — 'Do people in your work group swap opinions and ideas about work problems?' — is responded to on a five point scale from Definitely Yes (5) to Definitely No (1).

5. The clusters of items representing areas of common content were obtained by running a components analysis separately for:

(i) Items 1 — 42 (Motivation to work)
(ii) Items 43 — 100 (Perception of the employing organizations, ODQ)
(iii) Items 147 — 174 (Alienation)

The group of items relating to the personality domain were used as they appear in the questionnaire, *i.e.*

(iv) Items 105 — 114 (Self image)
(v) Items 115 — 125 (Dogmatism)
(vi) Items 126 — 135 (Ideal self image)
(vii) Items 136 — 146 (Psychosomatic anxiety)

The number of components retained, and thus the number of potential scales, was decided on the basis of the size of their eigenvalues (greater than 2.0), with some regard to the theoretical issues related to the measurement areas. It should be emphasized that there can never be a unique name which encompasses all the subtleties of meaning covered by the items within any one scale though good approximations may be obtained by inspecting items that demonstrate the greatest degree of collinearity with the underlying dimensions.

6. There are no significant between group differences at the school level for this item: this also applies to items 16 and 21. Significant differences in the same direction as that reported here occur for school leaver responses to the remaining items.

7. Significant differences between school leaver groups, in the same direction as those reported here, were found for these items with the exception of items 18 and 42. Bearing in mind the cross sectional nature of the sampling strategy it would thus appear that the differential group emphasis to these items is already well established prior to the transition to the work situation.

8. No significant difference between school leaver groups for this item and for item 11. Differences in the same direction to those noted for the remaining three items.

9. A reversal of the between-group difference for item 6 occurs at the school level; the stable group being more confident and less uncertain than the unstable group. This reversal also applies to item 26; the stable group having more confidence in the skills of supervisory personnel than the unstable group. A difference in the same direction occurs for item 12 while there is no significant difference between school leaver groups for items 27 and 38.

10. A similar pattern of responses to items 158, 167 and 171 is apparent at the school leaver level. There is, however, no significant difference for item 147.

11. The pattern of responses to both these items and to item 162 is similar at both school and employment levels. There are no significant differences between school leaver groups for the remaining three items.

12. Item 161 discriminates between the school leaver group in the same direction but there is no significant difference between the group on the other two items.

References

BYNNER, J.M. (1969). *The young smoker.* London: HMSO.

CRITES, J.O. (1971). *The maturity of vocational attitudes in adolescence.* Washington: American Personnel and Guidance Association. p.14

HALL, D.T. (1971). A theoretical model of career subidentity development in organizational settings. *Organizational Behaviour and Human Performance.* 6. 50-76.

HEIM, A.W. (1970). *AH4 Group Test of General Intelligence.* (Rev. ed.) Windsor: NFER.

JOHNSON, F. (ed.) (1973). *Alienation: concept, term and meanings.* London: Seminar Press.

MANSFIELD, R. (1973). Career and Individual Strategies. In Child, J.G. (ed.) *Man and Organization.* London: George Allen & Unwin.

MURRAY, C. (1974). Item analysis of the elementary school from the dogmatism scale. *Journal of Experimental Education.* 42. 50-54.

MURRAY, C. (ed.) (1978). *Youth in Contemporary Society: Research Perspectives on Work with Young People.* Windsor: NFER.

OSIPOW, S.H. (1968). *Theories of Career Development.* London: Appleton Century Crofts.

SCHACHT, R. (1971). *Alienation.* London: George Allen and Unwin Ltd.

WEDGE, P. and PROSSER, H. (1973). *Born to Fail?* London: Arrow Books.

Chapter 4

The Effects of CI

In this chapter we will initially draw on qualitative information which bears directly on the effectiveness of CI. In this regard our attention is drawn to the mechanisms which are involved in the allocation of young people to projects and to what actually happens or is perceived to happen in particular work situations. Employers' perceptions of CI are also relevant and consequently some additional material is presented under this head. The second section of the chapter draws on various statistical analyses in an effort to generalize about likely shifts in the attitudes and characteristics of the young people arising from their experiences with CI. As in previous chapters we conclude with a theoretical discussion of some of the issues involved but in this case the discussion is extended somewhat in order to bring together points raised in previous chapters.

Allocation of Young People to Projects

Decisions are made during the recruitment and selection procedure which determine what will initially happen to the young person. The young people are recruited for particular projects, are told that the work might change in the future and are asked whether they would like the kind of work which is available. The CI staff say that they attempt to ensure that the young person will be accepted by the work team and will be able to fit in with the group and with the scheme consultant. Thus the staff might avoid putting an articulate and seemingly quick-witted youngster with a team composed mainly of mentally slow youngsters, lest he become frustrated and bored. Similarly they might not locate a YE who is said to have emotional problems with a SC whom they feel does not have the ability to handle this effectively or who already has responsibility for several young people who have similar problems. Alternatively it might be judged that a team is sufficiently skilled, cohesive and resilient to accept a particularly uncommunicative person or someone likely to have epileptic attacks. Thus in allocating young people to projects, several considerations are said to be borne in mind:

ASM: 'Well I take into consideration the type of work they want to do. Some consultants couldn't handle a difficult kid, so I'm very much aware of who I put with who . . . If a young person is asking to work outside then I wouldn't automatically put him inside!'

Thus in allocating young people, their interests and preferences are considered as well as the desirability of achieving compatability with the scheme consultant. The staff also consider the existing composition of work teams particularly where members are considered ESN; the introduction of 'fly' lads to such a group might result in complete disruption. An attempt is made to give each youngster a 'fresh start', details of his previous 'career' being a matter for him to relate to the SC if he wishes.

ASM: 'I don't tell a consultant if a boy has a record. If the boy's going to tell him then that's up to him, but I won't let it go. Each consultant's given eight boys and it's up to him to work them as a team . . . I'll only tell them if somebody is very badly handicapped or has a health problem in some way.'

Attempts to match particular young people with particular projects are also constrained by their geographical location and the pre-existing composition of a work group. One staff member summarized the conflicting pressures:

ASM: 'I would like to be able to say that at all times we place the YE in an environment where he would have suitable YEs to work with and a suitable SC . . . the answer to all that would be no . . . very often it's a question of "who's one short" . . . the projects determine so much . . . where they are and what skills they require . . . sometimes we can place them more appropriately but in the end the project and the recruitment area are central . . .'

The allocation of young people to projects appears not to reflect subtle attempts to construct work groups on social-psychological principles but rather the person is allocated to the team in which there are vacancies and the staff do something at a later stage if the person does not 'settle down'. A range of indicators is used by the staff to judge whether, in fact, the young person is 'settling in'.

ASM: 'Most of the kids settle in without much bother. 'Course, a lot of 'em haven't worked for a long time. Some not at all. So their attendance might be poor at first. You can't expect a lad to come off the dole where he's used to getting up at dinner time because there's nothing to do if he gets up earlier and suddenly start getting to work on time every morning. But gradually their time-keeping and attendance improves.'

RO: 'Are there any other initial things that happen?'

ASM: 'Well, you might get the consultant saying he's having problems with a kid. You know, not doing as he's told, messing about or something, or he might be withdrawn into himself, sitting by himself at lunch or not speaking much to anybody.'

There seems to be at least two main classes of behaviour which provide clues as to whether a person is 'settling in': conforming to the basic rules of the work situation and evidence of accceptable interpersonal behaviour with respect to the SC, staff and other employees. If, over the first six or eight weeks, the person is seen as not settling down, then an initial effort is made to find out why things are not going according to plan. The SC talks to the person to find out 'what's wrong' and the staff may talk to the young person and to the SC to discover the reasons which have given rise to the situation. Questions posed may include the following:

> Are the problems relating to events outside CI? If not are there conflicts between the group and the young person or between the SC and the young person?
>
> Is the work itself unsuitable by virtue of being too hard, too easy or otherwise not acceptable to the young person?
>
> Is the young person simply a 'difficult person' or is the SC being too hard or too lenient?

The SC tends to account for the young workers' difficulties in terms of the attributes of the person concerned and his background in such terms as 'he has no self-confidence; he is lazy; he comes from a bad home; he is aggressive; he doesn't get on with the other kids; he is no good at the job; he can't seem to get the hang of work'. The staff tend to use a somewhat wider frame of reference than this which incorporates elements of lay psychology; typical statements would be: he is withdrawn, he rejects authority figures; he comes from a difficult home; he is ESN; but also incorporate other explanations which involve such notions as: 'the team find it difficult to accept him; there is a clash of personalities with other young persons or with the SC; the SC is being too lenient; the SC is expecting too much too soon'. Thus the staff use perceived characteristics of the young person too, but also draw upon their beliefs relating to individual adjustment and group functioning.

In particular, the 'clashes of personality' issue is deduced by the staff in various subtle ways. The young person may be absent or late fairly frequently; the SC may complain to the staff about the YE's lack of skill or discipline; there may be problems of discipline within the team as a whole which occur at regular intervals. In such cases the staff may initially discuss matters with the SC and young person and attempt to encourage the former to adopt different 'coping' strategies. If this fails, they may decide to move the young person to a different team, the rationale for the move being usually that a different SC who has a different approach may be more successful in fitting the lad into his team, or changing the young person's behaviour. With regard to the final circumstance of 'nothing much happening', a change of team is about all that can be done, apart from applying the 'encourage him to get a job' strategy. In this case a person may be seen as 'not yet ready for outside employment', and showing no progress towards 'being ready' and the staff explain such a move in terms of 'presenting a challenge' to the young person and they watch to 'see how he copes with it'. They may also see it as bringing the young person into contact with different supervisory practices.

By way of illustration two members of the staff discuss a YE who they thought was 'not getting on' in CI, his SC having reported that he was 'no longer getting anything from CI'.

ASM 1: 'It's the consultant that he's not getting anything from.'

ASM 2: (to RO) 'He's a big, well-built lad who bursts into tears when anyone says anything to him (*i.e.* tells him off).'

ASM 1: 'Yes . . . SC was a bit soft with him at first and now it's got established it's very difficult for him to change his approach. . . . (the YE) has also slipped into the role in the team of the one who never does anything. I think, actually, a change of team, you know, a new scheme consultant would do him good.'

ASM 2: 'Perhaps . . . (SC) should go round and have a chat with his parents. That might help. It often gets the consultant to see what the kid's problems are.'

Thus a change of team is being considered as a possible means for providing the basic conditions for changes in the YE's behaviour; the assumptions being that the old behavioural pattern will be partially broken up in the new situation as it will be seen to be less appropriate in the new circumstances. It is hoped that the new situation may force the young person to try out new behavioural strategies and so develop a different orientation. The importance of the SC's behaviour is also brought out in this interchange and is underlined by the following quotation; in terms of allocating young people to projects it was stressed that:

ASM: '. . . you've got your consultants to consider; there are some consultants who cope better with big, beefy, cheeky lads who'll perhaps respond to a bit of hard work and there are other consultants who'll respond to little meek lads. One SC copes very well with the backward kids or kids who are a bit funny one way or another because of his experiences in working with mentally handicapped kids . . . there are two consultants who both cope with bigger, tougher kids and are not averse to taking them round the back of a shed and giving them a kick in the pants if necessary! ('Course I don't know about that!) and they get the real respect of the kids.'

The overall composition of the squad is also said to be a factor in deciding whether or not a particular young person should go to work on a particular project. There are 'boys only' and 'girls only' squads but notions about the compatibility of different 'types' of young people also play a part in making decisions about allocation to the work situation:

ASM: '. . . if you happen to have a group, even if it's doing quite light work, which is composed of large kids, then you're unlikely to put a little squirt in because he's probably going to get picked on . . . I've got one squad which is mainly made up of "intellectual" sorts of kids, it's an odd squad; there's three kids on it who are really quite bright and they're "hairies" as opposed to "skin-heads" and they play guitars and write their own songs

. . . and in that squad there's also a couple of ESN kids who've taken on the same interests. So I wouldn't go and shove in a tough ''skin-head'' type because they'd be as different as chalk and cheese.'

There are various reasons for moving a YE to a different project which seem to be unrelated to the official CI position that the young people should experience a variety of work situations in order to enhance their personal development: there is no formal procedure for ensuring that everybody has a change of team at intervals. In practice the variety of work experience obtained by a given individual depends on the projects which become available and to which the team as a whole is moved; this in turn is related to some extent to the SC's skills and the sort of projects which CI is offered. Movement of YEs from one team to another appeared to be essentially a 'problem-solving' device, whether the problem be located in staff, SC or the YE. For example, a discipline problem associated with SC/YE relationships might lead to a move:

RO: 'Why was he moved to another squad?'

ASM: 'You'd just go in and find him swinging from a lampshade or something! . . . (the SC) was obviously not in control of the situation. He (the YE) was off on the sick and when he came back he asked could we shift him.'

What sequence of events covered 'he asked could we shift him' is not clear. No doubt degrees of choice, request, negotiation and 'encouragement' are involved but without direct observation of such situations the actual process cannot be established. Offers of a transfer can be made in an attempt to deal with conflict between SC and his YEs and sometimes a person may be moved to a project which he may not like in order to 'encourage' him to make a decision to leave.

The following extract from an area staff meeting is a case in point. It refers to a girl who had been absent frequently and to whom a letter had been sent indicating that if a sicknote was not forthcoming her employment would be terminated; the hope being expressed that she would not send a sicknote:

ASM 1: '. . . (YE) — bother the woman! — brought in a sicknote.'

ASM 2: 'What was the complaint?'

ASM 3: 'Chest complaint.'

ASM 1: 'However, I don't believe she's been in work this week and I haven't had a sicknote from her.' (For this absence.)

ASM 2: 'Are we of the opinion then that if there's no sicknote this week then we should terminate her employment?'

Staff: 'Yes.'

ASM 1: 'I'm of the opinion that she should definitely be taken out of the schools project . . . And I think that she will decide then to leave.'

ASM 2: 'Fair enough. So given that she's going to be moved out of school in any case, where is she going to go if she stays with CI in the interim period before she leaves?'

ASM 3: 'She's going to join . . . painting.'

ASM 1: (Amused) 'If she's got a chest complaint I think that's definitely what she should do (*i.e.* with the intention of forcing her resignation).'

ASM 2: 'So . . . (YE) is going painting?'

ASM 4: 'Yes. Officially she's going painting.'

ASM 2: 'She *is* going painting!' (Mock indignation at ASM 4's irony.)

ASM 3: 'She *is* going painting!' (Heavier irony.) 'And *then* she'll leave. Good!'

It was clear that there was no intention of endangering the health of the YE for the prediction was:

ASM 1: 'She won't go to it either. She won't stay for more than a day! . . . I mean, the fact is she's just hanging on here until this other job comes up anyway. She's just getting her stamp.'

ASM 4: 'Yes. A stamp on her card and that's basically it.'

A YE may also be moved if his attendance, behaviour or lack of skills is detrimental to a project or team. In this respect 'requests' for transfers may or may not be entirely spontaneous and the readiness with which they are granted may vary in relation to the particular circumstances of a case. The following extract from a Review of Progress meeting involves a case where a request for a transfer is handled with organizational requirements in mind:

ASM 1: 'Her (YE) attendance has been bad lately.'

ASM 2: 'She came into the office on Monday morning "Can I go back to the workshop?" So I said "What for?" She said "(cough) The paint's (cough) getting on my chest (cough, cough)." So I said that if she could get a note from the doctor to say she couldn't work with the paint I'd at least move her somewhere else . . .'

ASM 3: 'She's getting to the stage where she's no longer interested.'

ASM 2: 'I think the other tactic I'll employ is that she can't go back to the workshop because she's leaving.'

ASM 1: '. . . I'd be very much against her going back there.'

ASM 2: 'Well, I don't want her back with . . . (another YE) 'cos they don't do each other any good (*i.e.* there are discipline problems).'

There was one example of transfer discussed which involved a whole team. In this case the transfer was carried out because of problems of attendance and interpersonal relations which were seen as arising from characteristics of the SC:

ASM: 'Periodically, kids seem to get too much for him and the only way to deal with it is just really to get rid of his whole squad (*i.e.* disperse them to other sites) completely and give him new kids altogether.'

In some cases the SCs may request that a young person be transferred; an example which occurred during an area staff meeting concerned a request from a SC that a boy be transferred for health reasons (the boy was epileptic):

ASM 1: '. . . (SC) was on to me about that new boy — he's a bit concerned about him because he's taken about three 'turns' since he started and I don't know whether it's the strenuous work or what. But he asked me if we would consider at the next staff meeting having him moved . . .'

ASM 2: 'Well, we've got two choices . . . either sacking him or I would suggest . . . (name of project) because the work there is not as heavy at the moment as the work he is doing.'

'Sacking' is perhaps a misleading term for the person is not usually summarily dismissed. What normally happens in the relatively rare cases of unresolvable situations is that the young person doesn't come to work and if, after due efforts have been made to find out the reasons for this and to rectify matters, the YE still fails to attend, a letter is sent indicating that if this persists it will be assumed that after a given date he no longer wishes to work for CI and consequently his employment will be terminated.

The Work Situation

Once a YE has 'settled in' to the extent of coming to work regularly and being on time the SC shows him how to undertake the various tasks involved in a particular project and tries to ascertain his abilities and limitations. In the groups observed this was not done in terms of formal teaching, rather a SC would do part of the job, show one or two boys the technique involved and then let them have a try providing correction where necessary. The SC would check on his charges at intervals and point out mistakes, giving correction or praise according to performance; since new tasks or new aspects of current jobs arise from time to time this tends to be a continuing process. Within any team there will be a range of ability and the SCs tend to give the YEs jobs which they feel is consonant with their skill level. When they show themselves able to do a particular job, they may be tried with a rather more difficult one. Some boys possess a particular skill and tend to be given jobs related to this: for example, one lad in a team did the plastering, he had done this kind of work in the past and was particularly good at it. In one of the areas observed there were no 'specialist teams' in the sense that one team did all the joinery, one the painting and one the landscaping. However, there is some work group differentiation which reflects the various skills of the SCs whereby if a particular SC is unable to do a certain job himself another SC might come in to help. In general, however, the teams do all the work on a particular project and undertake projects requiring different kinds of skills. Thus one team, whose SC was a painter and decorator by trade, had done landscaping, bricklaying and joinery as well as painting. As has been previously noted a team tends to do one type of project which is related to the scheme consultant's own skills and if a large part of a project involves other skills, a different team, with a scheme consultant who can do that sort of job, is brought in.

ASM: 'It's unfair to the scheme consultants (to ask them to do unfamiliar jobs). You can't really expect a painter to be capable of taking the boys and showing them joinery. The boys especially have got to have every confidence in the scheme consultant. You couldn't have a painter doing joinery — not getting any decent projects and for them (the boys) to feel that they're doing a good job . . .'

The young people do tend to develop a loyalty to their scheme consultant and to identify themselves with a particular team. Even if a scheme consultant sees that a boy is good at a different kind of work, which is done by another team, the boy's own views are put foremost and he is not moved unless he wants to be. Needless to say, he is unlikely to want to move.

ASM: 'Any time I've suggested a transfer it's been ructions: "I'm not doing that! I'm a joiner! I'm staying with the joinery lot!" They're not interested in being moved.'

Within the work group, the boys receive a training in the basic aspects of the scheme consultant's skills and this seemed, from observation, to be an *ad hoc* matter. If a young person was given a job to do and the scheme consultant noticed he was having difficulty with it or tackling it in the wrong way, the scheme consultant would go over and show the person how to do the job. Often the scheme consultants would work alongside the boys, doing one or other of the jobs involved in the project. During the working day, in the teams observed, the boys go on with their jobs without much need for the scheme consultant's intervention. There were occasions, as in any work situation, when the boys 'lost enthusiasm' for working, or a subgroup stopped for a smoke which developed into a longer chat or 'horseplay' session. In such circumstances, the scheme consultant would engage in a mixture of badinage, cajoling and threats of varying intensity, in order to get the boys back to work.

When a boy came to the end of a job or a problem came up, he would call upon the scheme consultant for instructions and assitance. A simple illustration involved two boys who were painting a stairway. They could not find a ladder long enough to enable them to reach the highest parts and asked the consultant what to do next. He told them to get a short ladder and wedge it between the wall and the stairs and then lay planks from the ladder to the stairs as a base for a second ladder. The boys did not appear to understand, so the consultant took them in hand and helped them set up the steps and planks. It was on a similar sort of basis that training in trade skills took place: for example, a situation might arise in the course of a job where the young person did not know how to set about a task and so would ask the scheme consultant for assistance; alternatively the scheme consultant might notice that the YE was not doing a job properly and so would intervene. There were thus no formal 'lessons' as such at least where there was an established team; more formal teaching situations might occur with completely new teams. Some training has to be at a very basic level as the skills of the young people may be quite limited. A consultant whose team had all been to special schools made this point:

SC: 'When I first started with them they hadn't a clue. They didn't know how to work . . . They hadn't any idea how to use a shovel or a pick. I just moved in and showed them what to do. And they hadn't the strength to put a spade or a shovel down into the ground. They were standing and jumping up on the spade to *force* it down. But gradually, as time went on they got more confident and more adept at using a spade and pick. What I haven't got through to them yet is the idea of keeping a straight line or keeping things level.'

From this rather hesitant beginning, this team had completed some joinery work, fitting seats round window bays in a church hall, and at the time of observation was doing an excellent job of tidying up the church grounds and gardens.

In general CI sites tend to so closely resemble other 'real' work situations in appearance that is it difficult for the young people, the consultants, and possibly the staff to see the work situation as being anything other than that. This is particularly true of the consultants who may have spent many years in such situations. The 'meanings' of a CI site are connected to the SCs' past working lives and it is difficult for them to think about the situation in any terms other than that of doing a job. Thus as far as the consultants are concerned, a CI site *is* a work situation and means doing a job. It seems reasonable to suppose that consultants are unlikely to distance themselves from their past experiences to the extent of seeing the site as a means to an end; a means of developing not only trade skills, but the wider social skills written into the scheme. In one of his basic daily tasks, arranging the disposition of young people on the site, the SC's concern was with maximizing work output and minimizing disruption:

SC: 'You might pick one boy and say ''He's good at papering'' so I put him on papering. ''This boy's not so good'' so I let him paste the paper. That keeps him occupied. ''This boy and this boy when they are together cause trouble'', so I put them apart and try and pick a boy who doesn't cause trouble and put a trouble-maker with him. That's part of this job — thinking how to place the boys according to how skilful they are and how much trouble they cause.'

The consultant's past experience makes the work aspects of the situation highly salient. Work is in the foreground and it is unlikely that it could be seen as the background scenery for some other kind of activity. The sense in which the consulants are aware that the CI work situation is different from others which they have experienced tends to be limited to their realization that the young people are unskilled and are unable or unwilling to adopt work roles:

SC: 'I myself fell into this trap when I first started: I was demanding a certain amount of work, but it was only after two or three weeks I realized that these were boys and not men: I had been in the habit of supervising men.'

A wider 'education' tends to be limited to the giving of advice and the transmission of values during those parts of the working day which are clearly separated from work such as tea breaks and lunch. Informal and *ad hoc* 'counselling' tends to occur during conversations at these times which sometimes touches on personal problems. Sometimes it is not possible for the scheme consultant to offer more than sympathy and consideration with the problem being communicated in an oblique fashion:

SC: 'The boys will come up to you and they won't tell their problems sort of asking for fatherly advice. They will use another method . . . I was giving one boy a row for being late one morning and his exact words were ''I couldn't help it (name of SC). My mother's still lying in bed with that man she came up from the pub with last night and the two of them were drunk and never wakened me . . .'' What can you do?'

These conversations and daily relationships between SCs and YEs for example, when a scheme consultant makes disparaging remarks about a YE's untidiness or suggests in a friendly way that he might like to wash his hands before lunch are said to lead to some changes in the young people over and above changes in their work-related behaviour. A scheme consultant whose team is drawn from special schools and who lives in one of the city's 'roughest' areas said:

SC: 'They're beginning to take a pride in their appearance. When I got them at first they were rather ragged and down-at-heel . . . they're better dressed . . . their language has been modified to a great extent . . . especially when there are ladies about. I think the mere fact that they've got a job has . . . increased their confidence. And their hygiene has improved greatly — they're beginning to wash their hands after going to the toilet and before lunch. The only trouble I have with them is their eating habits — they'll just take a cup and pour tea into it without washing it out.'

It is interesting to note the views of the young people themselves about what happens in the work group; what they think about their job and what they get out of it. The boys in the main enjoy their jobs and feel they have settled down into work:

YE, 'This is my first job. I feel it has got me into the way of working, you know. Before I started working here, I was maybe out of one job and into another, you know. This is the first one I have stuck at and got into the way of working.'

RO: 'Do you enjoy doing it?

YE: 'Yes.'

One boy provided his perception of the 'induction process' and some aspects of the way initial training in a job proceeds:

YE: 'When you first come (the SC) will give you something real tight to do and he will watch — but he will not come up to you and say "What are you doing there?" if you are doing it wrong. He will come up to you and ease you into it slowly and say "Look, when you are painting you should use the brush like this, and watch for these runners" and things like that. And how to cut in, he'll just watch from a distance and if he doesn't think you are doing it good he will put you onto something else and he will keep changing you about to see what you can do.'

This points to the fact that in CI the staff are provided with the time for assessing what the YEs' capabilities are. CI may be different in this way from other jobs the boys have done. Certainly, in one aspect they see it as clearly different and this emerges in the following extract from a group discussion:

YE1: 'That's one thing: you are trusted. You are put into places where there are valuable things and you are trusted!'

YE2: 'Just like in the houses, painting the houses. You are trusted. See, I've been caught for house breaking and that and they sent me into the houses you know.'

YE1: 'If you went to other jobs they wouldn't trust you, that's what I think, this job is good in that way.'

RO: 'You think that's a good thing for them to do? That encourages people to . . .'

Several YEs: 'Yes, it is, yes.'

YE1: 'They will give you another chance and take you on. I mean, you could do something wrong once, but it doesn't mean to say you will do it all the time.'

Three major impressions were gained from these discussions with the young employees. Firstly, they enjoy working for CI because they have friendly relationships with their 'gaffers', are not excessively pressured to achieve high output and a certain amount of respect and concern is expressed for them as individuals. Secondly, the young people were more articulate about a whole range of topics both to do with work and with the wider society than is generally held. This is interesting for the reasons generally given for the demise of the industry council was the lack of articulacy of the young people and their inability to make a contribution. Perhaps the kind of things they were asked to discuss and the way in which discussions were run contributed to this impression; perhaps too much progress was expected to occur too quickly. Certainly when given the opportunity to discuss matters of concern to them on their own terms the YEs displayed sufficient verbal skills in discussion to form a basis upon which to build. The third point is related to the second. The young people are not merely articulate in discussing subjects which might be close to their interests, such as football; they are also very aware of wider matters which impinge upon them. The following quotation indicates an unexpected degree of insight and a realistic assessment of their own position:

RO: 'Would you like it to be a permanent job?'

YE1: 'If the wages are better. If they paid better wages, this would be a cracking job.'

YE2: 'And then the prospects aren't good. Like for the boys who have been in here so long; they could build them up and they could become a consultant; then there are chances, there is something in it. But just now there are no prospects. You are just here to work and you will always be.

YE1: I think the whole idea is to take the boys off the dole to cut the unemployment down.'

YE3: 'Yes. The reason is to keep the numbers down at the dole.'

Since CI is in some senses a 'treatment agency' which is not directed towards making a profit, many of the normal industrial incentives and sanctions cannot be used: there is no bonus scheme, no overtime can be worked and there is a reluctance to sack YEs since this would defeat the object of rehabilitation. The SCs therefore tend to use informal methods of establishing authority and control because formal alternative procedures are limited:

SC: 'I have a good team, and I treat them right. I give them a little bit of time off at times . . . Sometimes they (*i.e.* the staff) haven't agreed about it here. But if I turned round and said to the lads "Listen, I want a job done today, you get it done then I will let you go home". This is the only incentive I can give them. They cannot get any more money. They cannot get overtime. Well, you can't have them slaving their guts out everyday for nothing which is not right. You've got to give and take a little bit . . . If you kept them there until half past four everday, and expected anything you wouldn't get it, you wouldn't get the work out of them. Because they have come to me and said "Oh, I didn't like working for that fellow (*i.e.* other SC). Keeps you there until a minute past half past four and expects you to do this, that and the other. And we just don't do it."And they *don't* do it.'

The young people do not see themselves as in need of 'help' or 'treatment' and observation suggests that they do not see CI as a 'helping' or 'treatment' agency. Consequently they are not prepared to automatically accept CI's limitations, in terms of available incentives, as being a necessary part of the 'treatment' process; unlike, for example, a patient who goes to a hospital and is prepared to 'fit in' with its routine because he believes he is being helped. However, the young people have no formal authority or power. Thus, they cannot formally withdraw their labour or 'work to rule' or exercise the various other industrial sanctions normally available to a labour force. The only available sanctions are informal, walking off the site, non co-operation, aggression and disruption. These actions are not used in any organized way, nor are they brought to bear on matters of collective importance to the young people. Rather, they tend to be idiosyncratic, unarticulated expressions of conflict or disagreement sometimes reflecting incomprehension, frustration or boredom. As in other work situations of a similar type, involving manual labour, there is a coalition of differing interests which is maintained in part by exchanges and compromises. Since this can be only partially accommodated in an organizational sense such exchanges and compromises operate in half covert fashion with intermittent official admonitions aimed at keeping disruptive practices within limits rather than removing them. The SC may rely on his ability to 'get on with the young people' in order to maintain control or, in certain situations, may employ more basic methods:

SC: 'I said "I see I'm getting all the rough lads again". Well this has happened all the time I've been here. If they have had any of the toughs off anyone else they have just pushed them along to me, you see, and I don't treat them *roughly*. But I talk to them, *tell* them. And I have had a few little bits of do-ups with two or three of them, you see. If there is a laddie amongst them who is making a laughing stock of everybody else, you pick him out and you watch him until he does something wrong and you make an attack on him and if he back-chats you, you get a hold on him and you do something.'

These more direct methods are not often required but are thought to be necessary on certain occasions in order to establish control in terms which are clear to the people involved. Shared experiences and informal relationships are the more usual basis for control, being occasionally buttressed by manipulation of positive and negative santions.

This may be illustrated by reference to a work group where the SC needed to exercise control over a diverse and varied number of young people on an open site stretching for over three-quarters of a mile with group members often out of sight. The importance of informal relationship to control may be highlighted by the actions of a trainee scheme consultant who was left for part of a morning in sole charge of the group. During this time he made frequent reference to the need 'to keep at it', often singling out the 'slackers' by name. After a sequence of horse-play, exhortation, barely concealed verbal abuse, mockery from the YEs and further exhortation, the trainee SC had exhausted his stock of threats and attempted to move a ring-leader to another part of the site. The YE

YE:
(Male) 'We were told.'

The reasons given for the young people's non-involvement in decision-making refer either to their lack of appropriate experience or to their lack of ability and initiative:

RO: 'Do the YEs make suggestions about how to do jobs?'

SC: 'Sometimes they do. They will argue with you about how to do a job. Once they have got started (*i.e.* arguing) they don't want to stop. So you might give way to them. Usually they just want to waste a bit of time and not work. You let them have their way and then if it doesn't come off, they know they should have listened to you and if it does, then it builds them up a bit. You have to keep going and checking up on them all the time. At (names site) you would get two started laying bricks at one corner and go and get two more started at another corner and the first two would be shouting you to come over and check nearly every brick they had laid to see if they were doing it right. They have no self-confidence, you see. No confidence in their ability to do a job.'

Further questioning revealed that in the past the young people had been more involved in the execution of projects; for example, they had thought up designs for the construction of an adventure playground and had helped in designing the obstacles on a crazy golf course. The dilemma facing the scheme consultant in terms of the young person's 'participation' is pointed up by the following exchange:

SC: 'Well, this scheme, when it first set off — now it's changed. They said "Well, let the lads participate in what is said and done". Now it's reversed.'

RO: 'What happened at first?'

SC: 'Well like A (names a site) for instance, we let the lads create — I mean, it were all right. They were building a play area for kids — let the lads create something that they think kids will play on. So they erected those things. Did you see them? The lads said "We'll do this", you know. Let the lads participate in jobs that they are doing — but if you went on like that it would fall flat. You know, they would not get on with it kind of thing . . . they had them filling their own time sheets out, or one lad filling time sheets out at first. But the consultants had to fill them out again because they were in a mess. Now anything else that they had been left to do probably would end up in a mess after a while so there had to be somebody there to put them on the right way . . .'

RO: 'You said it had changed since then, how?'

SC: 'You had lads participating in the job. Putting their own time sheets in. Well, they used to fill these time sheets in but they were in such a mess sometimes we had to do them. In some jobs you couldn't let them participate. It all depends on the job you have got . . . on some jobs you could not let them participate because they would not know what they were doing, kind of thing.'

The special circumstances of one work team observed provides an illustration of the degree of participation of the young people in the decision making process. The team in question was split into two groups, doing separate jobs on sites three quarters of a mile apart. The consultant had to travel from one site to the other to ensure that the work was proceeding in an orderly fashion. On one of the sites, 3 boys were laying the foundations of a concrete playground and, without supervision, were industriously barrowing bricks and laying them in the space to be concreted. One boy, (A), was removing bricks from a derelict wall, another (B), was barrowing them onto the site, and the third, (C), was laying them in orderly rows. The supply of bricks from the wall ran out and (A) came over to (B) and (C) and suggested that they knock another derelict wall down. (C) objected 'We'll get lifted by the police'. The boys therefore stopped work and sat on a wall. After several minutes of inaction, (C) had a change of heart and suggested that they should knock down the derelict wall, which they duly did, and work commenced. It appeared that the boys had simply been left to get on with the job as a group, without anyone being specifically delegated to supervise the work. The YE who emerged as leader in this setting 'naturally' organized the others without specific authority from the SC. This was corroborated by observation on another occasion when the SC left a site, having merely told everybody what to do until he came back. No direction was given that a particular individual was 'in charge' or had to make sure that the work was completed.

The degree of YEs' involvement in decision making is limited to this sort of participation; their authority for suggesting courses of action being derived from informal peer-relationships within the work groups. The following illustration points up the kind of situation in which YEs exercise this kind of decision making with (E) being the individual who usually exercised peer leadership in this particular sub-group of the work team. On the day in question the SC had visited another site to oversee the laying of a playground; the three boys making up the sub-group in question were building a brick store behind the CI offices and erecting a fence and gate. (D) was building a low wall inside the store building and (E) was putting up a gate. (F) was bringing tools and materials to each of the others when required. (E), who was setting up the gate and deciding on the positions for the hinges, called to (D) to provide assistance with the hanging of the gate on its posts. (C) and (D) held the gate in position while (E) fixed the hinges to the gateposts; (F) handed screws to (E) when asked for them. When the gate had been hung it was catching slightly and not closing properly so (E) sent (F) to the stockroom for a plane. These informal exchanges characterize the extent of the YEs' involvement in decision making. The following conversation, about the small wall which (D) was building inside the store just mentioned, whilst being an isolated incident, is illustrative of this degree of involvement:

RO: 'What is this for?'

(D): 'I don't know. (To E) What is this for?'

(E): 'I think it's for small tools and bits and pieces.'

(D) (to RO) 'That doesn't seem right. Anyway, I don't know what it is for, I'm only building it.'

The last remark was accompanied by a knowing grin as if to say, slightly cynically, that it was typical that the person doing a job should know little about it. Both (D) and (E) on this site seemed intelligent young people and (D) in particular was articulate and quick witted in conversation. This observation is mentioned so that the following remarks of an area staff member about another YE may be placed in context:

ASM: '. . . he, and some of the other lads, notably (D) (the same boy as above) along with a couple of other lads who used to work for us, attend a regular discussion group with a probation officer, and they have talks with him about CI and the sort of projects they would be doing in their own patch. And I sort of encourage them. The probation officer talked to me about it and I said that if possible, we'd try and get something off the ground and we'd give that sort of project priority if the kids had suggested it. But to date nothing has come to light.'

The interesting point here is that the discussion group is run *outside* CI, there being neither the facilities nor structures for it to occur on a regular basis within the area in question.

Two teams which did involve the young people were new teams that had been set up in an area where there were few job opportunities, and hence many of the young people had been unemployed simply because there were no jobs to be had. The teams therefore had something approaching a more 'judicious mixture' of young people than most others. These YEs made suggestions about the project on which they were working, organized outings for themselves in the evenings and at weekends with some help from their SCs and showed more initiative in these ways than most other teams in the area. An area staff member remarked that this kind of enthusiasm had been widely in evidence when the scheme first started, for then most YEs had merely been unemployed and there had not been such a large number of ESN and mentally handicapped recruits. It would seem that the lack of involvement of young people in decision making is related to: the background experience, expectations and values of the staff and SCs; the kinds of young people who are selected for CI; the fact that CI is not permanent employment which results in the more able young people leaving. It is possible that the last two factors combine to diminish the possibility that effective peer leadership or initiative will emerge; this produces a situation in which there are few, if any, models provided by peers of responsible involvement in decision making from which other young people might learn.

In terms of the effect of staff backgrounds and related beliefs we may remark that the encouragement of participation requires certain modes of thinking and skills on the part of the staff which are not at present available to them. Similarly an initial resistance to and lack of ability to 'participate' is to be expected from the kinds of young people recruited for CI. Both these elements interact in the following rationale for *not* involving the young people.

RO: 'In the "Aims of CI" it says they should "gain social organizational skill by participation in the work group".'

ASM: 'At the very beginning, this was done. Like the meetings once a month: we had a worker's council. It was a waste of time. They are just not interested. They want someone to *tell* them what they're to do. If you were to turn round and say to them, "Now what colour would you like to paint this place?" 'Some would say purple, some grey, you know. You would get no-where! You would end up with them saying "Oh, you just tell us and we'll get on with it!" Maybe in some areas they want to participate, but I'd say with our lot, no. They want to be just treated like an employee. I mean, their scheme consultant is their "gaffer", I don't care what name *we* call them. And we're still their bosses no matter first-name terms or whatever, we're the ones that rule it. The main thing is you can be as friendly as you like with them, you can be as lax, as long as they know how far they can push it.'

The matter of the YEs' power and authority is clearly a potential source of conflict with the YEs' position in the hierarchies of control displayed in this extract from a Staff Association meeting:

SC (A): 'We are going forward looking for more money, and the kids, the youngsters are not getting any increase. Surely their case should be fought if we can afford to fight our own?'

SC (B): 'Well, unfortunately, as the executive we cannot fight for the boys. But we have on our application that an increase should be considered for the young people, basing it on, from their starting with us there have been two increases at social security level or unemployment level. We're basing it on these two increases which we think should be payable to the boys and all. I think it works out at about a pound. But at least it's something, even if it only covers their bus fares.'

This extract illustrates the ambiguous position of the young employees: are they relatively passive 'clients' of a therapeutic agency or are they young employees doing a proper job in an industrially realistic organization? Certainly some of the young people themselves would like more say in decisions which affect them as we see in the following discussion with a team, which incidentally, revealed more articulacy, awareness and potential for development than is usually taken to be the case for the CI YE.

RO: 'Do you think you have enough say in what happens in the Area?'

YE1: 'I think they could ask you a bit more — like come round every so often and ask you what is going on. They came round about once every two months or something like that . . .'

YE2: 'I think the boys should have a union. Everyone should have a union, for the boys and the men.'

YE3: 'I agree on that point, but I don't know if you would get it.'

YE2: 'I don't see why we shouldn't.'

YE3: 'There are not a great deal of people in here, on the boys' side (of the job). I don't know how you could fit it. They would be sending somebody down here all the time, because there is always something going on! We would be getting our money's worth! I think it would be a bit of a risk putting boys in a union.'

The Industry Councils, essentially being the elements of CI structure designed to involve the young people in decision making, do not function for the reasons set out in Chapter One. The staff were of the opinion that such Councils were artificial exercises since the young people did not have the expertise necessary to contribute to decision making and the Council had no real functions and power. To run it for the sake of running it seemed unrealistic and was perceived as forcing a 'middle-class idea suitable for sixth form grammar school lads' on to a group of lads for whom it was inappropriate and threatening. Thus when issues concerning wages and tenure emerged it became apparent that the Council could not influence matters. An area staff member recalls:

> 'It never had a function . . . set up to encourage participation . . . they groused about the wages, I wrote off to London . . . then the reply would be "No increase" . . . everything they were interested in they had no say in . . . the decisions that concerned them were not taken at local level . . . perhaps there is a need for more local autonomy to overcome this.'

The cause of the failure of Industry Councils as an exercise in participatory management or as an educational exercise in responsibility, is difficult to untangle. The constraints associated with the formal structure of CI are, of course, important but at a more personal level of analysis the kinds of skills which could help the Councils to function effectively may not be available. This may be illustrated by reference to a Council Meeting called to reintroduce procedures involving consultation with the young employees. It transpired that the staff had not discussed where to hold the meeting, how it should be conducted and who should introduce certain topics. When the AM addressed PO2 at the beginning of the meeting it seemed that the latter constituted the formal 'Chairman' figure, but within a few minutes the Pr O had interrupted with a series of suggestions as to how the YEs should introduce themselves. Throughout the meeting PO2 and Pr O engaged in sequences of questions and answers while PO1 adopted a more dominant role in the second half of the meeting and brought the meeting to a formal close.

There were several sequences of open-ended questions, pleas for 'Anything else you want to discuss?' and exhortations to go back to work groups to collect opinions; the following concluding sequence indicates a staff unawareness of the views of the YEs:

Pr O: 'Anything else now?'

YE: 'So we cannot get any safety belts, no rise, no tools . . . (YE laughter)

(Interwoven explanatory phrases about having 'covered all that' and 'Anything else?' and going back to work groups.)

YE: 'We'll talk among ourselves.'

PO2: 'If there's anything you want to bring up, then do it now, surely?'

YE: 'There might be something someone's scared to say.'

PO2: 'You have got to bring it up sometime.'

Pr O: *'There is no reason to be frightened because this is your committee . . . this is your chance of having a say in what happens in CI.'*

With almost the last exchanges of the morning PO1 suggested 'Would you rather have the meeting without us? . . . maybe meet without us for the first half hour till you've gathered your thoughts together . . . let's all say Aye . . . well we'll do that next time . . .'

Throughout this 'pioneering' meeting the CI staff seemed totally unaware of how their own replies structured the whole development of YE involvement. When the two more articulate boys ventured to query matters of organizational detail, they were not allowed more than a few sentences of introductory description. There soon followed long statements by the three CI staff as to how all concerned were bound by legal constraints hence the inability of CI locally to implement change. At one juncture a YE was incredulous that they could not take the issue to 'higher authority such as the Mayor'. The staff response turned on the naivety of this view and perhaps unwittingly demonstrated an infectious fatalism, *i.e.,* 'Well, have a word with him . . . that'll be more than *we* (stress) can do'. Whereupon the YE accurately concluded 'So I'm really fighting a losing battle — eh?'. CI staff replied 'in many ways, yes . . . this is perhaps one of the disadvantages of the scheme . . . that we're dependent on the LA . . . we're just not being helped . . .' This exchange was punctuated towards the end by one of the POs referring to 'Any more moans and groans before we get onto better things?' thus characterizing over half the Industrial Council session as a negative safety valve.

The overall impression gained from on-site observation is that the hierarchy of control and decision-making operates in a less authoritarian way than might be the case in some industrial situations. However, the local CI system may be most readily seen as consisting of a manager, his assistant managers, foremen/supervisors and workers. It must be emphasized though that the manner in which this hierarchical system functions involves a great deal of consultation and persuasion arising from a greater concern for persons than might be found elsewhere.

The qualitative material presented in this chapter suggests that within CI discipline is not only a matter of maintaining work output; it may also be seen as a means of orientating the YE's behaviour in relation to work requirements. The work group may be viewed as a simulated work situation in which young people are expected to produce certain patterns of behaviour. They receive 'rewards' and 'punishments' which, because they do not involve the removal of the YE from the work group, allows the development of an orientation which is considered appropriate for a work situation. Thus the relative benevolence of CI's disciplinary procedures, compared with those in open employment where the person might be dismissed for taking a particular action, is not merely a matter of 'caring' about or for the young person. Rather, it is a key aspect of the socialization process whereby the YEs are taught to behave in accordance with a particular ideology and set of values about work.

The staff and SCs do 'care' about the young people in the ordinary sense of being concerned for their well-being, but in organizational terms this is largely expressed in the lenient application of disciplinary procedures. The staff and SCs automatically discuss 'the caring role' in these terms. The notion of 'caring' thus appears to serve a covert socializing function into work-related roles and therefore has a deeper significance than its overt meaning of a kindly concern for the well-being of the young persons would suggest. Such a process depends on the presence of adults who will apply discipline/feedback and serve as models for the desired sets of role behaviour. Since the scheme consultants are mostly skilled and semi-skilled manual workers, who are likely to use implicit models about traditional work roles in deciding the appropriateness of the YEs' behaviour, this condition seems to be satisfied. A further limitation is that of time in that sufficient time has to be allowed for the desired behaviour to develop and become patterned. It seems likely that a year would be sufficient in this respect especially if the person goes to another job without an intervening period of unemployment, since this would ensure the provision of a situation in which the acquired behaviour would be positively reinforced.

Employers' Perceptions of CI[1]

The extent of the employers' knowledge of CI varied from area to area. Five of the employers interviewed were unaware of the existence of CI. They did not know that it was a government sponsored scheme and they were not aware of its objectives. Some remembered having 'read something in the papers' or 'seen something on television', but, in general, this was the limit of their knowledge. As one employer said:

> 'My only contact with Community Industry was a young lady who came to work for us approximately a year ago. I am speaking without a great deal of knowledge; I have read the odd thing in the paper about it; I wouldn't even know where to find out about it. It's not generally known to employers.'

Several of these employers evidenced some confusion between CI and other social service agencies. For example, one remarked:

> 'Yes, I think it is one of those social welfare schemes.'

And another said:

> 'We've got a lot of these Community Action groups round here and I've not got much time for them.'

The remaining eight were well-informed about CI. They were aware of its operation and that it was government sponsored. They were familiar with its objectives and some had shown a keen interest in the scheme from its inception; as one company personnel officer said:

> 'I think it is an ideal system. I think it is first-class because otherwise you have this group of people who really are out on a limb, because you get the boy who misses out on an apprenticeship at fifteen and from our experience they have turned out to be good lads.'

The General Manager of a public works department was of the same opinion:

> 'It is a first-class scheme. We've had an awful problem with young unemployed people here, and anything that can provide them with jobs must be good.'

From the employers' point of view a young person who has had CI experience would have a distinct advantage over a young unemployed person in terms of obtaining a job. The mere fact of having been employed is an advantage in that the young person has had a chance to develop a 'work history' during his period of employment with CI. The prospective employer can consult references and take personal recommendations from someone who knows the young person and is familiar with his job performance, character and personality. This is important because although many employers are casual in regard to recruitment policies and selection procedures, they are reluctant to 'take a chance' on an unemployed young person of unknown or unproven ability. One personnel officer of a printing company pointed out:

> 'The only time I would take people on would be on a personal recommendation from the personnel officer that this person would be ready to adapt to a more pressurized atmosphere and that they are capable of doing an exacting day's work. I think I would really insist upon this. If someone came to me and said they had been with CI for six months, this would not particularly impress me; it is not by itself any recommendation. Then I would go back to somebody at CI to find out what this person was like as a worker. Recommendation and references are absolutely crucial. What is needed is personal contact with someone at CI. It is not a major factor one way or the other, where their last job was. What really matters is the personal assessment of his previous managers.'

Another Local Goverment officer said:

> 'If two people came to be interviewed by me, and one was unemployed and one was from Community Industry, I would invariably select the one from Community Industry because at least I know what sort of jobs he has been doing.'

An additional factor which has to be taken into account is the concern which employers express as to why prospective employees have left their previous employment. In the case of ex-CI employees, any suspicions can quickly be allayed by a telephone call to CI Area Management.

Employers are also influenced by the person's self-presentation at interview. This may be illustrated at national level by reference to the results of a sample survey of unemployed young people and vacancies at Careers Offices contained in the report of a working party set up by the National Youth Employment Council (1974). We may quote from the report as follows (pp. 64-65):

'One further finding of considerable importance concerned the personal characteristics of the unemployed. It was felt that it would be worth while to find out whether, in the opinion of careers officers, unemployed young people appeared to have a smart appearance, or to be mentally alert, or to possess manual dexterity. Careers officers were also asked about some of the more obvious drawbacks which young people might have. It was possible to check careers officers' opinions by observing whether any particular group felt by them to have a particular characteristic performed badly or well in job-finding during the three-week survey period. The following table shows, roughly, what proportions of the unemployed were shown as having the characteristics listed; how far employers stipulated them when notifying vacancies; and how successful each group was in finding employment.

Table 6 *(a) Personal characteristics of young people.*

	Characteristic	*Number in Sample*	*Percentage in sample*	*Percentage entering employment*	*Median length unemployed weeks*
(a)	Smart appearance	2,163	26.0	33.5	4.9
(b)	Handicapped	303	3.6	12.5	13.4
(c)	Mentally alert	2,167	26.0	32.2	4.6
(d)	ESN	473	5.7	15.9	10.4
(e)	Illiterate	237	2.8	18.6	9.1
(f)	On probation, ex-approved school, etc.	679	8.1	22.8	4.5
(g)	Manual dexterity	1,784	21.4	29.2	4.5
(h)	None of those listed above	3,375	40.5	23.1	6.3
	Total	8,335	(144.1)	26.1	6.0

Table 6 *(b) Employers' requirements in terms of personal characteristics.*

	Requirement	*Number of vacancies in sample*	*Percentage of sample*
(p)	Smart appearance	3,432	33.3
(q)	Physically fit	3,158	30.6
(r)	Alert	5,272	51.1
(s)	Elementary literacy	2,306	22.3
(t)	Not on probation	1,195	11.6
(u)	Manual dexterity	3,101	30.1
(v)	None specified	1,897	18.4
	Total	10,319	(197.4)

Note: Numbers in the first column do not add to the total shown, and percentages in the second column do not add to 100 because many young people have, and many employees specify, more than one of the characteristics listed. The sample consisted of 5,996 young people who were unemployed on 20th November 1972 and a further 2,320 who registered as unemployed in the ensuing three weeks. Details were also obtained of 5,991 vacancies at careers offices on 20th November 1972 and of 4,328 further vacancies notified between then and 8th December 1972.

The person's appearance and 'attitude' thus have a significant effect on his chances of being offered a job. There is some evidence from interviews with employers that ex-CI employees are aware of the crucial importance of self-presentation.

A personnel officer said:

> 'You should see the state of some of the young people who come here looking for a job. They turn up late, their hair is uncombed and many of them look as though they haven't had a wash in weeks. They slouch in and out and most of the time they are wasting my time. At least with the people from Community Industry most of them come looking as though they want a job.'

Once they have entered employment, ex-CI employees are not dramatically dissimilar to other young people as far as the employers are concerned. It must be remembered that employers are accustomed to a high turnover of young people and that the young people, especially girls, are constantly coming and going.

One employer remarked:

> 'There is no difference in performance between ex-CI people and the other apprentices. We have had one leave out of three and as a percentage that is not bad at all.'

Another said:

> 'Well, let's face it, we have a considerable turnover in apprentices anyway. If I base it on the normal run-of-the mill apprentices, the CI people break even.'

And yet another:

> 'If I was to walk out now on that shop floor and look at the work done, I could not tell which had been done by the ex-CI people and which had been done by the rest.'

When the method by which ex-CI leavers obtained further employment was discussed with employers, it was evident that in the majority of cases the young people had been placed in employment by informal means. Typical remarks illustrating this process are:

Employer 1: 'Yes, (Name of ASM) is a very good friend of mine from way back. I admire what he is trying to do, and when he 'phoned me up and asked me would I be prepared to take two of his boys, I was dubious at first but now I'm glad I did and everything has worked out okay.'

Employer 2: '(Name of ASM) used to work here with me, and we were friendly then. When I wanted an extra couple of blokes, I 'phoned him up and asked him had he got a couple of suitable lads that would be interested in working here.'

Employer 3: 'It's funny, really, how I came to take on these Community Industry lads. I used to have my own do-it-yourself shop, and the CI people used to buy most of their material from me. When they found out I was starting this factory up, they said to contact them because they had some good lads doing joinery work on some of their projects.'

Employer 4: 'This was the thing, the people we started were well recommended by the people at CI, and they were all doing well when they started.'

This point about informal mechanisms would seem to be in accord with the earlier point concerning the importance of personal recommendations. Employers like to know the opinions of people who have worked in close contact with prospective employees, and respect the opinions of someone who they feel appreciates the employers' problems. There is added advantage if the recommendation comes from someone who is known to the employer.

A number of employers offered criticisms and suggestions based on their experience of employing CI's employees backed by their general expectations of young people in industry. One employer expressed the view that the reliance on team working within CI raised the danger of over-dependence upon the group which might stifle an individual's initiative. He commented in this respect:

> 'I appreciate that working in groups has a great benefit for these young people, in that it teaches them to work alongside other people, but unfortunately there comes a time when a person has to stand on his own two feet and make his own decisions. I just feel that too much reliance on the group could inhibit a person's initiative and individuality.'

He did, however, emphasize that this was a personal point of view and that he had not noticed any lack of individuality in the CI people now in his employ.

There is a type of employer to whom schemes like CI will always be 'unworkable' and 'impracticable'. The following would seem to be a fairly representative view illustrating this school of thought:

> 'I always think schemes like this (CI) are rather "make believe". The general idea seems all right, but these people lose their way for a bit sometimes, instead of getting a job and getting down to basic facts, they continue in this job, which I was almost going to say was a waste of time. It seems unfair when they are doing some good for someone, but it is not a real job. I think anyone who takes it on can only be taking it on as a "fill in" and never really put their best into it, unless they are really public-spirited. If they are not public-spirited, it can only be a fill-in until such time as either they think it is time to get a job or until they get turfed off the job. So I think that the basic idea is quite good, but this constant turnover of individuals might be bad for some of the individuals. I suppose this experience in CI could be beneficial if these people go into similar types of jobs as they have been doing in CI but apart from a bit of discipline, I can't see any benefit it would give them if they go and leave that job and go and take something different.'

To put this viewpoint in perspective it should be mentioned that only two of the employers interviewed held these beliefs. Other criticisms from employers were in a more constructive vein. In this respect an employer outlined the problem of ex-CI employees going into apprenticeships at eighteen, two years 'late' as it were, with their earnings being far less than their unskilled contemporaries. He explained:

> 'The difficulty we have found is that they are are a bit older. When they started, I explained to them the apprentices rates, etc. I discussed with our Managing Director the position of these boys and we agreed between ourselves and with the boy that if he showed he was making the grade by his second or third year, he would by this time be touching 20, we would advance him a year salary rise. Because we felt, as I explained to the boys, their pals are working as labourers, bus-drivers picking up £30 or £40 a week, he was prepared to sacrifice a bit of cash for his future, so we were prepared to meet him half way.'

By far the most insistent of the employers' criticisms was that CI could not provide a 'realistic industrial environment'. They all indicated the pressures that exist in modern industry with regard to individual performances, the meeting of deadlines and other demands. It was felt that CI's concern with punctuality and related issues were minimal requirements of the industrial situation. One personnel officer remarked:

> 'I just don't feel that Community Industry can offer a "realistic" industrial environment. We all have a deadline to meet here and if we don't meet it, someone has to "carry the can". They just don't experience any similar pressure in Community Industry and if you want to construct a more realistic replica of industrial conditions, considerably more pressure should be introduced.'

And another said:

> 'No wonder nobody wants to leave CI because it bends over backwards to keep them happy.'

The manager of a small joinery company who had taken a considerable number of CI's young people discussed the need for discipline and respect for authority in terms of the exigencies of business:

> 'These lads are basically good lads, but what has been wrong is that nobody has given them any guidance with things like discipline and respect for authority. They've not had it at home, they don't get it at school, and perhaps this is the

root of the problem and I don't think they get it in Community Industry. Whether they like it or not, when they come here they've got to accept that what I say goes. I am the boss and if anything goes wrong, it's my time and money that is at risk. There's no time for discussions as to the rights and wrongs of a thing. I have far more experience than they have, and what I say goes.'

Another employer suggested that Community Industry might benefit from the introduction of incentives:

'I think that if they do a particular job well or they finish it in the appropriate time, then they should get some kind of bonus. This is what happens here, and it would give them some idea of the pressure that exists in industry and also reward them for doing a job well and quickly.'

From these comments it would seem that the transition from Community Industry to other branches of industry could pose some problems for some CI leavers, although direct evidence of this is not readily available.

A person who probably has had more experience than any other as an employer is the superintendent of a zoo near area B. He employs about eight or nine CI employees on a more or less permanent basis and could be termed a particularly enlightened and caring employer. Some of his observations may be noted as follows:

'What needs to be stressed is the wide range of the types of young people that go through CI. There is not one particular type of CI leaver, and generalizations could be dangerous. At one end, I employ a young man here who has difficulty speaking and can hardly form his words. I've found him a job directing the contractors' lorries when they back up ready for unloading. He does his job conscientiously and diligently and never leaves until the last lorry has gone. Since he has been here his whole confidence has improved beyond recognition, and his parents have been round to thank us for the improvement he has shown. At the other end, I've got a bright lad who has become almost an expert in fork-truck driving. I won't be able to keep him here much longer because his earning capacity is considerable now in the building trade. I don't want to use jargon, but if I had to describe the effect of working in CI has on young people, I would call it a "mellowing" effect. When they come to us here, they are brash and insensitive young people. I've seen the change in them, and I have witnessed the development in them of a distinct awareness of other people's problems.'

Though generalizations can indeed 'be dangerous', it is necessary to have information of sufficient generality to inform policy decisions. It is to this general level we now turn by providing material arising from the quantitive aspect of the research.

Quantitative analysis; the general approach

In the planning stage for the quantitative aspect of the research a somewhat broad evaluative strategy was envisaged of attempting to isolate the effects of the CI experience upon the young people involved by drawing on the data from the various comparison groups involved in the research.[2] The rationale for this strategy is one of illustrating, rather than demonstrating unconditionally, the effects of the CI experience by means of a 'quasi-experimental' approach using the common measuring instruments previously described. Since the elements of randomization and repeated measures are not involved in this approch no simple comparison between groups can provide conclusive evidence, one way or the other, of the effects of the CI experience; what may be gained, however, by adopting this strategy is an insight into the possible effects of CI with the plausibility of any given interpretation being set against evidence from the qualitative aspect of the research which has been dealt with in the previous section. Thus rather than the classical design of a random division of a heterogeneous population into two groups where the independent (treatment) variable is experienced by one group but not the other, we have a 'quasi-experimental' design as illustrated below:

	Stage 1	Stage 2	Stage 3
Population A	A1	A2	A3
Population B	B1	B2	B3

——————— Time ———————→

For the purposes of illustration A is taken to be CI employees with A1, A2 and A3 representing length of time spent in organization (treatment); CI's employees being placed into three groups in terms of their length of employment with CI, *viz.* less than 4 months (A1); 4-9 months (A2); over 9 months (A3). Population B is taken to be apprentices who are similarly divided in terms of their length of time in their organization: analysis is conducted separately for males and females.[3] In additon to this preliminary cross-tabulation of our data a further series of analyses is offered for males only which dichotomizes the treatment variable and is repeated for two groups of geographical areas which appear distinctive in terms of CI young employees' ODQ scores.

Preliminary steps

The statistical treatment of the data attempts to account for the relationships between the teams of dependent variables previously described and the classificatory indices of group and length of time in organization which are adopted as independent variables. Age is introduced into the general linear model used to handle the analysis as a covariate. Our attention is focused on the interaction between the independent variables rather than each taken as a main effect, as this provides a pointer to differential changes over time between CI's young employees and the apprentices. This preliminary analysis was conducted separately for males and females.

Observation of the results indicates that there is a significant interaction effect for IQ (F 3.80, $P<.005$), attitude to work (F 3.86, $P<.005$), and perception of employing organization (F 3.01, $P<.005$), for males, but no significant interaction for any group of variables for females. Observation of the descriptive statistics accompanying the analysis suggests that with regard to IQ both verbal and non-verbal ability measures make a contribution to the significant result, and that this largely reflects an increase in IQ scores over time for the CI group as opposed to a falling off for the apprentices. Moderate contributions from all the three 'attitude to work' variables contribute to the significant interaction effect for this group of variables. It would seem that the apprentices see less meaning in work and have less commitment with length of time in the job while the CI group exhibits little change. Organizational care and work group support, particularly the latter, are the major contributing variables to the significant interaction relating to perception of employing organization. The CI group initially see their organization as exhibiting greater 'organizational care' and 'work group support' than do the apprentices; however, the difference is progressively narrowed as exposure of members to their respective organizations increases. Thus the apprentices who have spent more than 9 months in their organization score higher on organizational care than the equivalent CI group; a reversal of the situation at the under 4 months stage. We may draw together the points relating to these significant interactions by presenting graphically the differential changes over time for both groups.

Fig. 14: *Comparison of the changes in the CI and Apprentice groups with increased length of time in organization (males only).*

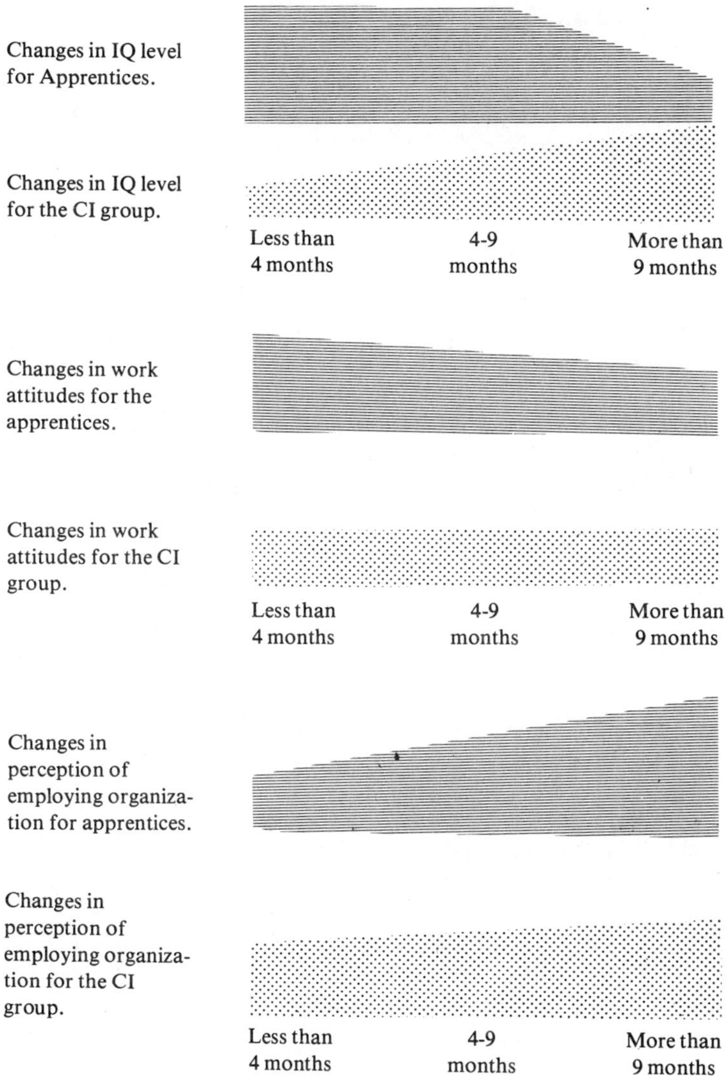

Increases indicate more favourable attitudes.

Further analysis

We may introduce at this point an analysis relating to differences between geographical areas in terms of CI young employees' perceptions of their organization. The ODQ variables were examined in an area by sex analysis and the difference between areas was found to be highly significant ($F = 2.0$, $P<.001$). Two dimensions adequately describe difference between the areas, accounting for 43 per cent and 35 per cent of trace respectively, with the first dimension being characterized by all four variables but being particularly well described by organizational care and task accomplishment. The first dimension may thus be described as perceived degree of 'organizational caring', and a 'caring' index was computed for each area by taking its average rank over the four contributing variables. Table 7 below shows the resulting rank order of areas in terms of this caring index:

Table 7: *CI's young employees' perception of their organization.*

		Rank Order on contributing variables (Means used to rank areas)			
Areas	*Index of Caring*	*Supervisory Satisfaction*	*Organ. Care*	*Work Group Support*	*Task Accomplish-ment*
A	2.5	3	2	4	1
C	2.5	3	4	1	2
D	2.7	2	2	3	4
E	2.7	1	1	6	3
H	4.5	5	6	2	5
G	5.1	6	5	4	4
B	7.0	7	7	7	7
F	8.0	8	8	8	8

It is apparent from this table that the areas tend to fall into two groups in terms of their perceived 'caring orientation'. This is shown by the dotted line in the table; areas A, C, D and E are perceived by the CI employees as 'more caring' than areas H, G, B and F.[4]

This identification of a basis for grouping areas affords a further means of investigating the effects of CI. We may suggest that because of the perceived differences in the functioning of CI in different geographical areas the CI experience may have correspondingly different effects on young employees. We now investigate the effects of the CI experience with respect to those areas which are perceived as stressing 'the caring role' and those areas that lay emphasis on the production of a 'realistic industrial environment'. The thinking associated with this analysis is that while the 'industrial' areas may be more successful in re-orienting the young employees towards a 'realistic' approach to work, the 'caring' areas may be more responsive to the social education aspect of CI and thus perhaps bring about some change in attitudes of young employees in this domain. The analyses undertaken were similar to those previously described and were run separately for the 'caring' and 'industrial' areas. Male CI employees were compared with male apprentices as before (group) and length of time in present organization was dichotomized into 'less than 7 months' and '7 months or more' to provide the second independent variable. Again our attention is focused on the interaction term. We find that the interaction for the IQ variables is significant in the caring areas ($F = 11.45$, $P < .001$) but not in the industrial areas ($F = 2.32$, N.S.). The position with regard to the 'work' variables is a reversal of that observed for IQ with a significant interaction being noted for the 'industrial' areas ($F = 2.62$, $P < .05$) but not the 'caring' areas ($F = 1.06$, NS); this pattern also holds for the organizational perception variables with the interaction term being significant for the industrial areas ($F = 4.43$, $P < .005$) but not the caring areas ($F = 0.16$, NS).

It is noticeable from the descriptive statistics accompanying these analyses that the increase in the mean IQ score of CI employees over time is in marked contrast to the downward trend for the apprentices. A possible interpretation of our results relating to this measurement area is that the CI experience brings about a positive shift in cognitive functioning due either to increased motivation to perform well on ability tests, which may be associated with the supportive role of CI, or due to the heightened interaction of the individual with adults and peers associated with the particular circumstances of his work situation. This interpretation is quite plausible in the light of evidence on changes in the level of intellectual functioning of individuals who move from a deprived to an enriched environment (Vernon, 1969; Nisbet, 1953; Wiseman, 1966; Cattell, 1963). However, one other explanation of this trend needs to be considered, namely, that as we are not dealing with the same individuals at different points in time the shift in intellectual functioning may merely represent fluctuations in CI's recruitment policy. It is possible that brighter teenagers were selected for CI employment before the survey was carried out, and that subsequent recruitment has concentrated on less able teenagers. The absence of a significant interaction effect for girls and its occurrence only in those areas whose perceived image is associated with conditions appropriate to such an influence, seems to argue against plausibility of the recruitment explanation. On the other hand, we might expect that the verbal component of the IQ test would make most contribution to the observed group difference: however, observation of the accompanying descriptive statistics indicates that both IQ components are making approximately the same contribution. The question must remain an open one as there is little supportive evidence from the qualitative aspect of the study for either interpretation, though, as we have seen, there is some suggestion that CI had, in fact, become *less* selective at the time of the research.

The dimension underlying the significant interaction for the attitude to work variables in the industrial areas is characterized by a major contribution from 'work meaning' with lesser contributions from 'work cynicism' and 'work commitment'. From the mean scores we see that the interaction is due largely to a shift in the scores of the apprentices with practically no change in the scores of CI employees. The items in the work meaning scale cover such aspects as 'work as a place solely to earn money', 'work affording the possibility of self-realization', and 'work as a purpose in itself', and we may note that mean score increases with length of time in job for the apprentices which, bearing in mind the direction of scoring for this scale, suggests a reduced feeling of purpose in work. The CI employees compare favourably with the apprentices on this variable since their mean score does not change. Similarly whilst 'work commitment' decreases for the apprentices it remains constant for the CI employees. Work cynicism tends to decrease for both groups.

Taking the pattern of scores for the apprenticeship group as the norm we may speculate that the CI experience has a 'holding effect' on work-related attitudes particularly with regard to the meaning and significance of work for the individual. The suggestion is then that the CI experience may offset the development of 'unfavourable' work-related attitudes which appear to occur even in such a highly advantaged group as apprentices with the caveat that an 'industrial' rather than 'caring' context be provided. The qualitative aspect of the research so far discussed supports this interpretation in that resource distribution tends towards a work rather than educational emphasis with little specification of appropriate forms of educational experiences.

Referring once again to our statistical analysis we see that in the industrial areas 'organizational care' is making the greatest contribution to the significant interaction effect with smaller contributions being apparent with regard to 'task accomplishment' and 'supervisory satisfaction'. In terms of the mean scores on 'organizational care' we may note that whilst apprentices' means increase with length of time, CI means do not change. This is consonant with an approach which is perceived as providing a 'realistic' industrial environment for its employees. A similar trend is apparent for 'task accomplishment' and 'supervisory satisfaction' but is not so marked as that observed for 'organizational care'.

The foregoing analysis has provided some pointers as to the likely effects of CI but, because of the deficiences associated with the cross-sectional nature of the design, these remain only suggestive. However, drawing upon both qualitative and quantitative material we may arrive at certain conclusions.

CI does appear to be having some beneficial impact on young people; an impact not merely in terms of 'work completed', the physical evidence of such an effect is to hand, but in terms of helping their young employees cope with 'open employment'. This beneficial impact operates essentially at two levels: (i) at the individual level CI helps to inculcate attitudes and behaviour patterns appropriate to obtaining and holding down a job in open employment for its male employees; (ii) at the institutional level CI helps break the vicious circle, whereby unemployment becomes self-reinforcing, through the provision of an occupational context which has associated supportive procedures. The quantitative aspect suggests that the conditions necessary for gains at level (i) involve the provision within CI areas of an industrial orientation, and the qualitative aspect indicates that the causative mechanism involved is the 'scheme consultant' who adopts a 'benign foreman' stance in relation to his young employees. With regard to level (ii),

CI provides a 'work history' for its young employees which, coupled with personal recommendations and references from the adult staff, may help the young person secure opportunities in open employment.

Both the quantitative and qualitative aspects suggest that CI has little, if any, impact on young employees in terms of their personal and social development; at least in so far as differences in test outcomes are concerned. The possible exception to this general finding is that CI, by providing a 'verbally enriched' environment for the disadvantaged youngster, may bring about a positive shift in measured cognitive functioning; the conditions associated with this shift appear to be related to the 'caring' rather than 'industrial' aspect of its operation. The qualitative aspect suggests that possible reasons for the ineffectiveness of the CI experience in this area of personal and social development lie in the backgrounds and skills of the scheme consultants and the amount of resources, particularly staff time, allocated to organizational structures designed to aid employee participation and development.

Theoretical overview and conclusion

The research described in this and the preceding chapters may perhaps best be put in perspective by referring to Keil *et al.'s* (1966) attempt to conceptualize the process of adjustment to working life by young people. This process may be summarized as follows:

(a) Socialization to work:	(Family, neighbourhood, school, peer group)
(b) Previous work experience	(Part-time jobs, work visits observation)
(c) Wider social influences:	(Media, religion, politics)
↓ Lead to	
(d) Attitudes and expectations about work:	(Intrinsic: extrinsic etc.)
↓ Explain	
(e) Actual job entry	Work situation, home situation, leisure situation

(f) Experience as a worker

Lead to

↓

(g) Adjustment/non-adjustment of the young worker

Job change or stability or reformulation of (d)

This above process is characterized by formal and informal influences at each stage and occurs within the context of a fluctuating labour market which varies in both space and time.

It is hoped that our research into youth unemployment and its attendant provision has thrown some light on the questions which are raised by Keil and co-workers by providing a glimpse into the life circumstances of such special groups of young people as CI employees. Though a considerable literature has developed around the theme of occupational preference, choice and attainment, it is distinguished by a lack of coherence and consensus which may in part reflect the relatively undeveloped state of empirical work in this area. This applies with regard to contributions from psychology (Kline, 1975) and sociology (Musgrave 1967; Coulson *et al.* 1967; Musgrave 1968) and at both normative and empirical levels of analysis (Vroom 1964). A re-occuring point which may be culled from this debate, however, is that relating to individual values, either as taken for granted phenomena (Ford and Box, 1967) or as dealt with in explicit fashion (Phillips 1964; Blaikie 1971). Thus differences in values, usually seen as arising from varying patterns of primary and secondary socialization which may in some sense be 'anticipatory', are often seen as furnishing the underlying criteria which account for differences in occupational preference, choice or attainment. A variant on this theme, associated with the work of Super and associates (Super and Bohn, 1971), stresses the maintenance of the individual's self-concept by matching the anticipated or actual satisfaction derived from a given occupation against needs. However we would agree with Cotgrove and Fuller (1972) when they comment:

> 'The theories we have been discussing imply that occupation is a general or typical means of implementing a self-concept . . . But it is only for a minority that embracing an occupational role is likely to provide a solution — that is, for that small minority for whom work is expressive and a major avenue of self actualization . . . In some cases, temporary and synthetic identities may serve

> as substitutes for the damaged and stigmatized identities conferred by society on those who fail the 11 plus, fail at school and are faced with the "choice" of a range of menial jobs . . . In such cases, occupation is not so much "chosen" as entered for instrumental reasons and without commitment. Indeed such individuals are characterized by the rapidity with which they change jobs. Meaning and a self-concept must be sought elsewhere: they cannot be conferred by alienating work.' (p. 60).

Though couched in somewhat emotive and heightened terms this quotation does draw attention to a point made by Haystead (1971) who argues that

> '. . . rather than constructing rational models of choice for testing, it is more useful to examine the types of rationality exhibited by different groups. This approach then focuses on the problems of, first, whether the subjects are "aware" of the fact that they are faced by competing alternatives. Secondly, it emphasizes the importance of examining their definition of the possible alternatives.' (p. 92).

Haystead's use of the concept of 'awareness contexts' to illustrate this point is not dissimilar to the notion of 'career' which we have used in this book as a sensitizing device to illustrate the CI experience.

Awareness contexts, as used by Glaser and Strauss (1964), draws attention to both the subjective experience of individuals and the structural constraints associated with their location in educational and/or occupational systems. The process of 'choice' in relation to the individual's awareness of it may be illustrated diagramatically as follows:

	Choice in 'reality'	*No choice in 'reality'*
Aware of Choice	A	B
Unaware of Choice	C	D

Where an individual has an awareness of choice, knowledge of job requirements and characteristics and knowledge of job demands in terms of personal characteristics required then an 'open' awareness context is said to exist (A). Where none of these conditions apply a 'closed' awareness context exists (D) with partial awareness contexts being represented by B and C in the diagram. Haystead remarks that

> '. . . instead of accounting for occupational entry solely in terms of choice within certain broad limits, we can study the process in terms of a "career", continually taking account of both the choices made by the individual which commit him in certain directions, and the decisions and actions of others (such as parents, teachers or youth employment officers) which affect him.' (p. 80).

We have seen that the individuals 'eligible' for entry to CI, at school and open employment levels, operate with relatively 'closed' awareness contexts in that they have rather different expectations with regard to the purposes and reward of work as compared with their higher achieving peers. We must stress, however, that this is largely a difference of degree rather than of kind and in this regard the sub-title of Ashton's article (1973), 'notes on the development of different frames of reference among young male workers', is somewhat misleading in that it suggests differences of kind rather than degree. The burden of his argument is that schools provide young people with different frames of reference which 'direct them towards different types of occupation'. At the structural level of analysis he suggests that young people who enter working class occupations are fed through two rather different channels:

(a) Lower streams of modern or comprehensive schools into 'careerless' occupations (semi-skilled and unskilled types of jobs).
(b) Higher streams of modern and middle of comprehensive schools which provide 'working class careers' (skilled manual work).

The 'distinctive properties' of these two channels are set out as:

	(a)	(b)
1)	Little chance of obtaining qualifications	Elementary forms of qualification
2)	Less chance for development of cognitive/manipulative skills.	Opportunity for development of cognitive/manipulative skills.
3)	Less chance of assuming responsible positions.	Chance to gain access to authority.
4)	Provide shortest school career.	Opportunity for lengthening careers.

The pen portrait of the jobs which these two feeder channels lead to may be given in shorthand form as:

(a) Movements between positions horizontal rather than vertical: discontinuous rather than sequential. Routine, simple nature of work tasks — high control of work by the organization: low level of earnings when averaged over the life course: insecurity and low status. No membership of an organized occupational group.

(b) Hierarchy of positions though only two to four steps: apprentice to skilled worker: chargehand to foreman or equivalent. Skills more varied and complex than in (a) and therefore greater control over the work process. Membership of an organized group based on 'the manipulation of transferable skills'. Higher life time income coupled with job security.

Ashton goes on to examine how young people acquire the different frames of reference associated with these types of jobs and how these function to prepare them for the world of work. The development of negative self-images resulting in commitment to semi-skilled and unskilled work is seen to begin for young people in the early stages of their movement through the schools and arises, it is suggested, from barriers associated with the following: (i) differences in language codes, 'elaborated' v 'restricted', between teachers and taught; (ii) the setting off, in an organizational sense, streaming or banding, of those not heading for formal qualifications; (iii) beliefs held by teachers which categorize such young people as 'louts, dunces and layabouts' which are reinforced by pupils in higher streams. This leads Ashton to conclude that

> 'In this way, by acquiring an image of themselves through their interactions with others as academically incapable, the pupils learn to see these occupations that require some form of educational qualifications for entry as beyond their reach. They may regard the apprentice as the one who had done best for himself, but not consider such an occupation as suitable for themselves.' (p. 109).

The experience of work in the secondary sector of the labour market is seen to reinforce this self-image for it is suggested that this type of work does not offer avenues for self advancement. The lack of training and specialized skill, and the competition for advancement lead to an absence of an 'occupational identity' and little involvement in work: thus work is seen to have little meaning for such individuals. The defining characteristics of the associated frame of reference are given as perceptual immediacy, a central concern with the concrete, absence of any short or long-term planning with work not a central life interest.

We have seen in a previous chapter that there are systematic differences between groups of young people, located within the same broad social strata, both at school and employment levels, but our examination of responses to individual items of the work scales indicates a considerable degree of 'overlap' between the groups; with a few exceptions it is a question of relative emphasis between groups rather than reversal of opinion. Ashton also tends to understate the importance of home background which may bring about differing, rather than different, frames of reference even before pupils enter the secondary school (Baumrind, 1975).

Carter's earlier work (Carter, 1962) illustrates the saliency of the family in orientating the young person towards particular types of jobs and points up the secondary influence of the school in this respect. In his later publication (Carter, 1969) he comments:

> '. . . basically they know that there *aren't* any really good jobs for the likes of them . . . perhaps it is as well that school makes such a small impact on these children — otherwise they would be due for a shock when they started work and found that they were little more than extensions to machines for example and required to do routine work unquestioningly . . . the transition for these boys and girls is smooth because they are moving from one world at school that does not hold much intrinsic appeal to a world at work which is of the same order, it is not a big jolt.' (p. 114).

Schools do certainly act in an allocative sense, distributing young people to various levels in the occupational structure but it is doubtful whether they *cause* the differing sets of values, attitudes and beliefs which we have seen to exist. The pattern of career-related influences is a complex one involving the individual young person as initiator as well as passive recipient (Phillips, 1973) and employers as well as school teachers (Maizels, 1970) within a given strata of that structure. Though the work of Thomas and Wetherell (1974) is an important step forward we would agree with Keil *et al.* that

> 'Much more research on the inter-relationship between home, school and industry is required.' (p. 127).

Such research can be both 'policy' orientated and academic; unlike Coleman (1973) we do not necessarily see policy research as a 'different animal' from disciplinary research. Certainly the policy orientated researcher has to cope with different sets of contraints on his work, particularly that of time, but may still hold to scientific values in executing his research. In the view of the author scientific knowledge is dependent upon generalizations which are generated by a consideration of the degree of 'communality' of events or actions and central to this idea is the requirement of objectivity. This implies that the conclusions reached as far as possible are independent of the values and beliefs of the social scientist. To acknowledge that we cannot be completely objective is no reason for discarding this value completely. As has been pointed out 'that women live longer than men in our society is a conclusion which should be reached by both men and women on the basis of available data'. Clearly, however, in putting forward policy recommendations based on his research the researcher relies upon his own values and it is in this light that the recommendations, arising from this evaluation exercise, should be viewed: they are given in an appendix in the form presented in the original report.

Notes

1. The material presented in this section was obtained from interviews conducted with the personnel of fifteen employing organizations distributed over eight geographical areas.

2. Analysis of differences in scale scores for the four groups shown in table 4 (chapter 3) plus an additional group composed of young people who had left CI was presented in the original report; here we focus only on CI employees and apprentices.

3. Due to insufficient cases for females the 'treatment' variable is dichotomized in terms of less than and more than 7 months in present organization for this group.

4. We may note that this grouping largely reflects the pattern revealed in relation to area staff's dissatisfaction with 'local support' as reported in chapter two. Those areas perceived as being 'most caring' by the young employees are on the whole those areas in which staff are most dissatisfied with 'local support'. (p. 89, Table 3).

   As previously pointed out, it should be noted that given CI is by definition and orientation a 'human organization', we have a different base line from that employed in most studies of industrial organizations where intervention by organization analysts is usually in terms of making the organization 'more human' and thereby more effective. We might expect, therefore, that the usual criteria of rated effectiveness is here reversed. Thus those areas occupying the highest ranks in Table 7, page 194, may be providing less of the 'realistic industrial environment' which is seen to be a desired characteristic of the CI experience. To test this proposition each member of CI HQ staff was presented with a set of 8 cards, each card having an area name written on it. Members were then independently asked to place the cards (areas) in rank order in terms of their 'effectiveness'; the request was deliberately phrased in a general fashion with no specific directions given as to the meaning of the term effectiveness. The ranks assigned to areas were summed over respondents to produce an average rank of judged effectiveness for each area:

AREAS	*Average Ranks* order*
B	1.4
G	1.6
F	3.0
H	4.4
C	5.0
D	6.4
A	7.0
E	7.2

* This represents the average ordering of the areas by five CI HQ staff.

It will be seen that judged effectiveness and caring are inversely related. ($r = -.81$, $P<.05$). It is also of interest to note that this ordering correlates significantly with the area staff's perceived lack of support reported in chapter 2. ($=-.86$, $P<.01$). The second dimension of difference is not referred to in the text but is described by 'Work Group Support' and shows area H as obtaining a higher score on this dimension than its overall rank would suggest; the reverse situation applies to area E. In the absence of other evidence we may speculate that the overall composition of the work force in each area may have an influence on peer group relationships as expressed in 'Work Group Support'.

References

ASHTON, D.N. (1973). The transition from school to work: notes on the development of different frames of reference among young male workers. *Sociological Review.* 21. 101-123.

BAUMRIND, D. (1975). Early socialization and adolescent competence. In Dragastin, S.E. and Elder, Jr. G.H. (eds.) *Adolescence in the life cycle.* London: Wiley.

BLAIKIE, N.W.H. (1971). Towards a theoretical model for the study of occupational choice. *Sociology.* 5. 313-333.

CARTER, M.P. (1962). *Home, school and work.* Oxford: Pergamon.

CARTER, M.P. (1969). *Into work.* Harmondsworth: Penguin.

CATTELL, R.B. (1963). Theory of fluid and crystallized intelligence: a critical experiment. *Journal of Educational Psychology*. 54. 1-22.

COLEMAN, J. (1973). Paper read at American Association for Advancement of Science meeting in Washington. Reported in *Report on Educational Research*. Jan. 17th, 1973.

COTGROVE, S. and FULLER, M. (1972). Occupational socialization and choice: the effect of sandwich courses. *Sociology*. 6. 59-70.

COULSON, M.A., KEIL, E.T., RIDDELL, D.S. and STRUTHERS, J.S. (1967). Towards a sociological theory of occupational choice — a critique. *Sociological Review*. 15. 301-309.

FORD, J. and BOX, S. (1967). Sociological theory and occupational choice. *Sociological Review*. 15. 287-299.

GLASER, B.G. and STRAUSS, A. (1964). Awareness context and social interaction. *American Sociological Review*. 29. 669-679.

HAYSTEAD, J. (1971). Social structure, awareness contexts and processes of choice. *Sociological Review*. 15. 79-94.

KEIL, E.T., RIDDELL, D.S. and GREEN, B.S.R. (1966). Youth and work: problems and perspectives. *Sociological Review*. 10. 117-137.

KLINE, P. (1975). *Psychology of vocational guidance*. London: Batsford.

MAIZELS, J. (1970). *Adolescent needs and the transition from school to work*. London: Athlone Press.

MUSGRAVE, P.W. (1967). Towards a sociological theory of occupational choice. *Sociological Review*. 15. 33-46.

MUSGRAVE, P.W. (1968). Continuities in the sociological theory of occupational choice: a note. *Sociological Review*. 16. 93-97.

NISBET, J.B. (1953). Family environment and intelligence. *Eugenics Review*. 45. 31-40.

PHILLIPS, B.S. (1964). Expected value deprivation and occupational preference. *Sociometry*. 27. 151-160.

PHILLIPS, D. (1973). Young and unemployed in a northern city. In D. Weir (ed.) *Men and work in modern Britain*. Fontana.

SUPER, D.E. and BOHN, M.J. (1971). *Occupational Psychology*. London: Tavistock.

THOMAS, R. and WETHERELL, D. (1974). *Looking forward to work*. London: HMSO.

VERNON, P.E. (1969). *Intelligence and cultural environment*. London: Methuen.

VROOM, V.H. (1964). *Work and motivation*. London: Wiley.

WISEMAN, S. (1966). Environmental and innate factors and educational attainment. In Meade, J.E. and Parkes, A.S. (eds.) *Genetic and environmental factors in human ability*. Edinburgh: Oliver and Boyd.

Unqualified, untrained and unemployed. Report of a Working Party set up by the National Youth Employment Council. London: HMSO.

Appendix 1

Recommendations

1. The experimental phase of Community Industry should now be regarded as ended. It is recommended that CI should be placed on a more permanent basis, an appropriate period of time being 5 years in the first instance with a review taking place during the fifth year. The timing of any announcement with regard to the continuation of CI should be made so as to ensure an orderly progression of work and the necessary budgetary provision at local level.

2. In recommending the continuation of CI for a given period we are of the opinion that a major modification be made with regard to existing methods of finance and organization. The scheme was set up very quickly and implemented through the NAYC which had generated the initial impetus for CI. Following on from this initiative we feel that some other arrangements are now necessary. A number of lines of development suggest themselves: either

   (a) the establishment of CI as a charitable organization with its own board of governors and financed directly by government grant, or

   (b) CI to come within the terms of statutory provision for training and become a section of a training agency financed by the normal agency vote, or

   (c) the responsibility for CI to be taken over by local authorities and financed through the rate support grant system or by direct grant either wholly or in part.

   Option (a) while preserving the greater autonomy for CI would result in considerable duplication of existing machinery in the employment/training field. Option (b) could make use of existing machinery and retain the distinctive 'social' and 'work' orientation developed by CI. The danger might be a loss of the will to 'experiment', extending or modifying activities with regard to particular circumstances and a tendency for CI to be seen as part of 'the establishment'. Option (c) would have the advantage of enabling LAs to set up CI schemes as and when they thought it appropriate and is ideologically acceptable in terms of the current stress on 'devolution'. The danger is that CI's commitment to the personal and social development of young employees might be neglected with the young people becoming part of the 'direct labour force' working for the authority. The essential 'dynamic' of the organization might thus be lost.

The weight of evidence from both aspects of the research leads us to recommend that CI should be regarded as another branch of the 'training field' helping to meet a deficiency in non-specialized provision below craft level. In so recommending we emphasize that CI should be regarded as non-specialized training with considerable emphasis on its educational aspects and support from local authorities. In making this reference to training we do not mean to imply that CI should cease to be an employing organization with training allowances substituted for wages. Rather we feel that the present 'employment' structure should be maintained and brought within the scope of the Manpower Services Commission which has recently been given responsibility for co-ordinating the employment and training services now run by the Department of Employment. We would thus favour option (b) with some experimentation during the five year period with regard to the maintenance of CI in one area under a local authority by means of the rate support grant. Provision for a small inspectoral/advisory team with some clerical support located near the areas is considered necessary for overseeing the scheme and maintaining a 'balanced orientation'; such a team might be chaired by a leading industrialist. Appropriate publicity would seem to be necessary to engender local support.

3. As a matter of some urgency we recommend that the pay and conditions of area staff be reviewed; positions should be salaried with an incremental scale adopted for the five year period.

4. CI has been successful in securing an ideological orientation of staff which seeks to balance 'educational' and 'work' aims with operational emphasis placed on the latter. In terms of the present orientation for the scheme the ideal background for staff appears to be one involving industrial experience coupled with a positive desire to help young people in difficulties rather than one involving social or youth work. In supporting this recruitment policy, however, we recommend that special emphasis be given to the training of scheme consultants in that aspect of their work concerned with the social and personal development of CI's young employees. Liaison with the education departments of Colleges of Education in CI areas particularly with those colleges offering courses for mature students would be beneficial in this respect.

5. In terms of recruitment of young people CI could easily be seen as an organization providing semi-permanent jobs for the handicapped and ESN. In this respect there is a danger that CI may spread its resources too widely and we feel that it may not be able to provide the specialized help required in such cases. We recommend that the 'judicious mixture' of youngsters which CI aims to recruit should be more closely specified and special consideration be given to the provision made for girls within CI. A close working relationship with the careers service is a necessary pre-condition for a satisfactory recruitment procedure.

6. Workshops, originally conceived as CI projects involving repair and renovation, might usefully be seen as a form of induction training for all new young employees prior to being assigned to projects. We recommend that their

use should constitute a very basic training in the care and maintenance of tools and equipment as well as providing an opportunity for an assessment of the individual's abilities and difficulties before attachment to a project. Such an assessment might be recorded on the young employee's file.

7. The review procedure should be simplified and become a major responsibility of the personnel officer whose original functions have been largely taken over by the scheme consultant. Close liaison should be established with careers officers with regard to placing youngsters in open employment. Additionally, CI might experiment more in terms of involving employers. In this respect a certain amount of paid secondment of young employees to local industries, particularly towards the end of a period of employment with CI is considered desirable.

8. The research has to some extent identified the characteristics of 'alienated' youth. The cross sectional nature of the design, however, necessarily limits the conclusions which may be drawn with regard to the shifts in the characteristics and employment related attitudes of such a 'special group' of young people. It is recommended that a programme of research, encompassing a longitudinal approach, addressed to the transition from school to work of such youngsters should be undertaken.

Appendix 2

Questionnaires

(a) Young Persons Questionnaire.

What to do:
We would like you to help us by answering some questions about a number of things. There are no 'right' or 'wrong' answers; it is your 'feelings' about the questions we want. The person in charge will explain how to answer the questions.

Do not write your name; all replies are strictly confidential.
Before you begin, please fill in the following:

			Office Use Only Cols.	Code
Write your card number here	______________________		1-4	—
			5	
			6 (Class No.)	—
			7 (Area Code)	—
What is your sex? (Tick the right box)	Male ☐ 1	Female ☐ 2	8	—
How old were you at your last birthday?	______________ years.		9-10	—

How many brothers and sisters have you altogether? ______________ 11-12 —
(If none put 0) (Add 1)

Which of the following is right for you? 13 —
(Tick the right box).

		Second born	☐ 2
Only child	☐ 0	Third born	☐ 3
First born	☐ 1	Fourth or later born	☐ 4

Below are a number of statements about work: we would like your opinion about each of them.

If you:- Strongly Agree with a statement, draw a circle around SA to the right of it.
Agree with a statement, draw a circle around A to the right of it.
Are Undecided about a statement, draw a circle around U to the right of it.
Disagree with a statement, draw a circle around D to the right of it.
Strongly Disagree with a statement, draw a circle around SD to the right of it.

For example: I like watching football (SA) A U D SD
In the example, the person Strongly Agrees with what is said in the statement.
If you find that you have changed your mind, or you make a mistake when drawing the circle, put a cross X through the first circle and draw in another circle.

For example: I enjoy walking SA ~~(A)~~ U (D) SD
In this example, the person first put a circle around A for Agree then changed his mind and so crossed out the circle around A and put in a circle around D for Disagrees.

Remember it is your opinion that we are interested in, so there are no "right" or "wrong" answers.

		1	2	3	4	5	
1.	I prefer to work on my own rather than in a group.	SA	A	U	D	SD	14
2.	I'm not much interested about how a job fits in with other people's jobs.	SA	A	U	D	SD	15
3.	I wouldn't like to be unemployed.	SA	A	U	D	SD	16
4.	I would like to feel that any job I had was important.	SA	A	U	D	SD	17
5.	I would only do overtime if I needed the money.	SA	A	U	D	SD	18
6.	I think that I could be trusted with any new important job that came up.	SA	A	U	D	SD	19
7.	Work gives you a sense of purpose.	SA	A	U	D	SD	20
8.	Any sort of job is better than being unemployed.	SA	A	U	D	SD	21
9.	I would feel lost if I were to be unemployed for any length of time.	SA	A	U	D	SD	22
10.	To work well, you have got to co-operate with your workmates.	SA	A	U	D	SD	23
11.	To get promotion you've got to do what you're told.	SA	A	U	D	SD	24
12.	I wouldn't mind if the person in charge of me didn't like my work.	SA	A	U	D	SD	25
13.	I think length of time with a firm counts for more than ability when it comes to promotion.	SA	A	U	D	SD	26
14.	I would sooner have a job where I had to work fast than one where I had to work slow.	SA	A	U	D	SD	27

		1	2	3	4	5	*Office Use Only* Cols.	Code
15.	Most jobs are dull and boring.	SA	A	U	D	SD	28	
16.	Even if I won enough money to live comfortably without working, I think I would still work.	SA	A	U	S	SD	29	
17.	There's no point in working except to get paid.	SA	A	U	D	SD	30	
18.	Work's a place where you make real friends.	SA	A	U	D	SD	31	
19.	When you start work, people begin treating you as a grown up person.	SA	AU		D	SD	32	
20.	If you bet bored with your job you should leave and try something else.	SA	A	U	D	SD	33	
21.	You should always choose a job that will lead on to a better job.	SA	A	U	D	SD	34	
22.	I would like a job that was always easy.	SA	A	U	D	SD	35	
23.	Management usually aren't interested in the ideas of the workers.	SA	A	U	D	SD	36	
24.	Workers would never get a pay rise if they didn't fight for it.	SA	A	U	D	SD	37	
25.	Many firms would be better off if they let the workers run them.	SA	A	U	D	SD	38	
26.	Most workers know more about the job than the foreman in charge of them.	SA	A	U	D	SD	39	

27.	If a foreman is going to be fair, he's got to be strict.	SA	A	U	D	SD	40
28.	Bosses tend to treat some people better than they treat the rest.	SA	A	U	D	SD	41
29.	Some people deserve more money just because of the conditions they have to work in.	SA	A	U	D	SD	42
30.	If you're going to leave a job it doesn't matter whether you hand in your notice or they give you the sack.	SA	A	U	D	SD	43
31.	Getting a good job depends on luck more than anything else.	SA	A	U	D	SD	44
32.	Once you've thought of one job you like, you should keep your mind on that job and not worry about other jobs.	SA	A	U	D	SD	45
33.	When all's said and done, the most important thing about a job is the pay.	SA	A	U	D	SD	46
34.	It's best to take whatever job you can get, and not be too choosey.	SA	A	U	D	SD	47
35.	The only way to get noticed at work is to work hard.	SA	A	U	D	SD	48
36.	Knowing the right people doesn't count for much these days in getting on in a job.	SA	A	U	D	SD	49
37.	I don't mind people criticizing my work if they could do any better.	SA	A	U	D	SD	50
38.	It's nice to know that you can be left to get on with something on your own without having someone breathing down your neck all the time.	SA	A	U	D	SD	51

39.	If you don't have a recognized skill, it's impossible to get on and do better for yourself.	SA A U D SD	52	
40.	It's worth going to evening classes to learn a trade.	SA A U D SD	53	
41.	Being able to take a rest when you feel like it encourages people to be idle at work.	SA A U D SD	54	
42.	I would like to work with people of my own age rather than with older more experienced workers.	SA A U D SD	55	

We would like to know what you think about the organization (firm, company, group etc.) which you work for. Please answer all the questions by putting a ring around the answer which is right for you: just as you did before.
If you feel that the answer to the question is:
Definitely Yes, draw a circle around DY to the right of it.
Yes, draw a circle round Y to the right of it.
Undecided, draw a circle around U to the right of it.
No, draw a circle around N to the right of it.
Definitely No, draw a circle around DN to the right of it.

It is important to answer how you really think: there are no "right" or "wrong" answers.
Remember that your answers will be CONFIDENTIAL — no one will be told what your answers are. Do not write your name down.
In the questions, 'work group' means all those who are under the same person.

Office Use Only Cols.	Code
1-4	
5	2
6 (Class No.)	
7 (Area Code)	
8	
9	

		5 4 3 2 1	
43.	Are you told enough about what is going on in other parts of your organization to meet your needs?	DY Y U N DN	10

44.	Do the people in your work group swap opinions and ideas about work problems?	DY	Y	U	N	DN	11
45.	Does the person in charge of you set an example by working hard himself?	DY	Y	U	N	DN	12
46.	Do you feel you can rely on members of your work group?	DY	Y	U	N	DN	13
47.	Is the person in charge of you a friendly person who you feel able to talk to about things?	DY	Y	U	N	DN	14
48.	Do you feel that you really ought to try hard to help your organization be successful?	DY	Y	U	N	DN	15
49.	Does the person in charge of you usually insist that work should be done so well that it is almost perfect?	DY	Y	U	N	DN	16
50.	In general do you have much say or influence about what happens in your organization?	DY	Y	U	N	DN	17
51.	Do you have a feeling of loyalty towards your organization?	DY	Y	U	N	DN	18
52.	Does the person in charge of you show you how to do your work better?	DY	Y	U	N	DN	19
53.	All in all, are you satisfied with those in your work group?	DY	Y	U	N	DN	20
54.	Do the people in your work group help you to work out how to tackle a task before your actually start?	DY	Y	U	N	DN	21
55.	Does the person in charge of you need to know more about how you see things in order to do his job better?	DY	Y	U	N	DN	22

56.	Does the person in charge of you usually want to listen to your ideas or suggestions?	DY	Y	U	N	DN	23
57.	When you talk to the others in your work group do they actually listen to what you have to say?	DY	Y	U	N	DN	24
58.	Do the people in your work group try to do their task so well it is almost perfect?	DY	Y	U	N	DN	25
59.	Do you and your work group decide together how a task should be done?	DY	Y	U	N	DN	26
60.	All in all, are you satisified with the person who is in charge of you?	DY	Y	U	N	DN	27
61.	In general does the person in charge of you have much say or influence in deciding what happens in your organization?	DY	Y	U	N	DN	28
62.	Are you satisfied with the progress you have made in your organization up to now?	DY	Y	U	N	DN	29
63.	Does the person in charge of you encourage people to do the best work they possibly can?	DY	Y	U	N	DN	30
64.	Are you satisfied with your pay?	DY	Y	U	N	DN	31
65.	Does the person in charge of you bring people together so that they can talk about problems to do with work?	DY	Y	U	N	DN	32

66.	Does the person in charge of you need to show more interest in and concern for your problems?	DY	Y	U	N	DN	33
67.	In general do different parts of your organization plan and work together?	DY	Y	U	N	DN	34
68.	Are the others in your work group friendly people who you can talk to about things?	DY	Y	U	N	DN	35
69.	Do the people in your work group emphasize a team goal?	DY	Y	U	N	DN	36
70.	When you talk to the person in charge of you does he listen to what you have to say?	DY	Y	U	N	DN	37
71.	On the whole do the people in your work group do their work well?	DY	Y	U	N	DN	38
72.	Does the person in charge of you organize things properly?	DY	Y	U	N	DN	39
73.	Do the people in your work group help to find ways to improve your work?	DY	Y	U	N	DN	40
74.	Do you enjoy doing the usual day-to-day things which make up your work?	DY	Y	U	N	DN	41
75.	Does your organization try to give people good working conditions?	DY	Y	U	N	DN	42
76.	Are you told what you need to know in order to do your work in the best possible way?	DY	Y	U	N	DN	43
77.	Do the people in your work group encourage each other to do the best work they possibly can?	DY	Y	U	N	DN	44

78.	Are the others in your work group willing to listen to your problems?	DY Y U N DN	45
79.	Do you and your work group get together and work out ways of solving problems to do with the task you are working on?	DY Y U N DN	46
80.	Are there things about your organization that make you want to work hard?	DY Y U N DN	47
81.	Does your organization care whether the people who work for it are happy or not?	DY Y U N DN	48
82.	Are those in your work group able to cope with difficult work tasks?	DY Y U N DN	49
83.	Are work activities sensibly organized in your organization?	DY Y U N DN	50
84.	Does the person in charge of you encourage those who are under him to work as team?	DY Y U N DN	51
85.	All in all, are you satisfied with the work you do?	DY Y U N DN	52
86.	Does the person in charge of you give you new ideas about how to get round problems to do with the work you are doing?	DY Y U N DN	53
87.	All in all, are you satisfied with your organization compared to how you think most other organizations are?	DY Y U N DN	54

88.	Is there much difference between what is intended to happen and what does happen in your organization?	DY	Y	U	N	DN	55
89.	Does the person in charge of you provide help so that you can plan what to do next?	DY	Y	U	N	DN	56
90.	Are the people who decide things in your organization usually the ones who know enough about them?	DY	Y	U	N	DN	57
91.	Do you look forward to coming to your organization each day?	DY	Y	U	N	DN	58
92.	Does the person in charge of you handle the technical side of his job well?	DY	Y	U	N	DN	59
93.	Does the person in charge of you encourage those under him to swap opinions and ideas about work problems?	DY	Y	U	N	DN	60
94.	In general do you get the equipment you need to do your own work properly?	DY	Y	U	N	DN	61
95.	When the person in charge of you has to decide about something are you asked for your views on it?	DY	Y	U	N	DN	62
96.	Do the people in your work group encourage each other to work as a team?	DY	Y	U	N	DN	63
97.	Do people in your work group give each other new ideas about how to deal with problems to do with a task?	DY	Y	U	N	DN	64
98.	On the basis of your experience and information how would you rate your work group, in comparison with other groups in your organization in coping with the work set?	My work group does: (tick one) 1. A very poor job ____ 2. A poor job ____ 3. Uncertain ____ 4. A good job ____ 5. A very good job ____					65

99.	Here is a list of ways that people might handle problems. Put a tick next to the one which is nearest to saying what usually happens in your organization.	1. Nothing is done about problems: they continue to exist. _____ 2. Nothing is done about problems: they sort themselves out after a time. _____ 3. Someone in charge higher up in the organization is told about the problem but nothing gets done about them. _____ 4. Someone in charge higher up in the organization is told about problems and they are sorted out there. _____ 5. The people who have the problems help each other to sort them out without asking somebody higher up to do something about them. _____	66

Please answer every question.
Remember: Work group means all those under the same person.

				Office Use Only Cols.	Code
100.	Here is a list of things that might happen when the person in charge of you has to make a decision. Put a tick next to the one that usually happens in your organization.	1. You are told what to do and there is no chance to ask questions or say what you think.	____	67	
		2. You are told what to do and then given a chance to ask questions and say what you think.	____		
		3. You are told what to do but if you suggest a different way of doing it, it is considered.	____		
		4. You are told what things you could do and then you say which one is best before the person in charge decides.	____		
		5. The person in charge does not tell you what to do instead you all talk about it and suggest things that you might do and then you decide between you which is best.	____		

Office Use Only
Cols. Code

We would like to know what kind of person your are. Here is a practice question about the kind of person you are.

Dare to take risks ☐ ☐ ☐ Want to be safe.

If you are the kind of person who dares to take risks, put a tick (like this ✓) in the box on the LEFT. 1-4

If you are the kind of person who wants to be safe, put a tick in the box on the RIGHT

Most people know which of these two kinds of person they are, but if you really cannot decide which kind of person you are, put a tick in the box in the MIDDLE. 6 (Class No.)

That question was just for practice. Now put a tick by each of these questions in the box which is right for the kind of person you are. Try to be as realistic as possible. 7 (Area Code)

8-9

		1	2	3		
105.	Good at my work	☐	☐	☐	Not so good at my work	10
106.	Good at sports	☐	☐	☐	Not so good at sports	11
107.	Often don't do as I am told.	☐	☐	☐	Usually do as I am told.	12
108.	Try to act 'big'	☐	☐	☐	Act my own age	13
109.	Plan and think ahead.	☐	☐	☐	Cannot wait, want everything at once.	14
110.	Scruffy	☐	☐	☐	Neat and clean.	15
111.	A bit of a bully.	☐	☐	☐	Do not bully.	16

112.	Like to do forbidden things.	☐	☐	☐	Do not do forbidden things.	17
113.	Spend my money.	☐	☐	☐	Save my money	18
114.	Often successful.	☐	☐	☐	Often a failure.	19

We would like your views on things in general. The following statements explain themselves. Read each carefully, decide how YOU feel about it, then ring the answer which is right for you; just as you did before.

Please answer every statement.

Remember: SA=Strongly Agree: A=Agree: U=Undecided: D=Disagree: SD=Strongly Disagree.

115.	Some people are always for what is true. All the rest are always against what is true.	SA	A	U	D	SD	20
116.	We must believe what important people say. If we do not we will not know what is going on in the world.	SA	A	U	D	SD	21
117.	Most people just do not care about others.	SA	A	U	D	SD	22
118.	There is no use to take time to listen to someone who will just try to change your mind.	SA	A	U	D	SD	23
119.	By saying things over and over you can be sure people know what you mean.	SA	A	U	D	SD	24
120.	People who think about themselves first are terrible.	SA	A	U	D	SD	25
121.	It does not matter much if you are not happy now. It is what will happen in years to come that counts.	SA	A	U	D	SD	26
122.	People seem to think that most of the things they do are bad.	SA	A	U	D	SD	27

123.	We are going against our own side if we listen to what the other side says.	SA	A	U	D	SD	28	
124.	People should not try to work together if they believe different things.	SA	A	U	D	SD	29	
125.	It seems like people I do not even know are always looking for the bad things in me.	SA	A	U	D	SD	30	

You have told us about the kind of person you really are. Here is something different. Think now about THE KIND OF PERSON YOU WOULD LIKE TO BE.

We want you to answer some of the same questions as before. But this time we are asking you about the kind of person you would like to be. This may not be the same as the kind of person you really are. So think carefully again about each question then put a tick in the box which is right for the kind of person you would like to be.

						Office Use Only Cols.	Code
		1	2	3			
126.	Good at my work.	☐	☐	☐	Not so good at my work.	31	
127.	Good at sports.	☐	☐	☐	Not good at sports.	32	
128.	Often don't do as I am told.	☐	☐	☐	Usually do as I am told.	33	
129.	Try to act 'big'	☐	☐	☐	Act my own age	34	
130	Plan and think ahead.	☐	☐	☐	Cannot wait, want everything at once.	35	

131.	Scruffy.	☐	☐	☐	Neat and clean.	36
132.	A bit of a bully.	☐	☐	☐	Do not bully.	37
133.	Like to do forbidden things.	☐	☐	☐	Do not do forbidden things.	38
134.	Spend my money.	☐	☐	☐	Save my money.	39
135.	Often successful.	☐	☐	☐	Often a failure.	40

Now tell us a little bit about yourself.

Please answer the following questions by putting a ring around the answer which is right for you: just as you did before.

Remember: DY=Definitely Yes: Y=Yes: U=Undecided: N=No: DN=Definitely No.

		5	4	3	2	1	
136.	Do your nerves often feel on edge?	DY	Y	U	N	DN	41
137.	Do you often have an upset stomach?	DY	Y	U	N	DN	42
138.	Do people say you are highly strung or nervous?	DY	Y	U	N	DN	43
139.	Do you often feel you can't sit still?	DY	Y	U	N	DN	44
140.	Do you often have headaches?	DY	Y	U	N	DN	45
141.	Do you often feel as if you want to scream?	DY	Y	U	N	DN	46
142.	Does your skin often break out in a rash?	DY	Y	U	N	DN	47
143.	Do you shiver sometimes, even in warm weather?	DY	Y	U	N	DN	48

144.	Do you feel you want to chew or suck something most of the time?	DY	Y	U	N	DN	49	
145.	Do you find it difficult to relax?	DY	Y	U	N	DN	50	
146.	Do you often have to take time off because you are not well?	DY	Y	U	N	DN	51	

Now here are some statements about things in general. We would like to get your feelings on each one of these.

Remember if you:—
Strongly Agree with a statement, draw a circle around SA to the right of it.
Agree with a statement, draw a circle around A to the right of it.
Are Undecided about a statement, draw a circle around U to the right of it.
Disagree with a statement, draw a circle around D to the right of it.
Strongly Disagree with a statement, draw a circle around SD to the right of it.

Office Use Only Cols.	Code
1-4	
5	4
6 (Class No.)	
7 (Area Code)	
8-9	

		1	2	3	4	5		
147.	If I decide to do something then I always succeed.	SA	A	U	D	SD	10	
148.	I find it difficult to believe in my abilities sometimes.	SA	A	U	D	SD	11	
149.	Shop-lifting is a serious crime and should be severely punished.	SA	A	U	D	SD	12	
150.	I don't mind admitting when I'm beat.	SA	A	U	D	SD	13	
151.	When I got out, I prefer going to the cinema than to dances.	SA	A	U	D	SD	14	

152.	If people tried hard enough, I know we could end wars.	SA	A	U	D	SD	15
153.	At times I think I am no good at all.	SA	A	U	D	SD	16
154.	In my case, getting what I want has little or nothing to do with luck.	SA	A	U	D	SD	17
155.	I've always felt close to my parents.	SA	A	U	D	SD	18
156.	I like listening to pop records with my friends.	SA	A	U	D	SD	19
157.	If someone stole something of mine because I'd left it lying around, I would feel that it was my own fault.	SA	A	U	D	SD	20
158.	No matter what I say or do, things seem to go against me.	SA	A	U	D	SD	21
159.	I feel that I've got to break the rules to get on.	SA	A	U	D	SD	22
160.	I'm sure strikes are inevitable.	SA	A	U	D	SD	23
161.	I'm not much interested in the TV programmes, films and magazines that most people seem to like.	SA	A	U	D	SD	24
162.	I stay out of other people's trouble because I know they won't stick their neck out for me.	SA	A	U	D	SD	25
163.	I often feel that people just don't like me.	SA	A	U	D	SD	26
164.	I often think it is no good trying to change things.	SA	A	U	D	SD	27
165.	I think it's better to admit my mistakes than to try to cover them up.	SA	A	U	D	SD	28
166.	It doesn't pay to trust people too much.	SA	A	U	D	SD	29
167.	People are always trying to stop me from doing what I want to do.	SA	A	U	D	SD	30

168.	I would do things differently if it was left to me.	SA	A	U	D	SD	31
169.	I have no doubt about what the future holds for me.	SA	A	U	D	SD	32
170.	I like to think that I get on well with people.	SA	A	U	D	SD	33
171.	I feel that what happens to me is not my own doing.	SA	A	U	D	SD	34
172.	I am able to do things as well as most other people.	SA	A	U	D	SD	35
173.	All in all, I feel that I am a failure.	SA	A	U	D	SD	36
174.	Instead of talking about life I just get on and live it.	SA	A	U	D	SD	37

THANK YOU for helping us:

check through and make sure you have answered every question.

(b) Adult Questionnaire

Please circle the appropriate number in the following statement.	*Office Use Only*	
	Cols.	Code
	1-4	—
(a) Your present position.	5	—
0. . .Office Manager		
1. . .Personnel Officer		
2. . .Projects Officer		
3. . .Scheme Consultant		
4. . .Area Manager	6	—
(b) Your CI Area:		
1. . .Dundee		
2. . .Glasgow		
3. . .Liverpool		
4. . .Newport		
5. . .Mexborough		
6. . .Teesside		
7. . .Sunderland		
8. . .Newcastle	7	—
(c) Your Age:		
1. . .20 — 24		
2. . .25 — 29		
3. . .30 — 34		
4. . .35 — 39		
5. . .40 — 44		
6. . .45 and over	8	—
(d) Your Sex:		
1. . .Male		
2. . .Female	9	—
(e) Your marital status.		
1. . .Single		
2. . .Married without children		
3. . .Married with children	10	—
(f) Your employment background		
1. . .Industrial (including building)		
2. . .Teaching		
3. . .Youth service		
4. . .Housewife		
5. . .Other (specify)	11	—

(g) Length of time with CI
1. . .Less than 3 months
2. . .4 to 6 months
3. . .7 to 9 months
4. . .10 to 12 months
5. . .Over 12 months 12 —
13 —

Now we would like to have your opinion as to what you think the aims of Community Industry should be. Listed below are a number of things which various people have said CI should be doing for young people. Read each statement and indicate the extent to which you think CI should be concerned by putting a circle around the answer to the right of it.

If your answer to a statement is:

Definitely Yes: draw a circle around DY to the right of it.
Yes: draw a circle around Y to the right of it.
Undecided: draw a circle around U to the right of it.
No: draw a circle around N to the right of it.
Definitely No: draw a circle around DN to the right of it.

If you find that you have changed your mind or you made a mistake when drawing the circle put and X through it and drawn in another.

Remember it is your opinion that we are interested in so there are no 'right' or 'wrong' answers.

			Office Use Only Cols.	Code
1.	Help the young people develop a will to work.	DY Y U N DN	14	
2.	Help the young people use materials properly and not waste them.	DY Y U N DN	15	
3.	Provide the young people with a source of support.	DY Y U N DN	16	
4.	Get the young people off the idea of not working and living on social security.	DY Y U N DN	17	

Remember: DY=Definitely Yes: Y=Yes: U=Undecided: N=No: DN=Definitey No.

			Office Use Only Cols.	Code
5.	Help the young people take good care of material and equipment.	DY Y U N DN	18.	
6.	Show the young people how to manage the money they are earning.	DY Y U N DN	19.	
7.	Provide a gradual introduction to open employment outside of CI for the young people	DY Y U N DN	20.	
8.	Enable the young people to communicate more effectively especially with those in authority.	DY Y U N DN	21.	
9.	Show the young people that swearing every other word can go against them.	DY Y U N DN	22.	
10.	Help the young people achieve high standards in their work.	DY Y U N DN	23.	
11.	Show the young people that the world does not owe them a living.	DY Y U N DN	24.	
12.	Help the young people develop a sense of self discipline.	DY Y U N DN	25.	
13.	Help the young people cope with realistic work experience.	DY Y U N DN	26.	
14.	Help the young people face work-related problems.	DY Y U N DN	27.	
15.	Involve the young people in decision making.	DY Y U N DN	28.	
16.	Demonstrate to the young people that work can be a rewarding experience.	DY Y U N DN	29.	

17.	Help the young people to understand and when necessary to assert their rights.	DY Y U N DN	30.
18.	Help the young people develop a sense of pride in holding down a job.	DY Y U N DN	31.
19.	Help make the young people cost conscious.	DY Y U N DN	32.
20.	Help the young people with all sorts of problems.	DY Y U N DN	33.
21.	Develop the young people's skill in a particular type of work.	DY Y U N DN	34.
22.	Help the young people accept responsibility for work-related tasks.	DY Y U N DN	35.
23.	Help the young people with personal problems.	DY Y U N DN	36.
24.	Provide the young people with varied work experience.	DY Y U N DN	37.
25.	Show the young people how to take work related problems through proper channels.	DY Y U N DN	38.
26.	Help the young people to make the most of their appearance.	DY Y U N DN	39.
27.	Help the young people to do a job as efficiently as possible.	DY Y U N DN	40.
28.	Help the young people to learn the proper way to voice complaints.	DY Y U N DN	41.
29.	Show the young people what to do if they get in trouble with the police.	DY Y U N DN	42.
30.	Provide the young people with *permanent* meaningful work.	DY Y U N DN	43.

Remember: DY=Definitely Yes: Y=Yes: U=Undecided: N=No: DN=Definitely No.

			Office Use Only Cols.	Code
31.	Get the young people to send in sick notes when absent.	DY Y U N DN	44.	
32.	Build up the young people's confidence.	DY Y U N DN	45.	
33.	Help the young people accept authority.	DY Y U N DN	46.	
34.	Help the young people to develop a concern for others.	DY Y U N DN	47.	
35.	Encourage the young people to obtain 'open employment'	DY Y U N DN	48.	
36.	Show the young people the necessity for keeping to set hours of work.	DY Y U N DN	49.	
37.	Help broaden the young person's outlook.	DY Y U N DN	50.	
38.	Help get as many youngsters off the dole as possible.	DY Y U N DN	51.	
39.	Show the young people how to follow established procedure.	DY Y U N DN	52.	
40.	Develop the young person's sense of initiative.	DY Y U N DN	53.	
41.	Equip the young people to hold down an ordinary job.	DY Y U N DN	54.	
42.	Motivate the young people to attend interviews for jobs.	DY Y U N DN	55.	
43.	Help the young people develop a sense of pride in a job well done.	DY Y U N DN	56.	
44.	Help the young people to become independent and stand on their own feet.	DY Y U N DN	57.	

45.	Help the young people develop their personalities and characters.	DY Y U N DN	58.
46.	Help the young people turn out work of a high quality.	DY Y U N DN	59.
47.	Help the young people accept justifiable criticism.	DY Y U N DN	60.
48.	Help the young people to appreciate other people's problems.	DY Y U N DN	61.
49.	Help the young people develop a more favourable attitude to work.	DY Y U N DN	62.
50.	Help the young people to accept 'the bad' as well as 'the good' aspects of work.	DY Y U N DN	63.
51.	Give the young people some form of self respect.	DY Y U N DN	64.
52.	Provide the young people with a *temporary* period of stable employment.	DY Y U N DN	65.
53.	Help the young people develop habits of good time keeping.	DY Y U N DN	66.
54.	Give the young people time to think about where they are going.	DY Y U N DN	67.
55.	Show the young people that adults can be friendly people with a genuine desire to help.	DY Y U N DN	68.
56.	Provide permanent work for those who otherwise wouldn't obtain a job.	DY Y U N DN	69.

Listed below are certain factors which may influence the performance of your work. Indicate how satisified you are with each by ringing the appropriate letter.

A = Very Satisfied.
B = Fairly Satisfied.
C = Either Satisfied or Dissatisfied.
D = Somewhat Dissatisfied.
E = Very Dissatisfied.

Underneath each statement briefly indicate reason for your satisfaction/dissatisfaction.

							Office Use Only *Cols.*	*Code*
57.	Projects of the right type. Reason.________	A	B	C	D	E	70.	
58.	Stress on 'throughput'. Reason.________	A	B	C	D	E	71.	
59.	General paper work which is required Reason.________	A	B	C	D	E	72.	
60.	Number of meetings which are scheduled. Reason.________	A	B	C	D	E	73.	
61.	Public 'Image' associated with CI. Reason.________	A	B	C	D	E	74.	
62.	Backing from the local authority. Reason.________	A	B	C	D	E	75.	
63.	Interest shown by sponsors. Reason.________	A	B	C	D	E	76.	
64.	Facilities and/or equipment. Reason.________	A	B	C	D	E	77.	
65.	Pay and conditions of service adult employees. Reason.________	A	B	C	D	E	78.	

							Office Use Only Cols.	Code
66.	Ratio of staff to young people. Reason.______	A	B	C	D	E	79.	
67.	Feedback with regard to job performance. Reason.______	A	B	C	D	E	80.	

Listed below are a number of statements that may be used to describe the behaviour of a Scheme Consultant as you think he/she should act. This is not a test of ability, it simply asks you to describe what an ideal Scheme Consultant ought to do in supervising the work group of young people. Read each statement and decide whether the Scheme Consultant should always, often, occasionally, seldom, or never, act as described by the statement. 1-4 —

Draw a circle around one of the five letters following the item to show the answer your have selected. 5 3 —

A=Always: B=Often: C=Occasionally: D=Seldom: E=Never 6 —

(Class Nos)

WHAT the IDEAL Scheme Consultant SHOULD do:

7 —

(Area Code)

8 —

9 —

126.	He lets group members know what is expected of them.	A B C D E	10.	
127.	He is friendly and approachable.	A B C D E	11.	
128.	He encourages the use of uniform procedures.	A B C D E	12.	
129.	He does little things to make it pleasant to be a member of the group.	A B C D E	13.	
130.	He tries out his ideas in the group.	A B C D E	14.	

			Office Use Only Cols.	Code
131.	He puts suggestions made by the group into operation.	A B C D E	15.	
132.	He makes his attitudes clear to the group.	A B C D E	16.	
133.	He treats all group members as his equals.	A B C D E	17.	
134.	He decides what shall be done and how it shall be done.	A B C D E	18.	
135.	He gives advance notice of changes.	A B C D E	19.	
136.	He assigns group members to particular tasks.	A B C D E	20.	
137.	He keeps to himself.	A B C D E	21.	
138.	He makes sure that his part in the group is understood by the group members.	A B C D E	22.	
139.	He looks out for the personal welfare of group members.	A B C D E	23.	
140.	He schedules the work to be done.	A B C D E	24.	
141.	He is willing to make changes.	A B C D E	25.	
142.	He maintains definite standards of performance.	A B C D E	26.	
143.	He refuses to explain his actions.	A B C D E	27.	
144.	He asks that group members follow standard rules and regulations.	A B C D E	28.	
145.	He acts without consulting the group.	A B C D E	29.	

Feel free to use this space to make any additional comments about CI which you may think necessary.

Continue opposite if required.

Thank you for your help and co-operation. Check all statements have been answered, place in envelope, seal and return to office.

Appendix 3

Identification of scales developed for the research

Notes

(a) A principal components analysis was performed on each of the following groups of items contained in the Young Person's questionnaire:

(i)	Items 1 — 42	(Motivation to work)
(ii)	Items 43 — 100	(ODQ)
(iii)	Items 147 — 174	(Alienation)

The component analysis for (iii) was performed on the responses obtained in a pre-test of the Alienation Scale. For the other two analyses the responses from the main sample were used.

(b) Figures in brackets to the left of each item refer to the number of the item in the questionnaire.

(c) For each component the two items with the highest loadings are asterisked(*).

Items	*Loadings*
Powerlessness	
* (158) No matter what I say or do, things seem to go against me.	0.56
(160) I'm sure strikes are inevitable.	0.30
(161) I'm not much interested in the TV programmes, films and magazines that most people seem to like.	0.30
(162) I stay out of other people's trouble because I know they won't stick their neck out for me.	0.51
(166) It doesn't pay to trust people too much.	0.48
* (167) People are always trying to stop me from doing what I want to do.	0.58

(168)	I would do things differently if it was left to me.	0.39
(169)	I have no doubt about what the future holds for me.	0.37
(171)	I feel that what happens to me is not my own doing.	0.42
(172)	Instead of talking about life I just get on and live it.	0.29

Moral Righteousness

* (149)	Shop-lifting is a serious crime and should be severely punished.	0.56
(150)	I don't mind admitting when I'm beat.	0.43
(152)	If people tried hard enough, I know we could end wars.	0.44
* (155)	I've always felt close to my parents.	0.52
(157)	If someone stole something of mine because I'd left it lying around, I would feel that it was my own fault.	0.33
(159)	I feel that I've got to break the rules to get on.	−0.39
(164)	I often think it is no good trying to change things.	0.31
(165)	I think it's better to admit my mistakes than to try to cover them up.	0.50
(170)	I like to think that I get on well with people.	0.42

Self Doubt

* (147)	If I decide to do something then I always succeed.	0.48
* (148)	I find it difficult to believe in my abilities sometimes.	−0.49
(151)	When I go out, I prefer going to the cinema than to dances.	0.30
(153)	At times I think I am no good at all.	Added item
(154)	In my case, getting what I want has little or nothing to do with luck.	0.33
(155)	I like listening to pop records with my friends.	−0.36

	Items	Loading
(163)	I often feel that people just don't like me.	−0.34
(172)	I am able to do things as well as most other people.	Added item
(173)	All in all, I feel that I am a failure.	Added item
Work Commitment		
(4)	I would like to feel that any job I had was important.	−0.45
(5)	I would only do overtime if I needed the money.	0.44
(12)	I wouldn't mind if the person in charge of me didn't like my work.	0.32
* (19)	When you start work, people begin treating you as a grown up person.	−0.49
(23)	Management usually aren't interested in the ideas of the workers.	0.44
(31)	Getting a good job depends on luck more than anything else.	0.39
* (35)	The only way to get noticed at work is to work hard.	−0.53
(42)	I would like to work with people of my own age rather than with older more experienced workers.	0.38
Work Cynicism		
(8)	Any sort of job is better than being unemployed.	−0.38
(13)	I think length of time with a firm counts for more than ability when it comes to promotion.	−0.41
(14)	I would sooner have a job where I had to work fast than one where I had to work slow.	−0.41
(15)	Most jobs are dull and boring.	−0.31
(24)	Workers would never get a pay rise if they didn't fight for it.	−0.40
* (25)	Many firms would be better off if they let the workers run them.	−0.56

(26)	Most workers know more about the job than the foreman in charge of them.	−0.43
(27)	If a foreman is going to be fair, he's got to be strict.	−0.36
(30)	If you're going to leave a job it doesn't matter whether you hand in your notice or they give you the sack.	−0.41
(32)	Once you've thought of a job you like, you should keep your mind on that job and not worry about other jobs.	−0.42
* (34)	It's best to take whatever job you can get, and not be too choosey.	−0.51
(36)	Knowing the right people doesn't count for much these days in getting on in a job.	−0.33
(39)	If you don't have a recognized skill, it's impossible to get on and do better for yourself.	−0.38

Work Meaning

(6)	I think that I could be trusted with any new important job that came up.	−0.39
* (9)	I would feel lost if I were to be unemployed for any length of time.	−0.58
(10)	To work well, you have to co-operate with your workmates.	−0.40
(11)	To get promotion you've got to do what you're told.	−0.39
(16)	Even if I won enough money to live comfortably without working, I think I would still work.	−0.41
(17)	There's no point in working except to get paid.	−0.34
* (18)	Work's a place where you make real friends.	−0.56
(20)	If you get bored with your job you should leave and try something else.	−0.38
(21)	You should always choose a job that will lead on to a better job.	−0.47

	Items	*Loadings*
(33)	When all's said and done, the most important thing about a job is the pay.	0.33
(38)	It's nice to know that you can be left to get on with something on your own without having someone breathing down your neck all the time.	−0.33
Supervisory Satisfaction		
(45)	Does the person in charge of you set an example by working hard himself?	0.64
* (47)	Is the person in charge of you a friendly person who you feel able to talk to about things?	0.71
(52)	Does the person in charge of you show you how to do your work better?	0.63
(56)	Does the person in charge of you usually want to listen to your ideas or suggestions?	0.59
* (60)	All in all, are you satisfied with the person who is in charge of you?	0.80
(65)	Does the person in charge of you bring people together so that they can talk about problems to do with work?	0.45
(92)	Does the person in charge of you handle the technical side of his job well?	0.37
(93)	Does the person in charge of you encourage those under him to swap opinions and ideas about work problem?	0.32
Organizational Care		
(51)	Do you have a feeling of loyalty towards your organization?	0.40
(64)	Are you satisfied with your pay?	0.46
* (75)	Does your organization try to give people good working conditions?	0.72
(76)	Are you told what you need to know in order to do your work in the best possible way?	0.34

(80)	Are there things about your organization that make you want to work hard?	0.41
* (81)	Does your organization care whether the people who work for it are happy or not?	0.74
(85)	All in all, are you satisfied with the work you do?	0.34
(87)	All in all, are your satisfied with your organization compared to how you think most other organizations are?	0.66
(90)	Are the people who decide things in your organization usually the ones who know enough about them?	0.36
(91)	Do you look forward to coming to your organization each day?	0.39
(94)	In general do you get the equipment you need to do your own work properly?	0.63

Work Group Support

(44)	Do the people in your work group swap opinions and ideas about work problems?	0.39
(46)	Do you feel you can rely on members of your work group?	0.67
(53)	All in all, are you satisfied with those in your work group?	0.30
(54)	Do the people in your work group help you to work out how to tackle a task before you actually start?	0.57
(57)	When you talk to the others in your work group do they actually listen to what you have to say?	0.52
* (68)	Are the others in your work group friendly people who you can talk to about things?	0.75
(70)	When you talk to the person in charge of you does he listen to what you have to say?	0.31
* (78)	Are the others in your work group willing to listen to your problems?	0.68

	Items	*Loadings*
Task Accomplishment		
(67)	In general do different parts of your organization plan and work together?	0.42
(69)	Do the people in your work group emphasize a team goal?	0.37
(72)	Does the person in charge of you organize things properly?	0.36
* (83)	Are work activities sensibly organized in your organization?	0.65
* (84)	Does the person in charge of you encourage those who are under him to work as a team?	0.70
(86)	Does the person in charge of you give you new ideas about how to get round problems to do with the work you are doing?	0.48
(89)	Does the person in charge of you provide help so that you can plan what to do next?	0.49
(96)	Do the people in your work group encourage each other to work as a team?	0.58

Index